Counter-Cartographies

Postcolonialism across the Disciplines 31

Postcolonialism across the Disciplines

Series Editors
Graham Huggan, University of Leeds
Andrew Thompson, University of Exeter

Postcolonialism across the Disciplines showcases alternative directions for postcolonial studies. It is in part an attempt to counteract the dominance in colonial and postcolonial studies of one particular discipline – English literary/cultural studies – and to make the case for a combination of disciplinary knowledges as the basis for contemporary postcolonial critique. Edited by leading scholars, the series aims to be a seminal contribution to the field, spanning the traditional range of disciplines represented in postcolonial studies but also those less acknowledged. It will also embrace new critical paradigms and examine the relationship between the transnational/cultural, the global and the postcolonial.

Counter-Cartographies
Reading Singapore Otherwise
Joanne Leow

Liverpool University Press

First published 2024 by
Liverpool University Press
4 Cambridge Street
Liverpool L69 7ZU

This paperback edition published 2026

Copyright © 2026 Joanne Leow

Joanne Leow has asserted the right to be identified as the author of this book in accordance with the Copyright, Design and Patents Act 1988.

All rights reserved. No part of this book may be reproduced, stored in a retrieval system, or transmitted, in any form or by any means, electronic, mechanical, photocopying, recording, or otherwise, without the prior written permission of the publisher.

British Library Cataloguing-in-Publication data
A British Library CIP record is available

ISBN 978-1-802-07447-5 (hardback)
ISBN 978-1-80596-574-9 (paperback)

Typeset in Amerigo BT by Carnegie Book Production, Lancaster

For my father,
who teaches me how to look
at the world around me with care.

Contents

Acknowledgments ix
Prelude: From Blueprint to Eden xiii

Introduction 1
    Of Maps and Other Fictions 1
    Mapped Singapore 4
    "You are here" 11
    The Arts in Singapore: Control, Co-optation, and Censorship 12
    Counter-Cartographical Reading: Excavate, Circumvent,
        Wayfind, Confabulate 18

1 Excavations 27
    "Sewn to the hardness of cement" 27
    SEA STATE 31
    Lost World 39
    Invisible City: In Preparation for Forgetting (beiwanglu, 备忘录) 44
    "A Fluid and Borderless Past" 54

2 Circumventions 61
    Circumscribed Realities 61
    To Singapore, With Love 69
    "National Day" 74
    And the Walls Come Crumbling Down 82

3 Wayfinding 89
    Grandma Positioning System 89
    Lost Roads: Singapore 94

Malay Sketches   106
"In Our Time"   114

4 Confabulations   119

"Past Conditional Temporality"   119
Hotel   125
The Art of Charlie Chan Hock Chye   134
Dream Storeys   143
SG50 and SG200: Jubilee and Bicentennial   148

Conclusion: Return to Eden   151

Works Cited   161

Index   171

Acknowledgments

This book took over a decade to come into being and thus owes many profound debts to scholars, friends, loved ones, and colleagues in Asia, North America, and Europe. There are many more of you than can be named here, so please forgive me for any glaring omissions.

Thank you to my editor Chloe Johnson, the series editors for Postcolonialism across the Disciplines, and the team at Liverpool University Press for believing in the importance of this work and shepherding this manuscript to its current form. Thanks as well to all the anonymous reviewers for asking the difficult but necessary questions to sharpen this work.

I began the writing of this book at the University of Toronto and have been generously supported by federal, provincial, and institutional funding in Canada. This included the Vanier Social Sciences and Humanities Research Council Graduate Scholarship, an Ontario Graduate scholarship, an Avie Bennett Award, a University of Toronto Fellowship, and a Department of English award. As a faculty member, I have also been supported for this work by funding from a Social Sciences and Humanities Research Council Insight Development Grant, the University of Saskatchewan, and Simon Fraser University.

In its initial iterations, the conceptualization and analysis in this work were guided by Philip Holden, Victor Li, Ato Quayson, and Karina Vernon. Much gratitude to them for their mentorship, generosity, conversations, and faith in my work. Thanks as well to Deidre Lynch for her initial belief in my project, and to Stanka Radović, whose graduate course gave me a foundation in spatial theory. Denise Cruz provided and still provides much-needed scholarly inspiration. My work was aided by the impeccable administrative assistance and warm support provided by Sangeeta Panjwani, Marguerite Perry, Tanuja Persaud, and other department staff and faculty in Toronto.

I want to thank my friends in Toronto for making us feel so at home in the city. Special mention must be made of Melissa Auclair, Rupaleem Bhuyan, Marc Clausen, Laura Cok, Laura Hartenberger, Kaelyn Kaoma, Katherine

Magyarody, Nathan Murray, Matt Schneider, Katherine Schwetz, Vicki Soon, Elisa Tersigni, Amanda Thambirajah, Phoebe Wang, and everyone in the safe haven of JHB916.

During my brief stint at McMaster for my postdoctoral work, I was so lucky to have been able to work with the late and dear Donald C. Goellnicht. Don's care and wisdom enabled me to navigate the positioning of this book in the world and helped me to understand its worth. Meeting the community at McMaster enabled transpacific connections and friendships that shaped my work. Thank you especially to Phanuel Antwi, Nadine Attewell, Vinh Nguyen, Thy Phu, Malissa Phung, and Danielle Wong for welcoming me into their circles. The late Y-Dang Troeung was a loyal friend, fantastic collaborator, and generous interlocutor. I feel honored to have known her for one all too brief moment.

My time at the University of Saskatchewan enabled me to write and revise major parts of this work. Thanks to colleagues and friends Sheri Benning, Tenille Campbell, Romain Chareyron, Jenna Hunnef, Kathleen James-Caven, Jeff Klassen, Ann Martin, Ella Ophir, Jeanette Lynnes, David Parkinson, Gabriela Prado, Wendy Roy, Jesse Stewart, Lisa Vargo, and the late Len Findlay and Peter Hynes. In times of bereavement and illness, I knew I could count on Jason Betke, Sean Bone, Sarah Buehler, Adeline Chu, Charlie Clark, Scott Davidson, Duc Le, Olga and Joe Lovick, Lisa Poon, Lisa and Lester Young, and my wonderful neighbors: Rose and Dave, Jean and Pete, Eddie and Linda. Cindy and Josh Wallace and the delightful Miriam and Pilgram were the source of so much light, love, and joy in the coldest and bleakest of times.

Simon Fraser University and Vancouver, BC have been wonderful new places to work from and complete this book. So much gratitude especially to Nadine Attewell, Cornel Bogle, David Chariandy, Christine Kim, Sophie McCall, Deanna Reder, my wonderful students and new colleagues for making me feel at home.

Much of this work was first delivered as conference papers, and the lively intellectual communities of Southeast Asian scholars at the Modern Language Association and at the meetings of the American Comparative Literature Association, Canadian Association for Commonwealth Literature and Language Studies gave me important and crucial feedback. Thank you to Nazry Bahrawi, Brian Bernards, Nadine Chan, Chan Cheow-Thia, Weihsin Gui, Shaoling Ma, Sheela Jane Menon, Cheryl Naruse, E.K. Tan, Ben Tran, and Mayee Wong.

The editors and rigorous reviewers of the *Journal of Commonwealth Literature*, the *Journal of Postcolonial Writing*, *positions: asia critique*, and *Verge: Studies in Global Asias* also helped to refine my writing and ideas. I am especially indebted to the Global Asias community at Penn State. Thank you to Jessamyn R. Abel, Tina Chen, and Cathy Schlund-Vials for pointing the way to the intersections between Asian and Asian American studies.

This dissertation could not have come about without the creative output of artists and writers from Singapore and its diasporas. I am so lucky to count so many of these brilliant, talented, and generous individuals as my friends. Doing scholarship on Singapore while out of the country is challenging, and I was fortunate to have access to films, plays, unpublished work, and artwork. Clara Chow, Lucy Davis, Tania De Rozario, ila, Sonny Liew, Charles Lim, Wild Rice, Alfian Sa'at, Tan Pin Pin, Tan Shzr Ee, Jeremy Tiang, Kelvin Tong, Li Lin Wee, and Li Xinli have all been attentive to my questions and gracious with my interpretations of their work. I am so grateful to Dr. Ang Swee Chai who gave me permission to quote her late husband Francis Khoo's original song lyrics. The collective of Singaporean academics in AcademiaSG have been a bulwark against the sometimes absurd nature of knowledge production and freedom in Singapore studies. Thank you to Ian Chong, Cherian George, Linda Lim, Corrie Tan and Teo You Yenn. You've made the long and winding journey of a Singaporean academic abroad feel much less lonely. I've learned so much as well from Sim Chiyin, Dan Feng, Faris Joraimi, Sai Siew Min, Hong Lysa, Madeleine Thien, and Jason Wee.

My dearest and oldest friends in and from Singapore, Sze Chan, Marilyne Chew, Usha Das, Luigi Ferrandi, Ernie Gao, Sylvain Guilbon, Laura Kho, Wendy Loh, Colette Wong, and Laurel Wong have always welcomed me with open arms and made me understand the stakes of my work.

My Italian family Daniele Gullotti, Bina Sapienza, Lisa and Thom, my father Lucas Leow, my late mother Josephine Phun, and my grandmother Philomen Chin have been a source of constant love and stories. Their sacrifices have enabled me to complete this work.

Finally, I want to thank my treasures: my sons Luca and Dante and my husband Giuliano, to whom this culmination of over a decade of transnational upheaval, long days, and working summers is dedicated. I have so much gratitude for your unstinting loyalty, love, and affection—without which nothing would be possible.

Prelude: From Blueprint to Eden

> Doesn't the permanent transformation of Singapore's territory by the state represent an unprecedented effort at creating and maintaining legible landscapes?
>
> (Rodolphe De Koninck, *Singapore's Permanent Territorial Revolution: Fifty Years in Fifty Maps*, 2017, 133)

> Singapore is already a fully conquered island in the imaginary, in that every foot of space is already assigned to a particular use, as signified by the multicolour coded planning maps. No space has been left to chance and even nature has to have the permission of the planning agencies to survive.
>
> (Chua Beng Huat, *Political Legitimacy and Housing: Stakeholding in Singapore*, 1997, 50)

I begin at the southern Singapore coastline where the Singapore river opens up into the Singapore Straits. The 1970s witness the beginnings of an ambitious land reclamation project that will see sand, earth, and soil taken from hills in the island's interior and dredged from islands belonging to Malaysia and Indonesia, and moved to this site. The coastline advances incrementally until we are looking at approximately 350 hectares of new Singapore land. Over the next few decades the land must sit quietly while the reclaimed soil settles and stabilizes. Then, a barrage is built across the mouth of the Singapore river to create an artificial bay where there was none before. This is the site of Marina Bay, an empty piece of new land – giving a new lease of life to the architect Rem Koolhaas's description of Singapore as a "tabula rasa" (1995, 1031). This land is zoned and demarcated by urban planners: part of it will play host to the island's first casino and integrated resort, while the rest will be given over to an ambitious horticultural project: Gardens by the Bay.

Counter-Cartographies

In the first few years of the new millennium, the Singapore government holds an international design competition to attract the world's best architectural and landscaping firms. A British firm, Grant Associates, is selected to be the lead designer in the project. Their plan culminates in two enormous cooled conservatories – one replicating a Mediterranean climate, the other a tropical mountain range; these conservatories, the Flower Dome and the Cloud Forest, each contain some 1,000 species of plants from every continent except the Antarctic. These are flanked by the Supertrees, giant concrete structures some 9 to 16 stories high, girded by purple steel branches that support vertical gardens of ferns, orchids, and climbers – 163,000 plants, 200 species from 30 countries. These are surrounded by the "themed gardens." They most notably include "heritage gardens": racialized, codified spaces that classify the main ethnic groups of Singapore and their related botany as scholarly Chinese, artistic Indians, rural Malays, and enterprising colonials – a reflection of the colonially inherited, strictly demarcated categories of race that the Singaporean state uses as a governing tool. The entire project costs 1 billion Singapore dollars (UD$720 million) to construct and continues to cost approximately 50 million dollars to maintain each year (Cheong, 2012). This is a space that has been produced with immense human and environmental capital: from exploited foreign labor to the ecological impact of importing and sustaining hundreds of thousands of species of nonindigenous flora.[1]

Fig. 1 Gardens by the Bay under construction at Marina Bay, Singapore in July 2011. Credit: Fieldafar, Wikimedia Commons, licensed under the Creative Commons Attribution-Share Alike 3.0 Unported license.

---

1 Statistics and details about the Gardens are taken from Koh (2012).

Perhaps the most visible representation of Gardens by the Bay is in the 2018 film *Crazy Rich Asians*. Based on the bestselling novel of the same name by the Singaporean-American author Kevin Kwan and touted as a milestone in Asian-American film-making, the film further cemented Singapore's status in the global imaginary as a clean, safe, and technologically advanced island paradise. A.O. Scott in his *New York Times* review of the film quips: "if there is any part of Singapore that is less than dazzlingly picturesque, we don't see it here" (2018). More significantly, he notes the imperialist longings of the film:

> Without betraying any overt nostalgia, "Crazy Rich Asians" casts a fond eye backward as well as Eastward, conjuring a world defined by hierarchies and prescribed roles in a way that evokes classic novels and films. Its keenest romantic impulse has less to do with Nick and Rachel's rather pedestrian love story than with the allure of endless luxury and dynastic authority.

The "dynastic authority" that Scott refers to is distinctly anglophone and wealthy, the lead role of Nicholas Young being played by newcomer Henry Golding, a half-Iban, half-British actor with an appealingly plummy accent. *Crazy Rich Asians* charms global audiences with its careful retention of colonial hierarchies and flamboyant displays of wealth, tracing the marriage plots of the most quintessential Victorian novels, and further adding a frisson of the tropical exotic to the mix. The characters cannot help but glide through these rarefied spaces. The text depicts the actual reality of the wealthiest of Singaporeans with the silent maids, cooks, chauffeurs, guards, and gardeners who move invisibly through a series of scenes in ostensibly walled-off and guarded spaces. The mansions, jewelry stores, churches, and hotels of the film underpin a universe that is deeply racialized and elitist.

When Gardens by the Bay appears in the film, it has been closed off for a private event. Intertwined in the text and essential to its depictions of extreme wealth are carefully pruned forms of vegetation, imported plants, and extreme ideas of climate control. The set pieces of the novel include a lavish flower-bedecked wedding, a matriarch's English garden with exotic and rare blooms, and architectural meldings of tropical botany and futuristic structures. Many of these long descriptive passages find uncanny resonances with the fantasy performances of Gardens by the Bay. Reading the film's source material, Kwan's novel, it becomes apparent that the orderly and verdant plant life in the text camouflages the immense ecological cost of its acquisition and maintenance. While resisting the novel's attempts to treat Singapore's manufactured tropicality as a mere backdrop to the eccentric lives of the hyper-rich, what we might consider in its place is how forms of gendered, heteronormative, and class-based controls are inextricably bound to spatial, climatic, and botanical ones. Placed in the context of developments like Gardens by the Bay, the somewhat satirical depictions of surreal landscapes in the novel *Crazy Rich Asians* (2013) refract the construction of tightly controlled, exclusive spaces.

Counter-Cartographies

A visit to Gardens by the Bay is a curious experience – one marked by a sense of unease at its performance of highly planned wildness, the ubiquitous signage exhorting visitors to keep away from the plants, and the telling absence of insect life. Discreetly, gardeners and workers toil to keep the plants from growing past clearly demarcated borders and zones. They enact an amplification, an intensely managed microcosm of spatial control and curated tropicality.

The two passages that begin this prelude from geographer Rodolphe De Koninck and sociologist Chua Beng Huat underscore the sweeping changes and intense control over the lived spaces of the city-state that made a space like Gardens by the Bay possible. Their language suggests the underlying colonial histories of cartography and conquest that haunt modern methodologies of city planning in Singapore. They tie the visual and proleptic modes of cartography with lived realities.

With its long history as a colonial and transnational node for trade and finance in Southeast Asia, Singapore's urban spaces are direct realizations of over a century of maps, mapping, and the material productions of power

Fig. 2 The interior of the Cloud Forest conservatory, 2017. Credit: Joanne Leow.

Fig. 3 Rules and regulations in the Gardens by the Bay, 2015. Credit: Joanne Leow.

Prelude: From Blueprint to Eden

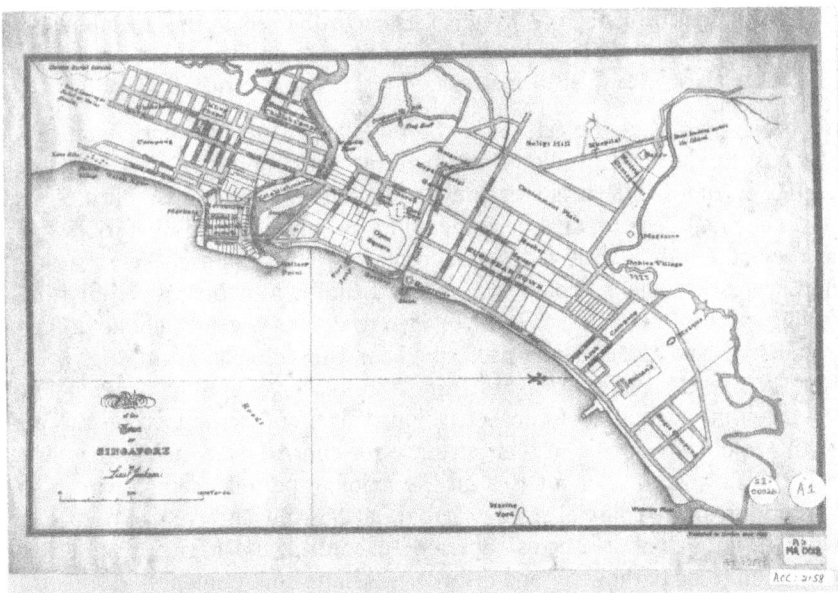

Fig. 4 Plan of the Town of Singapore by Lieutenant Philip Jackson, 1828. Credit: National Archives of Singapore. Used with permission.

that these maps have planned for. This process began with the 1822 Jackson Plan – a colonial map imposed on the new colony by Sir Stamford Raffles, who was "dissatisfied with the haphazard development" (Eng, 1992, 165). The plan "evinced a strict regularity in the layout of the streets and incorporated provisions for the separation of indigenous and European inhabitants along racial and social lines [...] with the aim of achieving political and economic control over the indigenous population" (Eng, 1992, 165).

This first plan, after over century of more ad hoc development under the colonial government, was followed by Master Plans in 1955 and 1958.[2] While the colonial government had neither the will nor the resources to implement complete control over its subjects, its ability to legislate development and its view of the rights colonial subjects should have in terms of their living spaces are crucial to understanding contemporary Singapore's urban planning history. In her seminal book on colonial Singapore, urban planning, and popular resistance, Brenda Yeoh argues that

> The colonial urban landscape is [...] not simply a palimpsest reflecting the impress of asymmetrical power relations undergirding colonial society, but also a terrain of discipline and resistance, a resource drawn upon by different groups and the contended object of everyday discourse in conflicts and

---

[2] See Yeoh (1996) and Eng (1992) for more detailed accounts of the colonial years of planning.

negotiations involving both colonialists and colonized groups. It embodies the negotiation of power between the dominant and the subordinated in society, each with their own version of reality and practice. (1996, 10)

Yeoh's study details the refusal of the population to cede spatial control of the city to the British colonizers, in terms very similar to de Certeausian tactics or James C. Scott's ideas on infrapolitics. Yeoh details their attempts to "drag their feet or dig their heels into requests for co-operation" even as they adopted "an outward attitude of apparent acquiescence (or at least non-protest)," where "compliance was withdrawn unobtrusively, without calling attention to the act itself or upsetting the larger symbolic order of dominance and dependence prescribed for the colonial world" (1996, 15). Her theorizations offer insights from a cultural geography "from below," documenting evidence of conflict, compromise, and resistance on the part of the colonized people in their struggle for control over their living space. Yeoh's study, even as it focuses on the colonial period, plainly evinces the limitations of the colonial state's cartographical view and control of the city, with its municipal strategies "devised to control and regulate what were perceived to be pathogenic and disorderly 'Asiatic environments'" (1996, 312). These strategies were essentially spatially based: surveillance, modification of built form, systemic regulation, increasing environment legibility, and so forth. The colonial maps and plans had clear impacts on everyday lives, social expression, and behavior and they provoked particular forms of resistance.

After 1958, this colonial legacy of the spatial relationship between state and citizen was cemented in a series of post-independence Master Plans that have mapped and zoned urban Singapore and Singaporean life in ways that cannot be underestimated.[3] Abidin Kusno sees this as a commitment to "an exceptional form of state modernism," a focus on "social engineering – with emphasis on cleanliness, the disciplining of the public, and the planning of the built environment" (2017, 234). Singapore's experiences of colonial and postcolonial mapping are more intense versions of a world that John Pickles describes where "cartographic institutions and practices have coded, decoded and recorded planetary, national and social spaces [...] They have respaced the geo-body. Maps and mapping precede the territory they 'represent'" (2004, 5).

In mapping out and manufacturing a "Tropical City of Excellence," the Singapore government has sustained colonial-era transformations and extreme recalibrations of the island's ecologies, even as it touts this development as a plan for sustainability and "greening." It is impossible to disambiguate colonial-era urban planning with the mass terraforming it entailed, as 95 percent of

---

3 The continuity with the colonial era is demonstrated by the preservation of the statue of Sir Stamford Raffles, who is seen as the legitimate founder of modern-day Singapore and how, for 2019, the Singaporean government mandated a set of celebrations for the 2019 bicentennial which ostensibly sought to commemorate the colonial founding of the city.

Singapore's indigenous flora was eliminated for plantations and development. In the second half of the twentieth century, the transformation of the island continued as the city "underwent a massive project to ensure the presence of vegetation throughout the island that reflected the tropical fecundity of much of Southeast Asia combined with the planning of the modern developmental state" (Barnard and Heng, 2014, 282). By 2011, botanists estimated that some 56 percent of the island was covered in some form of vegetation, about half of it being actively managed (Yee et al., 2011, 205). Singapore's colonial and (post) colonial development with its extensive land reclamation (the island increased its territory by 25 percent) and construction has eliminated virgin coastlines and forests both in Singapore and in the region.

This destructive and wholly unsustainable development has been funded in part by money derived from oil refining, and has been disguised and camouflaged by the construction of a controlled and engineered tropicality throughout the island. Historians Timothy P. Barnard and Corinne Heng argue that nature in Singapore has been "contained, discipline and manipulated to a point that conservation and state control have become one and the same. Nature has become a human construct" (2014, 283). The World Wildlife Foundation's *Living Planet Report* (2014) noted that Singapore had the seventh highest per capita ecological footprint in the world – no small feat for such a tiny island state but a clear reflection of the prodigious resources it takes to sustain the air-conditioned, manicured spaces of the city. Singapore's reputation as an ecologically friendly city, per the official narrative, is predicated on the disappearance of its own native coastal wetland ecologies, the denuding of its neighbors' beaches and river estuaries, and the exploitation of migrant labor.

Many of the dramatic (post)colonial transformations were helmed by the founding prime minister and "gardener in chief" Lee Kuan Yew, who deemed this necessary "to distinguish Singapore from other Third World Countries" by transforming it into a "tropical garden city" that met "First World Standards" (Lee, 2000, 175). Lee's vision of a tropical garden city was an authoritarian fantasy of a "clean and green Singapore" (Lee, 2000, 173), in effect marrying the lushness of an ideal tropics with the purity and orderliness of a regimented and regulated society. A corollary to urban planning and zoning, the tropicalization of Singapore's built environment was directly linked to Lee's mission to cultivate the populace itself. As he saw it, the frenzied planting of millions of trees, palms, and shrubs was part of a strategy to educate and exhort the populace to self-regulate while they "legislated to punish the willful minority" (Lee, 2000, 184). In his 1995 speech for the opening of the National Orchid Garden, the man himself opined: "Singapore today is a verdant city, where abundant greenery softens the landscape. This was no accident of nature. It is the result of a deliberate 30-year policy, which required political will and sustained effort to carry out" (Lee, 1995).

Infrastructure and planning in Singapore are thus central to not only its national project but to the core message and tenets of the ruling People's

Action Party (PAP). Jini Kim Watson argues that these projects make the authoritarian state's success legible to its population and other countries:

> The national scale of the built environment's reconstruction allows the PAP's commitment to the national project to be read symbolically and internalized by the population. Such "powerful signs" also signify the path of Singapore's future through the assumption of consent, that is, the population's desire for freedom through material improvement. (2008, 696)

With the construction of ever more ostentatious developments on seemingly virgin, new land, the significance of infrastructure as emblem, message, and material promise of authoritarian rule in Singapore has become almost completely inextricable from national myth.

In a speech at the opening of the state's latest techno-botanical project, the US$1.25 billion glass-domed shopping mall named Jewel at Changi Airport, featuring the world's largest indoor waterfall and imported flora, Prime Minister Lee Hsien Loong pointed out that remarking on infrastructure projects in his speeches was not "too cold, impersonal." He said that he:

> wanted Singaporeans to understand that Jewel and Changi Airport were not only an infrastructure story. Instead, they represented an idea; they were a symbol. They epitomized how Singapore, here, we must dream boldly to create possibilities for ourselves. It was an act of faith to believe that Changi could do this, and that Singaporeans, working together, could make amazing things happen. (2019b)

Lee's speech is characteristic of how the authoritarian People's Action Party government's ideologies of relentless development and pragmatism have produced a dominant narrative where, for both individuals and larger society, "economic success has become the emblem of the nation" (Chua, 2011, 31).

Yet one might ask, Whom this economic success is for and to what end? Away from obvious examples like Gardens by the Bay or the Changi Jewel, Singapore's much-lauded standardized housing projects belie the tensions, inequalities, and panoptic suppression that exist to keep its landscapes and citizens in check. Gavin Shatkin points out to other states who would adopt the real Singapore model as their goal that this might mean a lot more even than a ruthlessly centralized urbanization plan:

> While many of Singapore's achievements in the areas of economic growth and provision of basic needs have been laudable, the consequences of the means through which these achievements have been realized raise pressing questions. Singapore's transformation has been premised on the following: the subjugation and co-optation of civil society to the interests of the state; the severe curtailment of alternative claims to urban space outside of the state and the corporate economy; the imposition of a comprehensive regime of state social control; the assertion of state hegemony in determining the aesthetic and functional form of the city; and the bending of the meaning of history and culture to the interests of the state. (2014, 135)

Prelude: From Blueprint to Eden

The control of material, symbolic, and discursive spaces in Singapore is inextricably linked in the way the state exercises its power. Dissenting literary, filmic, and artistic texts that seek to complicate and challenge the overly one-dimensional narratives and authoritarian laws dispensed by the state have been the most vulnerable to the long arm of censorship and oversight.

I begin with Gardens by the Bay, its genesis in authoritarian state planning, and its materialization through literal terraforming to demonstrate the intense connections between cartographical control and material reality in Singapore. A specific vision of Singapore, linked to its colonial past, has become so powerful that it is capable of altering the territorial boundaries of the island state. In charting a course for its spaces, the (post)colonial Singaporean state has engineered history, society, and its future. The carefully pruned urban spaces are a reflection of planning and control, and one with the state's attempts to quell dissent in bodies or artistic expressions. The pressure of this power and rigidity is not often outwardly visible. The objective of this book is to carefully pierce this cartographical vision by examining a series of counter-cartographical texts: literature, artwork, films, and cultural artifacts. This assemblage of texts attempts, as I do, to read Singapore otherwise.

Introduction

> Triangulation by triangulation, war by war, treaty by treaty, the alignment of map and power proceeded.
>
> (Benedict Anderson, *Imagined Communities: Reflections on the Origin and Spread of Nationalism*, 2016, 173)

Of Maps and Other Fictions

What might it mean to read against the mapped spaces of our time? To attempt to read against what Benedict Anderson has seen as an alignment of cartography and power? In a moment where we take for granted the acceleration and intensification of maps and mapping, of being able to geolocate ourselves and all our desired places, of having a wholly mapped view of the cities and spaces around us, this book argues for reading other texts that function in opposition to fixed conceptions of space. From colonial times, the advent, evolution, and entrenchment of mapping and maps have fundamentally altered the ways in which we inhabit and produce space. From city master plans to aerial views of cities as targets, from blueprints of buildings to seeing ourselves as moving dots on our phones – maps elide, misplace, or erase even as they seek totalities both spatial and temporal.

Mapping as an epistemology, as a way of ordering and making sense of space, has long been critiqued for its colonial associations of exploring, fixing, categorizing, and totalizing. For Walter D. Mignolo and Madina V. Tlostanova, "the modern foundation of knowledge is territorial and imperial," a history that arises from and is illustrated by the world map drawn by Gerardus Mercator and Johannes Ortelius in the sixteenth century that created "a zero point of observation and of knowledge: a perspective that denied all other perspectives" (2006, 205, 206). In *Imagined Communities*, Anderson points to

John Harrison's 1761 invention of the chronometer and the precise calculation of longitudes as an event that fundamentally altered the ways in which we conceive of space. Michel de Certeau sees the map as producing "the erasure of the itineraries" forming "the tableau of a 'state' of geographical knowledge" without acknowledging the multiple historical journeys and trajectories "the operations of which it is the result or the necessary condition" (2002, 121). Henri Lefebvre discusses the inadequacies of using just one or even a few maps to represent social space, coming to the conclusion that the mutable multidimensional, multi-perspectival, and multi-scalar aspects of this space mean that we are confronted with "a sort of instant infinity" (1991, 85). Map historian and geographer J.B. Harley has famously noted how

> Maps as an impersonal type of knowledge tend to "desocialise" the territory they represent. They foster the notion of a socially empty space. The abstract quality of the map, embodied as much in the lines of a fifteenth-yqcentury Ptolemaic projection as in the contemporary images of computer cartography, lessens the burden of conscience about people in the landscape. Decisions about the exercise of power are removed from the realm of immediate face-to-face contacts. (1988, 303)

More than ever now, we view our world as one of maps and mapping. With the advent and now ubiquity of technologies like Google Maps, the spaces we inhabit are inevitably overlaid and permeated with our interactions with maps on our computers, smartphones, and other devices. Navigating between two points on a map becomes an exercise of plotting a virtual route on a material one, with the former often preceding and superseding the latter. The surfeit of information that maps *can* provide us necessarily prescribes the ways in which we understand and interact with space. Their technological interpellation of our spatial existence has fundamentally altered our conceptions of space.

Online mapping tools like the ubiquitous Google Maps have been heralded as the democratization of cartography, the devolution of cartography from its history of colonialism. Proponents of these forms of participatory cartographies have credited them with creating a kind of "sprawling, networked atlas – a 'geoweb' that's expanding so quickly its outer edges are impossible to pin down" (Ratliff, 2007, 156). What this rush to embrace new mapping tools fails to consider is the continuing, unspoken acceptance of the logic and validity of maps and their new use in technologies of commercialization and commodification. Jeremy W. Crampton reminds us that though cartography has "been slipping from the control of the powerful elites that have exercised dominance over it for several hundred years," this does not mean that we can move beyond a critique of these maps as situated "within specific relations of power and not as neutral scientific documents" (2006, 12). The pervasive nature of digital maps and technologies like "street view" recalls Umberto Eco's "On the Impossibility of Drawing a Map of the Empire on a Scale of 1 to 1," which speculates on the impractical, absurd, and dangerous effects of constructing a map that would overlay the territory of the Empire. This map, Eco writes, would be "endowed with self-awareness [...] and would itself become the empire" (1994, 106). The conceit of this absurdist essay reminds us of the power of constructed nature of maps despite their inability to contain the evolving complexities of geographical and social space. More crucially, Eco points out that ever-present, ever-changing, inevitable gap between the map and mapped space.

In its abstract, philosophical manner, Eco's essay reveals the impossibility of universal control through a map. But beyond this conception of the inevitable failure of mapping, *Counter-Cartographies* seeks to understand how we locate ourselves through specific encounters with the planned spaces of the (post)colonial city and its cultural texts. My work begins with Lefebvre's injunction that there are intimate relationships between spatial practice, represented space, and representational space. Lefebvre theorizes that the production of space occurs through "the dialectical relationship which exists within the triad of the perceived, the conceived, and the lived" (1991, 39). His conception of space creates significant equivalences of the material, the textual, and the symbolic. In the context of urban spaces like Singapore, Lefebvre would likely warn us not to discount both "representations of space," which "intervene in and modify spatial *textures*," and "representational space" which "embraces the loci of passion, of action and of lived situations" (1991, 42; emphasis original). In other words, unmappable notions of affect, symbolism, haunting, and alternate futures must be considered even in mapped space. The texts that I consider in this book provide ways to locate the (post)colonial self and community despite the imposition of maps and mapping. The specific acts of cultural and spatial analysis, and close reading that I undertake transform these artistic and literary works into an active repository for other ways of understanding lived space. What is lost in translation between our lives and our maps? How can we better inhabit (post)colonial spaces in ways that remain attentive to how generations of colonial and (post)colonial planners have plotted power, racialization, inequity, and amnesia into reality? How might acts of *excavation, circumvention, wayfinding,* and *confabulation* relate to the practice of attentive cultural analysis and close reading?

With these questions in mind, we are reminded that the origin of today's "street views" are the colonial maps that were often prepared for the exercise of spatialized power over a colonized space. Streets, buildings, town squares, and other racially segregated spaces of a colonial settlement often existed first as fictions in maps before being built and enforced. For instance, the grid-like streets in colonial port cities in North America, Africa, the Caribbean, India, and other parts of Southeast Asia are clear manifestations of the material legacies of colonial desires for maximum spatial efficiency with regards to the mobility of raw materials, goods, and colonial subjects. Indeed, the idea of mapping is inseparable from planning and planned space. It is, further, a manifestation of the impulse to govern, regulate, discipline, and enforce space. James C. Scott points out that in authoritarian states obsessed with the legibility of their societies and the ideology of high modernist planning, maps "would enable much of the reality they depicted to be remade" (1998, 3). This book arises from the need to consider the legacies of these early colonial maps, their modern and contemporary iterations in state planning, and their ongoing presences in our spatial lives. These maps are *fictions* of coloniality and their triangulations, geometrical grids, and conceptions of space are aligned with the mapmakers, and those who would experiment within and enforce their boundaries.

In the specific context of Southeast Asia, Ryan Bishop, John Phillips, and Wei Wei Yeo point out that

> Colonial urban space (from the beginning global) has been used in different ways as space for urban experimentation. Economic and military uses involve experiments with civilian targeting, riot control, penalization, and policing. Southeast Asia begins to look like an intense and multidisciplinary laboratory in which some of the great developments of urban modernity (in anthropology, technology, visual culture, and mass media not least) were developed, to be returned to European and American urban state centers, often in unexpected ways. (2003, 23)

While mapmaking and mapped power was implemented by the metropole in the colonies, Bishop et al. point out that this power evolved in the uncertainty of the urban laboratory that was Southeast Asia and most intensely in the crown colony of Singapore. These spatial experiments in colonized space, all inextricably tied to the mapping and remapping of its space through various disciplines and technologies, in turn influenced city planning and discipline in Europe and North America. Mapping as an epistemology has ontological and transnational consequences.

Mapped Singapore

In Singapore, the spatialization of a (post)colonial authoritarianism is most evident in the Singapore Master Plan, which is online and hyperlinked down to each city lot. The plan is a contemporary record of a city planned from the colonial government to its contemporary authoritarian government, a document of state capitalism and biopolitical regulation. The map is predicated on the Land Acquisition Act of 1966, directly descended from the colonial Land Acquisition Ordinance of 1920. The former gives the Singaporean state the power of compulsory land acquisition in the name of public development while further regulating the amount of compensation to landowners. By 1985, the government owned 76.2 percent of the land in Singapore which enabled it to bypass any contestations of how the land should be developed. The Act gives the government the "power to enter and survey" – physical acts that enable the material alteration of the land to be acquired – even before it exercises the "power to take possession."[1] The entire process of (post)colonial development in Singapore follows David Harvey's vision of the urban process under capitalism, one of "displacement and dispossession" (1997, 18), that results in dramatic transformations of lives and values. If, as Harvey argues, "in making the city, man has remade himself" (2008), what kinds of cities and populations do authoritarian states produce?

Cartography in Singapore became ever more detailed and controlling when the post-independence (1965) ruling party, the People's Action Party (PAP), implemented widespread city planning that zoned and regulated every plot of land on the island for the purposes of economic efficiency and social control. This involved paradoxical issues of scale: even as the government took control of ever larger swathes of land, it micro-managed them in ever smaller plots and zones. Shatkin terms this the ultimate success in "urban planning under state capitalism" (2014, 116). The island state's extensive and comprehensive urban redevelopment program was most famously critiqued by the architect Rem Koolhaas, who controversially called the city state "the apotheosis of tabula rasa" (1995, 1031) – what he deemed as a blank slate for city planners and politicians. However, this is a critique that elides much of the complex histories and trajectories that Singapore is enmeshed in and produced by.

A far more useful and less hyperbolic guide to the city's transformations comes from the lesser-known work of De Koninck, Julie Drolet, Marc Girard, and Pham Thanh Hai. In three, consistently updated editions in 1992, 2008, and 2017, De Koninck and his collaborators produced a series of atlases documenting the extreme changes in Singapore's physical, social, and political landscapes. An extraordinary effort that belies Koolhaas's attempt to cast Singapore as simply a *tabula rasa*, the work of De Koninck illustrates the spatial and symbolic constructions of Singapore's pragmatic, modernizing statecraft in its attempt to "maximize the value creation from [the] land" (Economic Review Committee, 2003, 105). By examining selected facets of Singapore's development and providing a series of historical and contemporary maps, De Koninck's most recent atlas, *Singapore's Permanent Territorial Revolution* (2017), deconstructs the levels and processes of the island state's cartographic control of its territory. Further,

---

[1] Even before the land is acquired from a landowner or squatter, the Act is fairly detailed about the state's right to "mark" the land and render it legible for cartographical surveillance. The state can: "(a) enter upon and survey and take levels of any land in that locality; (b) dig or bore into the soil; (c) do all other acts necessary to ascertain whether the land is suitable for such purpose; (d) set out the boundaries of the land proposed to be taken and the intended line of the work, if any, proposed thereon; (e) mark those levels, boundaries and line by placing marks and cutting trenches; and (f) cut down and clear away any standing crop, fence or jungle, where otherwise the survey cannot be completed, the levels taken or the boundaries or line of the work marked" (Land Acquisition Act, Chapter 152; original enactment: Act 41 of 1966; revised edition 1985 (30 March 1987)).

Fig. 5 Photograph of a detail from Singapore's Master Plan at the Singapore City Gallery, 2018. Credit: Joanne Leow.

by juxtaposing the 2015 Land Use map at the end of the atlas with the chronological maps in the earlier chapters of the book concerned with Singapore's wholesale alterations of topography, ecology, demography, production, circulation, control, and entertainment, De Koninck lay bare the instability between map as fiction and map as record. It is by making Singapore legible that the state has been able to refashion it and control its spaces and population. De Koninck muses that the "territorial alienation" among Singaporeans and other residents may contribute to political resignation, since "permanent and unquestionable remoulding of individual and communal territorial markers is a tool of political control" (2017, 133).

This legal control over land in Singapore is manifest in the basic textual elements of the urban environment: signage that exhorts citizens to not litter, not smoke, not loiter, and so forth are ubiquitous. Sociologist Daniel Goh points out that in Singapore, "the state is everywhere in the social life of the country. Its commandments are interpellations of the social … the commandments are written into the urban fabric" (2015, 219). He pessimistically declares,

> In all my attempts to study Singapore society […] I end up facing the state's knowing pronouncements and rationalizations echoing through the symbolic and discursive materials *and material space itself*. And when I focus on the state and its archive, I end up looking at society and all its cultural exuberance transcribed, rationalized, *and spatialized*. (2015, 219, emphasis original)

It is this confluence of the symbolic, discursive, textual, and material spaces that is central to my theorizations on how the *pressure* of mapped space impinges on the lives and cultural productions of Singaporeans.

This mapped space translates into a controlled living environment for its inhabitants: post-land acquisition, Singapore is one of few countries in having rehoused almost its entire population (over 80 percent) in neat, Le Corbusier-inspired public housing flats. The government makes these flats available based on racial quotas, with heterosexual families given priority. As Lefebvre points out, "housing is the guarantee of reproductivity, be it biological, social or political [...] housing under the control of a state which oversees both production and production, refers us [...] to the family unit and biological reproduction" (1991, 232). These zoning policies have affected the vast majority of the country's population, particularly the approximately 82 percent who live in public Housing Development Board (HDB) flats. A succession of colonial and post-independence governmental agencies has zoned and rezoned the entirety of the island. There was a wholesale clearance of old rundown buildings and slums post-independence, and the state oversaw the construction of countless blocks of modernist multistory housing, factories, and shopping centers.[2]

As Loh Kah Seng (2013) and Chua Beng Huat (1995) have demonstrated, housing policy is an instructive way to consider how spatial politics in the country enables the government to consolidate its socio-economic power in the material aspects of its citizens' lives. Chua argues that the policy of standardized public housing that emphasizes homeownership[3] "contributes to transforming and disciplining the population into an industrial labor force [...] The visual homogeneity of the physical environment of public housing estates [...] hides the exclusion of the socially and economically disadvantaged Singaporeans who are the 'collateral failures' of rapid capitalist economic development" (1995, 45, 46). In her study of low-income households in Singapore, Teo You Yenn notes how they appear to be blended into middle-income neighborhoods in public housing but with key differences in the architectures of density for their rental flats. Teo points out that "It may be true that looking from afar Singapore does not have the housing problems that other cities do. But people don't live as if they are looking from afar or

---

2 Historian Loh Kah Seng complicates the governing PAP's dominant narrative that champions this urban redevelopment as a roaring success and evidence of Singapore's viability as a model for the rest of the developing world. Parsing the 1961 Bukit Ho Swee fire, which destroyed a squatter area leaving it ready for urban redevelopment, Loh reads the management of this narrative as one that produces the formal structures of the state and, consequently, "citizens" for the newly postcolonial Singapore. Loh argues that "kampongs" (villages) deemed slums by the authorities were "an alternative form of modernity" that was pitted against the "creation of a well-planned city of public housing estates" (2013, 2) and that "squatters were not inert, as depicted, but progressive and urbanised, and with effective social autonomy" (2013, 2). Thus, the clearance of these "slums" was also the destruction of alternative forms of modernity.

3 Or rather a 99-year lease. See Chua (1997).

above. We live every day, bodily realities. Inequality is experienced in the interior of hours and minutes of a day" (2018, 63). In effect, the standardized cityscapes of the suburban areas of Singapore with their homogeneous, model-like exteriors belie sinister social outcomes. This pragmatic and overdetermined view of the island has consequences that reach far beyond the superficial aspects of the built environment. Indeed, the very form of the built environment enables economic, social, racialized, and behavioral controls. Shatkin notes how Singapore's public housing enables the state to be involved in "a constant process of reengineering politics, society, culture, and identity" (2014, 126). This is achieved through "the design of the new towns, which have developed around the central principle of neutralizing urban space through the elimination of social claims to space outside of those mandated by the plan" (Shatkin, 2014, 127). In effect, the void decks and the streets are forms of public space that are too open to appropriation and have been de-emphasized in lieu of shopping malls and self-contained hawker centers (Shatkin, 2014, 127).

In visual and architectural contrast to these "heartland" estates are the spectacular downtown developments on reclaimed land that include a Moshe Safdie-designed casino, the world's largest cooled conservatories for temperate plants, and a gleaming financial district. This spatial narrative highlights the government's architectural conservation efforts – primarily for touristic consumption, and the protection of Singapore's historical assets (as a form of cultural investment). While specific swathes of the island have been redeveloped as densely populated residential areas to house its burgeoning workforce to drive economic growth, "urban renewal" has been emphasized in the downtown core.

The colonial legacies of this control are visible in the skyline itself. A great deal of the architecture of the old British colonial center of the city was left untouched by the government's policies of urban redevelopment. In selectively choosing which old buildings were to be preserved and which were to be demolished, Singapore's planners have inscribed in the city skyline a history that privileges official power over that of community-based life. Further, as Ryan Bishop, John Phillips, and Wei-Wei Yeo note, these very same colonial buildings have been exploited by capitalist ventures specifically for their commodified historic function:

> Singapore flaunts its colonial past and postcolonial/global present through the historical maintenance of these buildings' facades. The act of renovation preserves the colonial shell of the building while reworking the buildings from the foundation up to better suit contemporary use, whether as luxury hotel, bank, government building, or restaurant. Readable in the buildings, then, is a continuation, perpetuation, and multiplication of colonial richness into the present global order, while also using the striking juxtaposition of colonial buildings and modernist high-rise buildings to reveal a specific continuum and continuity. (2004, 2)

In this way, Singapore's urban planning produces a mapped city as a legible text, with obvious and fixed landmarks of power and history. Experiencing the city through sanctioned channels means being party to a schematized way of perceiving, conceiving, and producing city space. The contemporary uses of colonial buildings are tied with capitalist or governing functions whether "luxury hotel, bank, government building, or restaurant." Even the museums, art galleries, and performance spaces that have been housed in these former colonial buildings are part of a complex propagation of state versions of history and historicity. The old Parliament House becomes a multidisciplinary art and film space and the Supreme Court the National Art Gallery. The new versions of these seats of authoritarian power are constructed in designs that are an amalgamation of modernist, brutalist, and neoclassical styles. Architectural and spatial "continuity" in this context is really a form of neocolonialism that is geared towards "a mode of attracting global capital to Singapore" (Bishop et al., 2004, 2).

These developments only accelerated in the new millennium, the rapid construction of an entirely new downtown quarter on reclaimed land south of its original business district has added ever-new considerations to anyone reading Singapore as text. The $5.7 billion Marina Bay Sands project was designed by celebrated architect Moshe Safdie, funded by multinational gambling consortium the Las Vegas Sands Corporation, and built at great human cost by exploited laborers from Singapore's poorer regional neighbors.[4] Funded in part by the government and by projected revenues from newly built casinos in "Integrated Resorts," the Marina Bay area has been transformed from an empty patch of reclaimed land to a spectacular iconic waterfront geared to attract tourists and investors. In a more general critique of the trend towards "iconic architecture" in Asia, William S.W. Lim posits that "the present rush of trading in iconic architecture is doomed to fail, as their fashionable theme-park images are full of sound and fury, but signifying nothing" (2011, 30). Architect Pauline Ang points out the disturbing fact that "the most 'imageable' part of the city is now a casino and luxury hotel" (2011). Even more troubling is that the project has created fundamentally elitist, stratified urban spaces while seeking to redefine the city-state. The panoramic and engineered view of Singapore that it offers is precisely one of a spectacular, planned city cartography. Numerous publicity shots from the top of the Marina Bay Sands hotel, from its one hectare SkyPark and infinity swimming pool, attest to its iconic nature. Further, Safdie's press release claims that the SkyPark "celebrates the notion of the Garden City that has been the

---

4 Safdie's euphoric press release posits that "Marina Bay Sands is really more than a building project, it is a microcosm of a city rooted in Singapore's culture, climate, and contemporary life. Our challenge was to create a vital public place at the district-urban scale, in other words, to address the issue of megascale and invent an urban landscape that would work at the human scale."

underpinning of Singapore's urban design strategy" (2011) – suggesting that the project itself is a microcosm of the sweeping developments in the city. These new developments are ostentatious manifestations of global capital, expertise, and migrant labor.

In a metropolis where space is at a premium and capitalist time is of the essence, hyper-mapped Singapore is a beacon of (post)colonial success. The material and cultural spaces of Singapore represent an exemplary case study for the efficacy of colonial and nationalist city planning. Writing of Singapore's numerous long-term national projects including land reclamation, public housing, industrial and petrochemical hubs, and one of the world's busiest airports, Watson posits that "what is significant is the unparalleled capacity of the Singaporean government to produce and manage space, enabled by its 'single layer' of government combining city, region, and state levels" (2016, 546). Singapore's exceptionalism has implications that range beyond its narrow borders: it is often cited as an "aspirational city for the Global South" (Watson, 2016, 543), a "model" (Chua, 2011, 29) for other cities in developing nations. The "formula" for its success has been attempted in sites as diverse as Tianjin, Bangalore, Kigali, and Sao Paulo.[5]

Since the Malayan Emergency and its forced separation from a merger with its larger neighbor, Malaysia, Singapore has been in a constant state of exception – in his memoirs, Lee Kuan Yew makes a convincing case for the government's siege mentality:

> We faced tremendous odds with an improbable chance of survival. Singapore was not a natural country but man-made, a trading post the British had developed into a nodal point in their worldwide maritime empire. We inherited the island without its hinterland, a heart without a body. (2000, 3)

These "threats" to and "odds" against Singapore's survival have justified the authoritarian government that has been in power since its independence. Giorgio Agamben theorizes that a state of exception enables the existence of the modern totalitarian state, "of a legal civil war that allows for the physical elimination not only of political adversaries but of entire categories of citizens who for some reason cannot be integrated into the political system" (2005, 2). This state of exception made it possible to silence dissident voices through both legal and political means, but further to foster the production of what Lefebvre would call "abstract space" and a more compliant population. This extends as well to the very ecologies of the island, as land, flora, and

---

5 Chye (2018) notes how authorities from various states have used Singapore's rhetoric of top-down urban planning and direct references to Singapore itself as a way to justify deeply centralized, cartographically minded, high modernist planning. The Singapore Cooperation Enterprise's website, he points out, "reveals the international scope of the city-state's developmental footprint." See sce.org.sg/our-reach.aspx.

water are completely altered by development (even as these are concealed by tropical plantings).

As Lefebvre posits, this abstract space is "a product of violence and war, it is political; instituted by a state, it is institutional [...] with space performing the function of a plane, a bulldozer or a tank" (1991, 285). Indeed, for the purposes of my study, I have found it invaluable to draw clear connections with colonial and colonized space and Lefebvre's notion of abstract space. Reading Lefebvre in the context of (post)colonial Singapore, one cannot help but see abstract space made flesh, since it has

> homogeneity as its goal, its orientation, its "lens". And, indeed it renders homogeneous. But in itself it is multiform. Its geometric and visual formants are complementary in their antithesis. They are different ways of achieving the same outcome: the reduction of the "real", on the one hand, to a "plan" existing in a void and endowed with no other qualities, and on the other hand, to the flatness of a mirror, of an image, of pure spectacle under an absolutely cold gaze. (1991, 287)

In other words, abstract space is most keenly felt in authoritarian cartography in control and homogenization through mapping. In Singapore's case, this control extends not just to its material and natural spaces but to the psychological and social manipulation of its inhabitants. Scott similarly points out that "a prostrate civil society that lacks the capacity to resist these plans" is essential to the success of the "*imperialism* of high-modernist, planned social order" (1998, 5, 6, emphasis original). He, as do I, points out that it is important not to make a totalizing case against bureaucratic planning or high-modernist ideology. Where Scott makes an argument for "the necessary role of local knowledge and know-how" (1998, 6), I turn to other questions: What kind of art and culture can be made in such a space? How do they resist co-optation and censorship? What insights can they give us into modes of witnessing and resisting such authoritarian productions of space?

"You are here"

As a literary scholar born, raised, and partly educated in (post)colonial Singapore, these historical, imperial, and contemporary connections are no more evident to me than during a visit to the country's City Gallery. Housed in the first three floors of the Urban Redevelopment Authority building in downtown Singapore, the gallery is an urban planning visitors center in a (post)colony which flaunts a through line from the colonial city planning of the nineteenth century to the hyperlinked maps of the twenty-first. Recalling and challenging Eco, a visit to the urban planning nerve center of what *The Economist* has called the "exception" of Singapore leaves the visitor with the uncanny possibility of being subsumed into a city model as map *par excellence* ("Singapore Exception," 2015). The first encounter with a full-scale, regularly

Fig. 6 Photograph of a detail from the Central Area Model at the Singapore City Gallery, 2018. Credit: Joanne Leow.

updated model of the island implicates the viewer with a *mise-en-abyme* sign that notes "You are here."

Collapsing the boundaries between mapped space and the material space of the gallery in the city, the sign "You are here" speaks to one of this book's central concerns: that of locating the self and community as enmeshed within the politics and mechanisms of planned spaces. Eco points out the numerous paradoxes in attempts to draw and install a map that would perfectly represent the territory, since "at the moment the map is realized, the empire becomes unreproducible" (1994, 106) for the map itself alters the city by its very existence. For *Counter-Cartographies*, that gap between maps as powerful representations of space and lived experience in mapped space is a liminal place into which the fictional, the literary, and the imagined overlap and intersect with the material.

The Arts in Singapore: Spatial Control, Co-optation, and Censorship

In the latter part of the twentieth century, a crucial part of Singapore's transformation into a successful global city has been its decision to treat the arts as a significant component of its economic development. The commercialization and commodification of Singapore's arts scene were central to these efforts.[6] The multi-million-dollar investments in performing venues,

---

6 Angelia Poon notes that "while the Arts was previously viewed in the immediate post-Independence period as a 'luxury' that the Singapore nation, strenuously

galleries, museums, festivals, biennales, and grants began in the 1980s, and in 1999, a series of "Master Plans" for the arts and the "creative industries" were conceived and implemented. A corollary to the Master Concept Plans which attempt to rationalize, regulate, and zone the physical space of Singapore, the Renaissance City Plans were "developed to coordinate the strategies in the arts and culture sector to prepare Singapore for the transition from an industrial to a knowledge economy" (Kong, 2012, 287). In essence, with its stated goal of developing "cultural 'software' – capabilities, audiences and vibrancy" (Arts and Heritage Development Division, 2008, 6), the plan sought to map out Singapore's social and artistic spaces, to designate specific material spaces for artistic and cultural expression, to use funding to develop or stunt particular modes of artistic creation, and to produce "transnational" spaces in arts festivals that were designed to position Singapore as a regional and global hub for the arts.

In a system enamored of statistics and figures, these measures produced quantifiable successes. The metrics used to measure the "success" of these ventures are firmly grounded "in terms of consumption": attendance and visitorship, which showed major gains between 2007 and 2010 (Kong, 2012). Between 1990 and 2008 there was a "veritable explosion in writing across all three genres [fiction, poetry, and drama] in a mere eighteen years" (Poon, 2009, 359). While the advent of smaller presses like Ethos Books and Epigram Books has enabled the country's literary scene to become more diverse and, in some cases, more critical of the state's policies, literary output, boosted by government grants and campaigns like #buysinglit and the Golden Point Awards, has not been immune from the state's planning schemes.

In the late twentieth and early twenty-first century, Singaporean art, literature, and film continue to wrestle with the colonial legacies and (post) colonial practices of urban control, redevelopment, and regulation. The contemporary Singaporean state, post-independence, has become still more intolerant of forms of artistic dissent even as it seeks to foster what it calls the "creative industries." As many scholars have pointed out, cultural and artistic production was at first deemed a "luxury we cannot afford" in the early years of nation-building in Singapore. This evolved with the country's bid to transform itself from a "survivalist and developmental state into a creative global city" (Tan, 2016, 235). Even as it appears that more material and social spaces for the arts have been fostered and encouraged by the state, the latter's control of these designated spaces has been consistently authoritarian since the period immediately following independence. Major acts of censorship and harassment of the artistic community include the imprisonment of Chinese-language theater practitioners, artists, and intellectuals in the '60s and '70s,

---

committed to economic development and industrialization, could not afford to be distracted by, it now represented a potentially lucrative commodity around which an industry could be cultivated" (2009, 361).

Operation Spectrum which saw members of the theater group The Third Stage detained in 1987 accusing them of a "Marxist Conspiracy," and the decade-long ban of performance theater and forum theater from 1994.[7] The improvisational and spontaneous methods of performance and forum theater were obviously anathema to a state obsessed with spatial control. Social theater was seen as dangerous, since it transgressed the carefully drawn lines between political space and artistic space.

The level of control exerted over artistic performances is evident in the state's regulation of *where* art can be performed or exhibited, *which* words can be spoken in these spaces, and *who* can participate in these events. Theater scripts must still be submitted for vetting to the National Arts Council and the Public Entertainment Licensing Unit (a division of the Singapore Police Force), reflecting the extent of how public discourse is regulated within artistic spaces. Local writer and prolific playwright Alfian Sa'at intuits the violence of the regulation scheme as "the aggressor, a double-headed demon carrying two knives [...] the two knives not only symbolize a doubling of the arsenal but also the possibility of contingency. If one knife proves to be blunt, there is another one to inflict the wound" (2016, 167). The theater practitioner Paul Rae argues that censorship in Singapore enacts "a kind of phenomenological foreclosure: constraining some aspect of one's experience or interpretation of the world, and thereby of one's affective, embodied, sense of self" (2011, 119). Rae reflects on both the symbolic and material effects of this censorship – citing the fact that "interventions" by the state tend to occur late in the creative process, sometimes even after tickets for a performance have been sold. The effect is to isolate the artist "because when decisions that can directly affect one personally and materially are in the hands of a bureaucratic agency, the network of friends and colleagues one might ordinarily look to for support is essentially powerless" (2011, 119). This disempowerment and dispossession of the artist mirrors and amplifies the experience of the ordinary citizen whose everyday experiences are strictly regulated in the spaces of Singapore.

What can be marked, filmed, discussed, read, watched, and performed in Singapore has always been subject to severe restrictions, and *where* these activities can be performed has been circumscribed. The Public Entertainments and Meetings Act, first enacted in 1958 and revised in 2001, prohibits any public entertainment that is not "in an approved place" and "in accordance with a license issued by a Licensing Officer." Rae traces the establishment of this law not just to the Malayan Emergency which saw the enactment of numerous repressive laws in the name of security, but further again to the British colonial Theatre Ordinance of 1895. The state has used this law not

---

[7] See Peterson (2001), Chong (2012), and Kenneth Tan's numerous articles for detailed accounts of the suppression and resistance in the anglophone Singapore theater scene.

only to prevent performances from taking place (often at the last minute), but also to regulate where they can be performed to mitigate the effects of site-specific work.[8] Terence Chong (2010) argues that the PAP state has not scaled back its monopoly over power and control over the country's spaces. Chong draws a clear link between the state's control over artistic projects through funding, the encouragement of self-censorship, and regulation by proxy (usually a conservative element in society), and the ways in which it is always intent on forcefully quashing any form of civil disobedience, no matter how small.

Thus, even as the state attempts to "liberalize" to perform global norms of freedom of artistic expression and cultural vibrancy, its authoritarian tendencies mean that it continues to heavily regulate *all* forms of alternate space-making whether artistic, cultural, or civil. Kenneth Tan marks out how the state seeks a calibration of its control – allowing certain dissident artistic practices that do not overtly contest the hegemony of the official narrative, commodifying nostalgia to build an affective citizenry and, more chillingly, maintaining "an interdependent relationship with filmmakers in such a way as to be able to harness these transgressive instincts for critical acclaim" (2016, 245).[9] The state-based capitalist sponsorship of the arts opens the possibilities of a passive censorship where projects deemed unsuitable (or unprofitable, or both) are simply not funded or have their funding withdrawn. These range from entire theater groups like WildRice! in 2010 to individual authors like Sonny Liew and Jeremy Tiang whose work touches on sensitive subjects.[10] There is also a risk that works of art can be exploited as subtle forms of state propaganda.[11]

---

8 See Rae (2011) for a detailed examination of the intricacies of the Act and for more examples of its implementation and implications.
9 For a useful and succinct account of state censorship, instrumentalized nostalgia, and "The Singapore Story," see Tan (2016).
10 See Valles (2012) for an overview of government policies regarding the arts. He argues that there is "some tension in creative production, primarily between the Singapore-based artists' desire for individuality and otherness on the one hand and the drive toward conformity with state policies or Western market expectations on the other" (198).
11 Khoo (2013) interrogates the increasingly nostalgic and sentimental representations of public housing estates in government-funded Singapore cinema and multimedia projects, aligning them with the state's nationalist agenda. She points out that even ostensibly affective, emotionally complex projects like *Civic Life* must be "contextualized within [a] greater state discourse that produces affective and effective neoliberal citizens" (107) and was only allowed because it was not "perceived as threatening to the state" (108). Khoo argues, it is especially works like *Civic Life* and director Royston Tan's series of nostalgic films with what she calls their "popular aesthetics of affect and nostalgia" (107) that fit "an agenda to use affect in combination with economics to develop a stronger sense of civic nationalism" (107).

Tracing a legal history of various other controls in her book *Authoritarian Rule of Law: Legislation, Discourse and Legitimacy in Singapore* (2012), Jothie Rajah turns to the history of authoritarian lawmaking and legal precedents, among other methods, to convincingly argue that the Singaporean state has repeatedly used legal means in order to close down material and textual spaces for dissent, artistic and political.[12] These methods include detaining dissidents without trial, punishing citizens for marking public spaces, and restricting the freedom to assemble. The state specifically targeted civil society bodies like the press and the legal profession with legislation to prevent them from participating in the political life of the state. Rajah explicitly ties language to this implementation of authoritarian rule:

> Citizens are subordinated when the state denies the polysemantic capacity of language and attributes singular meanings to terms it defines, not within legislation, but through public discourse ... the state employs its hegemonic dominance of the public domain to assign meaning to opaque legislative text. This practice inherently subordinates citizens because it unilaterally excludes other possible meanings ... This subordination encloses citizens in a discursive world in which the state is the only social actor empowered to engage in interpretation, rendering citizens silent, acquiescent receptors of state meaning-making. (2012, 283)

The closing down of semantic and discursive spaces here is directly linked to the ways in which the authoritarian state maps out the spaces for acceptable and unacceptable behavior for its citizens – a map that is at once material and discursive, affecting almost every aspect of their lives, from housing to leisure, entertainment, arts, culture, and the law.

In the twenty-first century, the state has updated its laws to keep pace with new technologies that have enabled a wider dissemination of potentially "subversive" content. The changes to the Films Act in 2009 and 2018, for instance, reflect the ever-tightening vise on activist and artistic space. These amendments enhance the powers of the Media Development agency to enter private premises and seize suspected unlawful films without a warrant. In a "Community Position Paper" from an influential group of Singaporean filmmakers, great apprehension in particular was voiced on the licensing officers' authorization to "break open any door or window leading to the premises, or remove by force any obstruction" necessary to obtain entry (Chen et al., 2017). The actual destruction of material barriers to the enforcement of laws designed to criminalize the act of political filmmaking could not be clearer in this instance. The nature of this destruction demonstrates the intersection of legal, symbolic, and material realities. More recent legal

---

12 Rajah's book looks specifically at the 1966 Vandalism Act, 1986 Press Act Amendment, 1986 Legal Profession Act, 1989 Religious Harmony Act, and the 2009 Public Order Act as instances where the law was changed in reaction to expressions of dissent.

Introduction

developments like the Protection from Online Falsehoods and Manipulation Act (or, as it is colloquially known, "POF-MA") have further chilled online discourse and academic research (see "Singaporean Ministers," 2020).

Perhaps the most apt example of the overlapping control of artistic space, civil space, and ecology is embodied in the 2015 destruction and removal of a huge banyan tree that had become literally and figuratively entwined with Singapore's premier alternative arts venue, The Substation. Founded in 1990 by the celebrated playwright and organizer Kuo Pao Kun, the venue became a community space for artists and a site for experimental theater, art, music, and other forms of performance. The tree was witness to the evolving alternative art scene in Singapore as, one artist noted, a "darkly supportive presence," until it was taken away to allow the construction of a new section of the Singaporean Management University.[13] The documentary filmmaker Tan Pin Pin, whose oeuvre I look at intently later in this book, recorded the painful and difficult process of cutting down and transporting the tree on a rainy day, interspersing the footage in her work *In Time to Come* (2017). As rain pours down, the artists and curators of The Substation stand around the workers who are dismantling the tree limb by limb, as if mourning at a funeral. Coincidentally, the removal of the tree was subsequently followed by the closure of The Substation in 2021 after the National Arts Council arbitrarily decided to renovate the site and thereafter lease it to multiple tenants.

The works I examine in *Counter-Cartographies* must be understood in the context of this double-edged explosion of the arts and ecologies in Singapore: a growth in the provision of commercial space for the "creative industries" and the intense imaging of tropicality in Singapore, in tandem with the closing down of spaces for dissident art and film and the devastation of multiple ecological sites. With respect to the arts, I do not wish to create a false essentialism of an artist or their art as pure and untouched by the corruptions of capital or state ideology. Neither do I wish to hark back to some artificial and performative idea of Singaporean ecology. Instead I am interested in the negotiations and implications that are evident in the cultural forms of dissident work and as they engage with the rapid ecological changes in Singapore. These are works that are highly aware of the fraught landscape (political, symbolic, literal) in which they exist and function. Each of their texts has found its own idiosyncratic ways to depart from the overdetermined spaces of Singapore, while challenging what are its literal and figurative borders. This so often means finding a way to exist in relation to the spaces of Singapore despite its overmapped nature. These are ways that seek the buried and the lost, circumvent power and censorship, while finding their way to alternate ideas of the past and future. Throughout, these texts and trajectories produce spaces that sidestep the blueprint of Singapore as a globalized, capitalist success story.

---

13 See "Substation Malayan Banyan," *ROOTS*, https://www.roots.gov.sg/Collection-Landing/listing/1350799.

Counter-Cartographical Reading:
Excavate, Circumvent, Wayfind, Confabulate

> Loose ends and ongoing stories are real challenges to cartography.
> (Doreen Massey, *For Space*, 2005, 107)

Through its cartographical control, whether by designating only particular spaces for art and performance, censorship, heavily regulating public assembly, and/or the withdrawal of funding or a license to perform or exhibit an artwork, the Singaporean state achieves the control and reduction of available material, symbolic, and social space to the artist and their audience. By these levers, the state attempts to regulate national narratives that produce the histories, contemporary realities, and possible futures of the country. By tracing texts that excavate, circumvent, wayfind, and confabulate alternatives in the context of the social and legal controls, *Counter-Cartographies* does not just seek to document and theorize the means of artistic and imaginative resistance – it reveals the unseen boundaries imposed on acts of artistic performance and creation in the highly planned and regulated authoritarian city-state, and the methods used to suppress alternate, decolonial, anti-authoritarian productions of space. In the wider political context, artists, filmmakers, and writers are cognizant of the histories and contemporary realities of violence, repression, detention without trial, death penalty for minor offenses, discrimination against LGBTQ communities and racialized minorities, and the curtailed rights of migrant workers within the country.

In a global political context that is increasingly marked by a return to authoritarianism, the "minor literature" that is cultural production from Singapore provides an intense, microcosmic view of the conditions of artistic production in an overdetermined urban space, under duress and censorship – both spatial and political. These literary and cultural texts point to new and alternate spatialities that challenge the state's authoritarianism and imagine radical possibilities for living with the legacies of colonialism and the realities of authoritarian planning. Examining contemporary Singapore literature and film allows us to look intently at a (post)colonial space and culture that is among the most keenly affected by continual waves of authoritarian repression coupled with neoliberal globalization. Through counter-cartographical readings, this book traverses the urban spaces of Singapore through its literary and artistic productions. These include short stories that detail construction sites, conceptual art that bears witness to shorelines disappearing to land reclamation, graphic novels that reimagine streetscapes, psychogeographic memoirs that encounter forgotten pockets of wilderness, documentaries that reframe orderly public housing estates, flash fictions where lost *kampung*s (villages) are resurrected, autofictions that reveal hidden queer communities, and speculative fictions that imagine unbuilt architecture. These spaces are not figured in the intensely mapped and overdetermined spaces of the Singaporean state or in the glossy imagery of a global city with which it markets itself. The sheer generic plurality and polyphony of these texts are a testament to the potent and ever-evolving resistance to a nimble, efficiently calibrated authoritarian state. This is not to understate the reach of the Singaporean state's power and its calculated psychological and financial controls of its citizens. Yet an ever-growing, diverse number of texts and genres have produced an alternate affective and political geography of the city-state that must not be disregarded in the larger context of global anglophone literature and postcolonial studies.

My theoretical framework in *Counter-Cartographies* arises from this specific colonial history of urban mapping and subsequent (post)colonial authoritarian control to think through their effects in our contemporary moment. I pay attention to writing and art about planned and regulated urban spaces and develop methodologies to read that gap between planned space and spatial practice. Crucially, while these ways of reading resist and contest cartographical and authoritarian conceptions of urban space, they nevertheless occur *against* the backdrop of these maps and laws. For to excavate, circumvent, wayfind, and confabulate these spaces means being *pushed up* against histories and legacies of mapped power, even as acts of reading, writing, and art making seek to *push against* these conceptions of space.

The terms excavate, circumvent, wayfind, and confabulate are spatially oriented and reflect both the ways in which I read the texts, and the artistic and imaginative moves that are being made in the texts themselves. Tracking these movements allows us to develop an awareness of the ways in which power has shaped the spaces in which texts are produced, how they interact with and resist these planned spaces, and, further, how they reveal invisible and hitherto hidden aspects of the (post)colonial city. These four spatial and theoretical movements deliberately enmesh the space of everyday life in time: in historical contexts, in ongoing social relations, and in contemporary political realities. If the state sees only what it wants to see and shapes material reality in its vision, this study seeks other ways of seeing that are not panoptic, reductive, or restrictive. It asks us to see and read conscious of our memories, our bodies, and our imagined futures.[14]

---

14 Work on building connections between (post)colonial development and cultural production in Singapore has already begun. For instance, considering texts from the pioneer generation of post-independence poets, Jini Kim Watson points out how paying attention to the state's postcolonial historical development means being aware of a "spatial and architectural transformation, a process most clearly registered in the figures and displacements taken up in various fictional texts" (2011, 8). Arguing for a more active and contentious role of the arts, C.J.W.-L. Wee's analysis of work by filmmakers and playwrights from the city-state in the 1980s and '90s considers their intimate relationship to the homogenized urban environment of the regulated and zoned state. He argues that their work

In Chapter 1, I begin with a theorization of excavation that draws from Doreen Massey's insight that a conception of space must take into account the ongoing reality of "trajectories which co-form this space" (2005, 110), whether these be material, symbolic, or textual. Excavation, when exercised in a counter-cartographical way, becomes a risky, shifting business. In this chapter, I examine texts by conceptual artist Charles Lim, documentary filmmakers Kalyanee Mam and Tan Pin Pin, and artist and writer ila. Their works seek to depict how Singapore's ground is unstable and impermanent. What acts of excavation allow is not just an understanding of how spaces were in the past, what was there before, but how the present space is a concentration of intersections and relations. Excavating as praxis is bearing witness to the material, the passage of time as it is implicated in spatial change, and the attention to records and record-keeping. My reading here reveals and extracts, asking what material realities and unspoken lives are colliding in the literary and artistic texts. It is a remedial process as Lim, Mam, Tan, and ila's works insist on digging up what seem to be the illegible spaces on the map: the intertidal zones, the archipelagic nature of Singapore, the seas that surround it, the caverns it gouges out from its bedrock, and the ruins and demolished buildings that underpin so much of its infrastructure.

In Chapter 2, I move from excavation that delves and remembers to circumvention, which asks what the artist does in the presence of real and present obstacles in mapped space. These take the form of borders, maritime barriers, or domestic walls as they suggest political exile, detentions, and demolitions. In literary and cultural terms, the contours of power further manifest themselves in the restrictions on archives, censorship from the authorities, or a withdrawal of funding for spaces of creation and art. What acts of subterfuge and evasion must happen for works of art that are created in the context of colonially mapped, neocolonially planned space? The *Oxford English Dictionary* defines the act of circumvention as "the act of overreaching, outwitting, cheating, 'getting round', 'taking in'" or the acts of "evading or finding a way around, going round, making the circuit of." The acts of overreaching, outwitting, and making the circuit, or finding a way around, become necessary as acts of counter-cartography when faced with subjects that are banned, histories that are erased, and spaces of the state that are out of bounds. I consider what is entailed for those who must orient themselves differently in Singapore, who must circumvent the state's authoritarianism or fail in their attempts to do so. If colonial and (post)colonial maps and zones require specific and regimented "orientations" and correct ways for bodies to act within these spaces, what happens in texts by Tan Pin Pin, Jeremy Tiang,

---

represents a "reinvention of locality in reaction [...] to the social and cultural costs paid by the citizenry for economic success," a cityscape that was more than just its "sterilized surfaces" (2007, 91). Wee sees the possibility of art's role in some limited way altering urban spatializations of a specific historical period.

and Tania de Rozario when minority subjects in Singapore cannot or will not adhere to the proper orientations, whether political, economic, or sexual? In these cases, circumvention becomes a tactic of survival against the erasure and regulation of alternate spaces in the (post)colonial city.

While excavation and circumvention directly grapple with and confront the spatial authority that is wielded by the state, the second half of this book will attempt theorizations of alternative, decolonial space-making. In Chapter 3, I consider how to wayfind, as Timothy Ingold has argued, is *not* to navigate by a map. To wayfind, one must specify a current location in relation to "where one has been, or where one is going" (Ingold, 2000, 237). Wayfinding as an element of counter-cartographical reading is to see each literary and cultural text's trajectory in space as profoundly intertextual and interdiscursive. Wayfinding as a methodology is an attention to a narrative unfolding that is always conscious of the unexpected and of the intensely sensorial and emotional experience of the text as it is moving through space. Mikhail Bakhtin famously defined the literary artistic chronotope as one where "spatial and temporal indicators are fused into one carefully thought-out, concrete whole" where "Time, as it were, thickens, takes on flesh, becomes artistically visible; likewise, space becomes charged and responsive to the movements of time, plot and history" (1981, 84). I envisage a subversive wayfinding in the routes, paths, moments, and landmarks of Kelvin Tong's short film, Tan Shzr Ee's experimental memoir, and Alfian Sa'at's collection of flash fictions. These movements complicate the spectacular, highly planned, and regulated spatio-temporalities that the Singaporean state produces.

In the final chapter, I turn fully to the possibilities of speculative fiction to imagine otherwise. The *Oxford English Dictionary* defines to confabulate as "to fabricate imaginary experiences as compensation for loss of memory." In the Singaporean context, my theorization of the term points to the role of fiction in the production of powerful imagined and symbolic spaces. If the mapped state began with colonial and (post)colonial bureaucratic fictions based on racialization, the disenfranchisement of minorities, and the exploitation of space, how might we imagine otherwise? Confabulatory literary urbanisms produced by Singaporean artists, architects, and writers raise intriguing possibilities about the role of the literary text in the planned (post)colonial city. Confabulation creates a social space in the Lefebvrian sense, while it compensates for collective losses of memory in an urban setting through fabrication and imagination. In paying attention to the ways in which texts by Alfian Sa'at and Marcia Vanderstraaten, Sonny Liew, and Clara Chow encounter and depart from historical sources to project potential futures, whether they are the untold stories of a historic hotel room, an imaginary artist who provides a cheeky counter-narrative to Singapore's official history, or unbuilt and unbuildable buildings on the island, considering confabulatory gestures enable us to see the unmappable aspects of Singapore's mapped spaces.

Counter-Cartographies is a consideration of how art and literature are produced in the reality of massive physical alterations in a planned (post)colonial urban landscape with its concordant regimes of censorship and regulation. Artistic and cultural production in Singapore reflects and refracts the material, symbolic, and textual conditions that produce this space. Through a careful reading of these texts, it becomes possible to trace the contours of authoritarian power that is exercised through amnesia, omission, censorship, punishment, surveillance, dispossession, and the production of dominant narratives of nation building in a state of exception. This complex circulation and imposition of power to maintain hegemonic dominance is of central importance to my study, and the alternate geographies and ways of seeing that are produced by plays, films, poems, novels, and artworks allow us to recognize the existence of this power and to imagine other ways of being.

My readings consider a diverse range of anglophone and multilingual texts created in contemporary Singapore and in its diasporic community. These works are being produced in an unprecedented surge of creative output spanning the late twentieth and early twenty-first century. There is a vibrant, growing body of countercultural resistance to an overmapped existence by Singaporean writers and artists at home and abroad that must now be viewed in its complicated plurality. In this (post)colonial context, their work is akin to what Gilles Deleuze and Felix Guattari called a "minor literature," one whose "cramped space forces each individual intrigue to connect immediately to politics," producing "an active solidarity in spite of skepticism" (1986, 17). Dissident Singaporean artists, writers, and filmmakers use colonially inherited cultural and literary traditions, and work within a regimented urban space produce this political body of work.

In many ways, Lefebvre's assertion that the combination of conceived, perceived, and lived spaces *produce* space as we know it continues to confound and perplex. Are we truly holding textual and symbolic representations of space to be equivalent to actual material space? What are the dangers and possibilities of these slippages between fiction and so-called reality, between blueprint and construction, poem and everyday life? *Counter-Cartographies* is profoundly interested in these questions as it unsettles the boundaries between how we plan space, how we use space, and what we imagine it to mean. By focusing on one of the most consistently planned urban environments in our (post)colonial moment, I seek to unmap the colonial legacies of (post)colonial space and to consider the important work of writers and artists in the (post)colony as excavators, circumventers, wayfinders, and confabulists of the planned, authoritarian, capitalist spaces they find themselves in. While my work is not a formal literary history of Singapore's contemporary cultural production, encountering a diverse selection of writing and filmmaking from this global city-state in the new millennium provides invaluable insights to how authoritarian hyper-development is seen and challenged by a multiracial, hybrid, syncretic cultural imagination.

This interdisciplinary mode of reading also allows us an active form of decolonial praxis in our (post)colonial moment. For if postcolonial studies as a field is about speaking truth to power and revealing the connections between the "successes" of Empire and its brutal abuses and exploitation of the colonies, counter-cartographical reading offers us active and grounded ways in which to delve into the contemporary spatialities of (post)coloniality through the voices and perspectives of writers and artists living with its legacies. As Jini Kim Watson and Gary Wilder argue in the introduction to their collection *The Postcolonial Contemporary* (2018), as critics of the contemporary moment, we must "reckon with new and persisting postcolonial predicaments by reconsidering the relationship between geographic/spatial configuration and political imagination" (2018, 19). Indeed, as they posit, "we cannot grasp the way that local, regional, and global politics are unfolding without thinking them in relation to colonial legacies and ongoing imperial arrangements" (2018, 9). The Singaporean dissident imaginary that I trace in this book is not only deeply concerned with the politics of censorship and repression in the city-state, but further with how politics, aesthetics, infrastructure, and ecology are inextricably entwined in the country's governance and spatial production. The map that dominates and figures in much of the country and my study is at once symbolic and material, exacting pressures on the poetic, the political, and the physical.

As a Singapore-born academic working in Canada and cognizant of my adopted country's contemporary Indigenous and settler relations, I have used the term "(post)colonial" with a pointed parenthesis consistently in this introduction, as Ann Laura Stoler does, to acknowledge "the temporal and affective space in which colonial inequities endure and the forms in which they do so" (2016, ix). The kinds of spatial readings that are possible through my theorizations are both material and textual: colonial inequities endure in planned, built, absent, and symbolic spaces. Reading these contours and what Stoler calls the "deep pressure points of generative possibilities or violent and violating absences" (2016, 5) in the landscape, architecture, fiction, poetry, film, and urban planning documents of an exceptional, accelerated (post)colonial space like Singapore gives us the tools with which to begin to dismantle the cartographical conceptions that coloniality has bequeathed to us.

But it is not enough to dwell on these "deep pressure points," revelatory as they may be. In my theorizations of the material, textual, formal, and symbolic movements that are made by these artistic texts, I am likewise recalling their agency in urban space. Their agency is part of what Massey would see as the unfinished, ever-mutable nature of space that is "a simultaneity of stories-so-far" (2005, 10). She urges us to be fully cognizant of its "contemporaneous plurality," of how chance and the chance encounter are "intrinsic to spatiality" (2005, 10, 8). She argues that it is in "the happenstance juxtaposition, in the unforeseen tearing apart, in the internal irruption, in the impossibility of closure, in the finding of yourself next door to alterity, in precisely that possibility of being surprised [...] that the chance of space is to be found" (2005, 116).[15]

Specifically, this concept of chance as extrapolated to urban spaces is one that "makes them the ongoing constructions which are our continuing responsibility, the ongoing event of place which has to be addressed" (Massey, 2005, 180). They are not spaces that can be mapped, since they cannot be fixed or accurately predicted. Massey's theorizations speak to "the instability and potential of the spatial" (2005, 116) and, I would argue, for my purposes, to the instability and potential of literary texts about urban spaces as they are read and interpreted individually and collectively. *Counter-Cartographies*, aside from reading the pressure points of Singapore's (post)colonial urban spaces, allows for the recognition of the ruptures, contradictions, and unforeseen beyond its planned materiality. Excavate this space and there will be ghosts, materials from other spaces, traces that have effects on the contemporary. Circumvent the loci of power in the state-controlled city, discover the contours of its power, and find other ways of seeing the country and its inhabitants. Wayfind to discover lost, unmapped, and unmappable paths, and ways of being in a zoned and regulated city. Confabulate when all seems overdetermined to envisage alternate histories and futures.

Singapore's planned nature can seem debilitating to many of its artists and activists. Even more telling is how states like China and North Korea seek to emulate its authoritarian urbanism. Restoring the unforeseen in this sense, then, would mean an attempt to carefully reconsider how lived, conceived, and perceived space are intertwined, and to consider a different way of seeing the temporal. It would entail an acknowledgment of how the imaginative and the unexpected are crucial components in our spatial practice, wresting control of the urban narrative from the authoritarian state. The texts that are examined in this study precisely and consciously point to the agency of the artistic and the literary in the production of space – it is the text's ability to draw connections between seemingly unrelated events, spatio-temporalities, and relations that restores complexity and sociality to the erstwhile abstract spaces of Singapore. Counter-cartographical reading is necessary in the context of the late capitalist urban space and its possible futures. In an era of rapid urban development and redevelopment, buildings, roads, and neighborhoods often disappear or are inaccessible – excavation, circumvention, wayfinding,

---

15 De Certeau similarly acknowledges the importance of "the unforeseen" in urban life, arguing that "to eliminate the unforeseen or expel it from calculation as an illegitimate accident and an obstacle to rationality is to interdict the possibility of a living and 'mythical' practice of the city. It is to leave its inhabitants only the scraps of a programming produced by the power of the other and altered by the event. Casual time is what is narrated in the actual discourse of the city: an indeterminate fable, better articulated on the metaphorical practices and stratified places than on the empire of the evident in functionalist technocracy" (2002, 203).

and confabulation are all ways of survival and spatial negotiation. It is through the artistic text's fictive and indeterminate explorations of these complex intersections of the sensorial and the temporal that a remediated space is produced. How can we move beyond the paradoxically overdetermined and uncertain future that haunts the conceived, perceived, and lived spaces of the (post)colonial city? How can we learn to see space beyond colonial and (post)colonial maps? I believe that it is a matter of urgency that we turn to examine the possibilities of counter-cartographical reading to reclaim future iterations of our cities.

CHAPTER 1

Excavations

"Sewn to the hardness of cement"

Singaporean poet Arthur Yap's 1974 poem "minimum excavation" (2013, 187) notes that "no intricate adornment / of fernroots, young shoots" can disguise the rapid development occurring in Singapore as "busy hands shift terrains, / lay down a horizon / dividing nothing / more than itself." Written in an era of ubiquitous construction and land reclamation projects on the island state, Yap's poem uses his characteristic stark imagery to depict the relentless transformation of the land and sea, utterly controlled to their horizons. Confronted with these changes, the poem suggests a certain numbness and apathy that the speaker feels, as they are "stony" in the face of "long-ago memories." "minimum excavation," along with other poems in Yap's body of work from the 1970s and '80s, returns again and again to images of sites of excavation, the expanding coastline, and the ironic definitions of "public" and "nature." Even in this early work, Yap critiques the Singaporean state's emphasis on the use of plants to camouflage the ecological devastation that is occurring as result of the rapid urbanization of the island, and the movement of land and soil itself.[1] Another poem by Yap, "public beach," immerses itself in the materiality of land reclamation as Singapore's most invisible yet most essential infrastructure. The poem hints at intimate connections and the possibilities of life amid relentless construction, there is "more of life / webbed up here by the sewer / sewn to the hardness of cement" (Yap, 2013, 176). These poems were early entries in a growing body of texts from and about Singapore

---

1 Singaporean literature has had a constant preoccupation with this strategic use of botany. Numerous poems from the post-independence period to the 1990s reiterate the themes of gardening as nation building, tree planting as a political act, and the artificiality of the garden city. Famous examples include Gilbert Koh's "Garden City," "expansion" by Arthur Yap, the final stanza of Lee Tzu Pheng's "My Country and My People," and Leong Liew Geok's "Trees Are Only Temporary."

that elucidate the impact of the country's complete remodeling of its spaces on the psyche of its citizens.

Land reclamation (the act of filling in the sea to increase the city-state's land area) in Singapore began with the British in 1822, as Charles Lim notes in his talk "First Hill Lost at Sea." *The Hikayat Abdullah* (1849), the autobiography of Abdullah bin Abdul Kadir written in the period of colonial rule and an influential Malay account of the time, refers to this process of geo-engineering in Singapore. It is entirely possible and necessary to see the reclamation of what would become downtown Singapore in the colonial period as laying the foundations and inclinations for Singapore's intensive development post-independence. These changes have culminated in highly (in)visible contemporary formations of power and ecological degradation. Singapore's landmass has expanded from 224.5 to 276.5 square miles in half a century, and most of the sand and infill has been from its regional neighbors: Malaysia, Indonesia, Vietnam, Cambodia, and Myanmar.

Lim Tin Seng notes that while fill materials were at first comprised of soil excavated from Singapore's own hills and seabeds, by the mid-1980s these sources began to run out and Singapore had to start importing sand from neighboring countries. This led to a tenfold increase in the cost of foreign sand and to Malaysia and Indonesia banning exports in 1997 and 2007, respectively (Lim, 2017, 19). Joshua Comaroff points out that Singapore's use of raw materials like sand "is not merely a matter of coastal reclamation" (2015) since Singapore's high-rise architecture also needs foreign sand (and foreign labor) for its supply of cement. Much of Singapore's infrastructure is predicated on reclaimed land. Many of its outlying islands have been expanded upon for oil refining, while its Central Business District, international airport, and Marina Bay Sands development have been built wholly on newly reclaimed land.

Singapore's highly planned built environment is a point of great pride and significance. The island state's infrastructural prowess has long been used as a symbol of and rationale for its status as an exceptional (post)colony and the preeminent business, oil refining, and financial hub in Southeast Asia. However, an excavatory reading of the reclaimed lands in Singapore and whatever is built on top of it – the so-called eco-development of Gardens by the Bay, the new skyscrapers of the New Downtown, Marina Bay – means envisioning these spaces as something quite different from architectural and engineering feats. I argue that they are ruins and ruination in and of themselves: "an active, ongoing process that disperses imperial debris differentially [...] that unites apparently disparate moments, places, people, and objects" (Stoler, 2016, 346).

Ruin, ruination, ruins. These words are anathema to conventional depictions of Singapore as a global city, a tourist hub, a tropical city of excellence, a "city in a garden." Yet, as Ann Laura Stoler reminds us, "Much depends on where we look for detritus, what we expect it to look like, and what we expect to see"

(2016, 355). On the one hand, the acts of land reclamation and construction are fundamental to Singapore's survival as conceived by the state, its urban planners, economists, and engineers. The city state's lack of physical space has, it is argued, necessitated the extreme acts of land reclamation that have been central to its nation-building project. However, these strategies of survival have been wholly reliant not only on the devastation of Singapore's natural coastlines, intertidal zones, and mangroves, but also an extensive network of disappeared islands and ecologies throughout the region.

Stoler writes of imperial formations that endure beyond the colonial era, that leave ruins: "the corroded hollows of landscapes [...] shattered infrastructures, polluted places, dispersed families [...] racialized markers on a global scale" (2016, 348, 353). In the work of Cambodian-American filmmaker and activist Kalyanee Mam, it is evident that the dredging of sand from Cambodia's river estuaries produces such ruins. This ruination is also (post)colonial, transnational, and transboundary. Mam makes explicit the connections between the ruination of Cambodia and Singapore's infrastructure: "Each year, millions of metric tons of sand are shipped to Singapore to enlarge this island nation's land mass, while Cambodia destroys its only natural protection against erosion, rising sea levels, tsunamis, and hurricanes and lays waste to a vital and fragile ecosystem that thousands of families depend on for their livelihood" (2018). The destruction of both the mangroves and estuaries in Cambodia and the indigenous flora of the Singaporean coastline are part of the same transnational ruins.

If we see these developments as ruins, what are the implications of the fact that infrastructure in Singapore is central to not only its national project but to the core message and tenets of the ruling People's Action Party (PAP)? Development and its associated ecological sequelae are intimately entwined with the political and social control of Singapore's populace. De Koninck points out that Singapore's perpetual alteration of its physical landscapes has always been in service of making it more legible and thus more controllable by the state. Turning a map into land. Like Yap, he muses about the effect of these mass infrastructural projects when he asks:

> Isn't the relentless overhaul of Singaporean living space – nearly always considered as a *fait accompli* yet always subject to being revised by the state – leading to territorial alienation among the City-State's citizens and permanent residents? Could this alienation possibly contribute to political resignation among the City-State's citizens and permanent residents? (2017, 133)

The disorientation and alienation that De Koninck theorizes find their counterpoint in the artistic, filmic, and literary texts that I analyze in this chapter. In an urban space that has been so thoroughly planned, excavated, and remodeled, what has been lost and forgotten? What forms of artistic and cultural strategies are necessary to document not just the immense territorial and ecological changes that have occurred in Singapore but to trouble the accompanying state-enforced amnesia about the ecological, political, and social costs of this development?

The artistic excavations that I examine in this chapter in the multidisciplinary conceptual art in *SEA STATE* by Charles Lim, the transmedial work of ila, and the poetic documentaries *Invisible City* by Tan Pin Pin and *Lost World* by Kalyanee Mam, go below the glossy, green skin of the "Tropical City of Excellence," as envisioned by the city state's planners. Lim's work lays bare the ecological cost of the raw materials used in the island's cartographical and material transformations. In dialogue with *SEA STATE*, Kalyanee Mam's devastating short film ponders the ethics of taking sand from river estuaries in Cambodia to expand Singapore, Tan Pin Pin's film returns to desire, nostalgia, and affect as a means to perform counter-excavations into what is unseen in the city. ila's text conjures the violence done unto land and communities that underpin the seascapes and infrastructure of the city. Artistic excavations such as these contest certain claims of Singapore's (post)colonial state: its siege mentality, its insistence on sterility and control, its exceptionality, and the singular narrative about its success.

By juxtaposing these texts and placing them in the context of the state's extreme reconfiguration of the physical landscape of the country, I perform, in my own critical praxis, an excavation of sorts. This doubled excavation – that of the artist and then of the critic – is essential in thinking through excavation beyond the removal of layers to reach some sort of buried truth. Edward Soja in *Postmodern Geographies* urges us to "spatialize the historical narrative, to attach to dureé an enduring critical human geography," to allow us to make more "'lateral' connections [...] a geography of simultaneous relations and meanings that are tied together by a spatial rather than a temporal logic" (1989, 1). This, Soja argues, is necessary since it is only through a thorough investigation of the spatial that we can understand "how relations of power and discipline are inscribed into the apparently innocent spatiality of social life, how human geographies become filled with politics and ideology" (1989, 6). What I seek to do in examining these works is to investigate the layers, the multiple spatio-temporalities that only artistic and imaginative endeavors can reveal in non-chronological, non-teleological ways.

Reading against the two-dimensional map, the act of excavation is inevitable. Lefebvre, thinking through the "formants" of abstract space, emphasizes the geometric and the optical (or visual), where the three-dimensional realities are reduced to two-dimensional plans and the visual "gains the upper hand over the other senses" (1991, 285–86). In his theorization of abstract space, what Lefebvre glosses over is the rigidity and fixity of abstract space. Its desire for "homogeneity" (1991, 287) has implications for its understanding of temporalities and trajectories. Singular, dominant narratives for space and time prevail, and the unexpected mingling or collision of various chronotopes are discouraged. In other words, in abstract space, there is only one way of interpreting the historical and the material. Lefebvre posits that "*there is a violence intrinsic to abstraction* [...] the violence of abstraction unfolds in parallel with what we call 'history'" (1991, 289; emphasis original). This violence closes down, attempts to destroy, hide, and render inert the possibilities of space.

In countering this authoritarian conception of space, my theorization of excavation is not simply an act of archaeology, a geological cross-section of excavated spaces, or a recourse to the concept of the palimpsest. As Massey argues, these conceptions of space take on a temporal fixity that does not allow for a heterogeneous view:

> In this story, the things that are missing (erased) from the map are somehow always things from "before". The gaps in representation (the erasures, the blind spots) are not the same as the discontinuities of the multiplicity in contemporaneous space; the latter are the mark of the coexistence of the coeval. Deconstruction in this guise seems hampered by its primary focus on "text", however broadly imagined. To picture this argument through the figure of the palimpsest is to stay within the imagination of surfaces – it fails to bring alive the trajectories which co-form this space [...] as the product of superimposed horizontal structures rather than full contemporaneous coexistence and becoming. (2005, 110)

Following Massey, my counter-cartographical analysis in this chapter seeks to show the imbrication of artistic and literary excavations in the physical reshaping of Singapore, and further to examine how what is unearthed mingles together as it is being excavated, throwing the relationship between past, present, and future into more complex arrangements. What has the mapping of Singapore space sought to destroy, misremember, or erase?

To answer this question, we move between seemingly incommensurable spaces and scales in this chapter whether cavern, reclaimed coastline, archaeological site, film archive, or body. Each genre, whether art piece, essay, performance, photography, or documentary provides a different methodology to excavate the mapped city. Artistic and literary excavations in Singapore are necessarily incomplete and fragmentary – the archives, tools, and freedoms that the artists have are circumscribed, censored, or absent. As wide-ranging and plural as these texts may be, what they have in common is this context of power, and a keen awareness of the material debris and temporal plurality of Singapore's spaces. They are counter-cartographical as they refuse the homogeneity of the disciplined, mapped, abstract, and legible space in favor of depictions of excess, of the unsettling and unsettled, and of the deep fissures of race, desire, ecological harm, and violence inherent in Singapore's (post)colonial spaces.

SEA STATE

In the enigmatic short film *SEA STATE 6: Phase 1*, the multidisciplinary artist and former Olympic sailor Charles Lim Yi Yong documents the excavation of the

Jurong Rock Caverns in Singapore, 130 meters underneath the petrochemical hub Jurong Island.[2] This development began in 2014 and will create 150-acre caverns to store almost 1.5 million cubic meters of oil, naphtha, and gas. The caverns themselves are as tall as nine-story buildings and 8 kilometers of tunnels were created to access them. Lim's contemplative and enigmatic film of the tunnels begins with an underwater shot, reminding us of the submarine aspects of these endeavors and, further, with a fleeting shot of a human body in the water making the scale of the excavation clear. We descend into the caverns via an industrial elevator and the camera remains static as the viewer takes in the slow, deliberate, downward movement into a space that is Singapore but somehow beyond it. We encounter the caverns on an immense, scarcely believable scale. The camera moves steadily towards its limits, sometimes filming only the back of a human subject as he walks, barefoot, in the waterlogged tunnel seemingly without purpose. Later, in the film, we encounter the foreign migrant workers who are tasked with the continual detonation of explosives to further excavate the cavern, and the maintenance of its boundaries, as their small bodies are contrasted with the towering walls that surround them. After the detonation, the film abruptly cuts to shots of barge after barge of sand being brought in for land reclamation and to shots of silt slowly melting into the sea. The film ends with an ascent of one of the shafts in a symmetrical shot but cuts out before we reach the surface.

In this experimental, conceptual video, Lim is simply *showing* the actual process and effects of geological excavation in Singapore for the purposes of creating more space in the city-state to store fossil fuels and to further its ambition of being a hub for oil refining and trade – to create "more infrastructural support to the major chemical companies operating there such as Chevron Philips, ExxonMobil and Shell ("Jurong Rock Caverns"). Singapore's lack of physical space has, it is argued, necessitated the extreme acts of excavation and reclamation that have been central to its nation-building project since its independence in 1965. Through the tactics of experimental documentary, Lim's work lets us consider the actual physical excavation of the caverns through his own artistic excavation. His art's repeated insertion of surreal juxtapositions and seemingly superfluous human bodies into the grand engineering feats of excavation, dredging, and land reclamation unsettle the smooth movements of capital, labor, raw materials, and geological rearrangements of the state.

---

2 Charles Lim studied fine arts at Central Saint Martin's School of Art and Design. He represented Singapore in the 1996 Olympics in sailing and co-founded the net-art collective tsunamii.net. In his own words, *SEA STATE* "explores the political, biophysical and psychic contours of the Southeast Asian city state, Singapore, through the visible and invisible lenses of the seas" (2015, 138). His work has been extensively exhibited in Singapore and internationally. In 2015, he represented Singapore at the Venice Biennale to great acclaim.

Fig. 7 Film still from *SEA STATE 9: Proclamation* (2017). Credit: Charles Lim. Used with permission.

Nowhere has the rapid reconfiguration of Singapore's territories been better archived and documented in an artistic form than in Lim's obsessions with the emptiness of caverns, the seemingly pristine and formless shape of sand, the anonymous shots of the tropical sea. In much of his work, Lim contrasts long meditative films on the movement and installation of sand with photographs of buoys and sea walls and cartographic depictions of the island of Singapore and its extensive land-reclamation projects. In effect, Lim's work bears witness to the actual production of conceived space, of space that is mapped even before its existence and then brought into existence as reclaimed land through acts of immense environmental manipulation and engineering. Tracing the limits and transgressions of these projects, Lim's larger project *SEA STATE* (2005–) is a ten-part multidisciplinary work that includes experimental film, photography, installation art, field research, and remedial cartography. It was first comprehensively exhibited at the Venice Biennale in 2015 as part of the Singapore Pavilion but is still very much an ongoing, long-term project.

Through its persistence and coherence, *SEA STATE* enacts a counter-excavation of the work that has extended the country's coast and deepened its reach underground. *SEA STATE*'s title is ambiguous: Singapore is a sea state, a maritime state, a state whose boundaries between sand and sea are suspect and shifting. But *SEA STATE* also plays on the acronym for Southeast

Asia State, which embeds Singapore in the larger regional body politic and geography. *SEA STATE* is highly cognizant of the fact that the sand that Singapore uses to expand itself comes from the region and further that this fundamentally alters the boundaries and relationship between sea and land. Lim, a former Olympic sailor, also points out that the structure of this work is inspired by the World Meteorological Organization's code for measuring sea conditions, which numbers the varying states ranging from calm, to moderate, to the phenomenal.[3] As he puts it on the work's accompanying website, "*SEA STATE* is an index of this extreme oscillation and a call to attention." In other words, *SEA STATE* registers the massive scale on which Singapore is altering its coastal borders and asks us to pay close attention to their ongoing, ever-evolving variations. In its multiple iterations, Lim's work gives us inverted, alternate perspectives of the Singapore's coast. These include: 110 water border markers of Singapore photographed from both sides, inverted 3D prints of the seabed, surreal footage of the 130-meter-deep rock caverns, installation art that recreates lost sea buoys, gardens of coastal plants salvaged from reclaimed land, and experimental films that trace the island's hydrological cycles and pathways.

SEA STATE is a wide-ranging, idiosyncratic, symphonic work – one that keeps pace with and yet diverges from Singapore's relentless excavation and

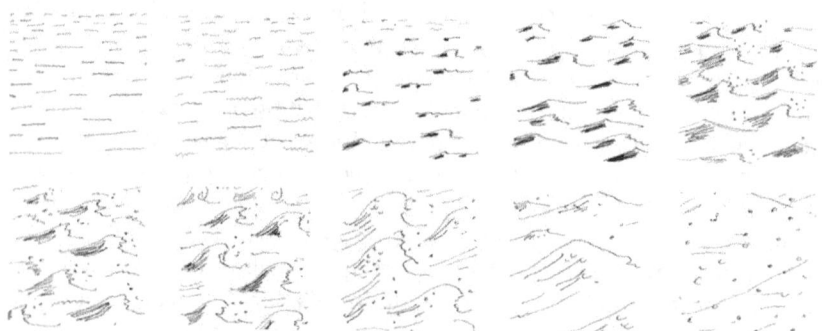

Fig. 8 *SEA STATE* illustration. Credit: Charles Lim. Used with permission.

---

3 The terms to describe sea states, including the word "phenomenal," come from the Douglas Scale which is used for supplying weather information and forecasts for shipping, publications, pilots and so forth. See https://www.wmo.int/pages/prog/amp/mmop/faq.html#douglas.

extension of its lands and seas. It pays attention to the periphery, the minor, the overlooked, the ignored. It attempts to provide a fragmentary, polyphonic articulation of the strange new world that Singapore has built on what was once sea. As David Teh puts it, "with his reiterative mapping of its dynamic coastline, Lim scrapes away at the island's gridded, terraformed surface to uncover its uneasy maritime unconscious" (2012, 5). The slow, contemplative pace of many sections of the work and their contrast with the accelerated and profound irrevocable changes to Singapore's land and maritime borders evoke the changing sea conditions from sea state 0, where the sea's surface is smooth and mirror-like, to sea state 9, where the air is filled with foam, waves over 45 feet tall, the sea is completely white with driving spray, and visibility is greatly reduced.

These mutable views of the ocean challenge the static, cartographical views of maritime Singapore – where the straits and the South China Sea are seen as untroubled, placid spaces for profit. Singapore's textbook history as first a "fishing village" and then a bustling colonial entrepot site is predicated on Singapore's strategic location on shipping lanes and its natural harbor. The offshore islands, coastlines, and marine ecologies that have been lost in its extreme acts of excavation, dredging, and land reclamation seem minor and forgotten concerns.

SEA STATE is as varied as it is enigmatic, with Lim refusing to provide overt commentary on the scenes that he is recording. One reason for this is the possibility of censorship and loss of access to the sites. But another is to allow space for the audience to interpret these unseen aspects of the island city in their own ways, to allow for different ways of seeing. In *SEA STATE 7: Sandwich*, for instance, where landscape-format videos of the coastline are turned on their side and pressed up against each other, we are unable to resort to the usual perspectival illusion of limitless sand and sea, but instead focus on the construction, industry, land reclamation, and disappeared coastal villages and islands.

All these sites, as they are pressed up against each other, sky to sea to sand to barge to lost island, testify to the bounded nature of the seas around Singapore. Lim focuses on how these layers of meaning are sandwiched upon each other, a perspective that recalls the structures of sedimentation and palimpsestic archaeologies, but rejects a linear or cumulative production of space. What we have is multiple spatialities, multiple temporalities all vying at once for our attention, all askew, asking us to pay attention to all layers at once, and not to simply imagine that we can discover them one by one. The

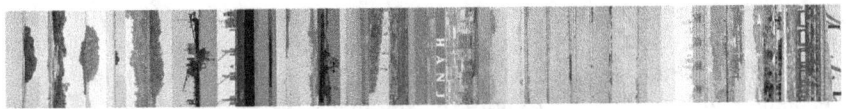

Fig. 9 *SEA STATE 7: Sandwich* (2015). Credit: Charles Lim.
Used with permission.

pace of Singapore's expansion and development, the government's enforcing of regimes of censorship and amnesia have shaped Lim's excavatory processes into ones that are sophisticated and subtle. *Sandwich* eschews any overt statements in its depiction of the coastline and forces the viewer to pay close attention to the shoreline, to tilt one's head to understand the visual image. The form of the piece compresses time and space in simple yet effective ways.

In *SEA STATE 9: Proclamation*, Lim contemplates the act of proclamation by which the President of Singapore legally "proclaims" reclaimed land to be part of the state. This legal gesture hovers between fiction and reality, turning that which was sea into land, and that which was sand from another state into territorial Singapore. The complexity and far-reaching consequences of this act necessitate the numerous transmedial iterations of *SEA STATE 9*: remedial cartography, experimental film, the collation of legal documents and archival newspaper clippings. The most recent part of the work is Lim's 2019 exhibition *Proclamation Garden*, which features living plants that began growing on reclaimed land in Singapore. *SEA STATE 9* attempts to think through the myriad consequences of Singapore's developmental politics through an attention to the legal machinery that makes it possible, the materialities of reclaimed land, and, most recently, the prospect of unexpected botanical tenacities.

While its parts may seem disparate, *SEA STATE 9*, as a multi-year, transmedial work, allows for a dynamic contemplation of the scale of sand reclamation in Singapore. The work begins with a simple reproduction of the "Foreshores Act":

> —(1) The President may, by proclamation published in the Gazette, declare any lands formed by the reclamation of any part of the foreshore of Singapore, or any areas of land reclaimed from the sea to be State land, and thereupon that land shall immediately vest in the State freed and discharged from all public and private rights which may have existed or been claimed over the foreshore or the sea-bed before the same were so reclaimed. (Singapore Government)

The legal formulations in the act allow the state to proclaim its ownership of reclaimed land regardless of any prior rights held by landowners at the old shoreline, and they also help elide the provenance of the sand and aggregate used to construct the new land. Its language reflects the attempt at imperial totality: it provides an inventory of all the possible substances that might exist in this land: "corals, stone, clay, sand, gravel, and other natural deposits, brine, petroleum and any other mineral oil or relative hydrocarbon, and natural gas" (Singapore Government). The legal precedents for this act come from colonial-era laws enacted in 1872 that were revised more than a century later, in the 1980s, at the height of (post)colonial Singapore's extensive reclamation work. Lim's citation of this act in his work is a conscious attempt to reveal the legal machinery through which Singapore enacts its territorial rights over reclaimed land and further to note the colonial roots of this process.

Simultaneously, Lim offers us a cartographic fantasy of what these reclaimed lands look like in their totality. He calls this new island: *Pulau*

Punggolsebaraokeastsamalunbukomsentosatuasviewdamartekongmarinajurong-covebranibaratchangilautekongsajahatsenanghantu, a satirical amalgamation of the names of the new plots and developments that have been built on reclaimed land. The name's impossible nature conveys the incommensurability of Singapore's territorial expansion. The use of speculative cartography to fuse all the reclaimed lands in Singapore creates a new map, a future state, a grouping that helps us understand the scale of this disruption and how, as Lim puts it, "Singapore reclaims and recreates itself constantly – this is the paramount expression of its will" (2015). The new map defamiliarizes and unsettles the shape of the island in ways that more conventional depictions of Singapore's expansion do not. The foreignness of the map reminds us of the alterity of the new shores and developments, hinting at their origins.

Lim's art pushes against the smooth surfaces of mapped power, excavating the troubling use of labor and raw materials, and the disciplining of a population. By placing the monumentality of these legal documents alongside speculative cartography, Lim's *SEA STATE 9* carefully walks the line between simply showing the reality of Singapore's new lands and a pointed political critique of the ramifications of Singapore's unbridled expansion. A short

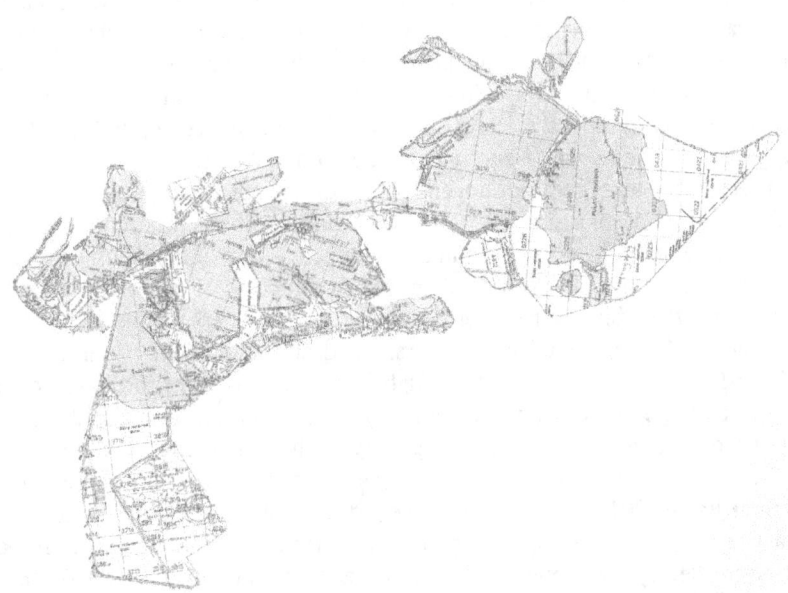

Fig. 10 Map art from Charles Lim's *SEA STATE 9: Proclamation* (2015), "Pulau Punggolsebaraokeastsamalunbukomsentosatuasviewdamartekongmarina jurongcovebranibaratchangilautekongsajahatsenanghantu prepared GSP1 chart, published by Maritime and Port Authority of Singapore (2014)." Credit: Charles Lim. Used with permission.

drone-shot film that is part of *SEA STATE 9* takes on a more sinister tone when read in the context of Lim's other representations of the legal act of "proclamation" and the scale of reclamation. It appears to simply document the process of the transport of sand, its release into the sea, its amalgamation into new shores, and its use to construct innumerable blocks of housing. The wholly aerial view of the process that it offers arguably mimics the god-like view of a planner or cartographer, in this case, one who seems to simply will new land into existence from maps and projections.

In this film, Lim relies primarily on drone footage of the process that takes on this map-like, stylized, impersonal, aerial view of the reclamation. The distance that the drone allows from the process enables the film to act almost like a map in time, to depict the scale of geo-engineering that Singapore is undertaking. Unlike a static, colonial cartographic rendering, Lim's use of drone technology enables him to track the temporality of Singapore's new territorial gains and, paradoxically, unsettle this large-scale view. Lim's short films begin with these all-seeing aerial views, showing the scale and grandeur of Singapore's land reclamation. Yet the overly long shots begin to unsettle the viewer, returning us to a consciousness of the scale and time required to produce this new land. Again and again, we are forced to confront a seemingly endless shot of sand pouring into a pile that first disappears into the ocean and then only later gains solidity. Herein lies the film's power: to allow one to contemplate the scale and materiality of the process. Lim cuts between the processes of land reclamation to images of semi-finished apartment blocks. This juxtaposition associates the land being reclaimed with the initial skeletal structures of incomplete housing. These residential blocks are presented as pure infrastructure, with the barest suggestion of the moving figure of a worker or an inhabitant.

Further, the exaggerated movements of the drone itself smoothly panning from side to side or rising into the air, remind us of the inherent artificiality of this viewpoint. It is not a human perspective but one that is prosthetic, mechanical, cyborg-like. Lim's self-conscious direction of the drone's panning movement destabilizes the naturalization of this perspective due to our familiarity with maps and aerial shots. His drone techniques recall Macarena Gómez-Barris's argument for a through line that runs from forms of colonial seeing through surveys and cartography to contemporary extractive states. The latter, she notes, operate through new technologies that link "capitalism, military technologies, and the parallel expansion of dispossession on the ground" (Gómez-Barris, 2017, 8). Lim's canny use of these same technologies reveals the scale of Singapore's alterations, even as it disrupts and undercuts the smooth space created by the drone. The human is deliberately omitted in *SEA STATE 9* as figures of migrant workers and Singaporeans are strategically dwarfed by vast tracts and dunes of sand and endless repeating concrete blocks. The omission of human figures in the bulk of Lim's work on the coastlines hints at the repetitive and mechanized labor that is required for Singapore's reclamations. His work shows a modernized cartographic view at work – one that erases the ecologies, textures, and histories of the land itself. Deterritorialized from its origins, the sand that is depicted seems to have no provenance and shows no signs of running out.

Lim's resolute, obsessive focus on the changes on the Singapore coast is admirable. But his is an impossible ambition to chronicle even a small fraction of the sweeping changes that have occurred since the nation's independence in 1965. Indeed, his conceptual artworks and his subtle critique may risk insularity. Still, Lim's excavation reveals Singapore's imperial history and its colonial legacies. His work recalibrates our view of the island not so much as a successful (post)colony but as a twenty-first-century iteration of a British maritime empire, another small island that disregards the sovereignty of other peoples and other nations, bolstered by its status as a rich US ally, and erstwhile base for US interests in Southeast Asia. And beyond the spatial sense of the imperial, we might also read echoes of the East India Company in Singapore's business-oriented, mercantile empire. What kinds of reconfigurations would it entail to consider Singapore's relations with the major imperial powers in the region: China with its own reclaimed islands in the South China Sea, and the US whose military presence in the Asia Pacific region is also dependent on its utilization of Singapore's strategic geography? What other transcolonial, inter-imperial modes would need to be considered when understanding its cultural production? Singapore's own national narrative as a nation under siege, a tiny, precarious, unlikely nation-state, would need to be set aside for it to see itself as the city-state heart of this minor empire, one that literally takes land away from its neighbors. Like all other empires, the Singapore empire does not just occupy the now vanished beaches of the Riau Islands, Cambodian riverbeds, Malaysian hills; it has further displaced Indigenous people within its ever-expanding borders – both the Orang Seletar in the northern coastal region and the Orang Laut in the southern islands.

Lost World

Lim's focus on the Singaporean state's resolute developmentalism finds a poignant counterpoint and corrective in the work of Cambodian-American documentary filmmaker and activist Kalyanee Mam.[4] All of the other artists, filmmakers, and writers in this book are Singaporean or based in Singapore. The inclusion of Mam's work is crucial because it provides a rare voice from Southeast Asia that forces a reckoning with Singapore's ecological exploitation of its regional neighbors. Borrowing some of Lim's drone footage in her short film *Lost World*, Mam carefully constructs her film around the perspective of

---

4 Kalyanee Mam is an award-winning filmmaker, activist, and trained lawyer who was born in Cambodia during the Khmer Rouge regime. Her debut documentary film *A River Changes Course* won the Sundance Grand Jury Award for World Cinema among other accolades. Aside from *Lost World*, her other documentary shorts include *Fight for Areng Valley*, *Between Earth & Sky*, and *Cries of Our Ancestors*.

a Cambodian fisherwoman, Phalla Vy. Phalla's home and fishing grounds have been ruined by sand dredging driven by Singapore's insatiable demand, and it is through her eyes, through the intimacy of her contact with the sand, that we begin to see the simultaneously minute and vast scale of the ruination wreaked by Singapore's infrastructure.

Two of the film's images seem particularly apt: a handful of sand running through a woman's fingers and a drone shot of a dredger spilling silt into the

Fig. 11 Film still from Kalyanee Mam's film *Lost World* (2018). Phalla Vy lets sand fall through her fingers. [Fair use.]

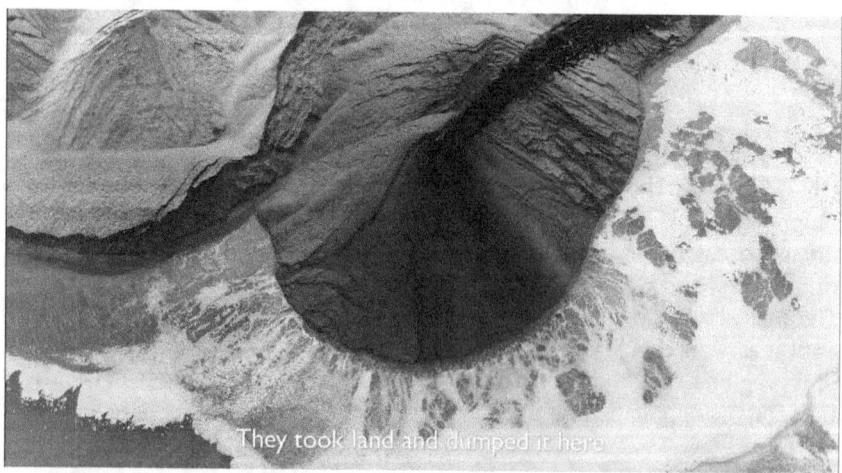

Fig. 12 A sand dredger pours sand into the sea as part of land reclamation processes. Film still taken from Kalyanee Mam's film *Lost World*. Originally part of Charles Lim's film *SEA STATE 9: Proclamation* (2017). Credit: Charles Lim. Used with permission.

ocean. These two scenes juxtapose the body of a Cambodian fisherwoman, Phalla Vy, with the impersonal aerial views of land reclamation works in the seas just off the island state: the familiarity of human contact with the creation of enormous coastal infrastructure. These sharp contrasts appear repeatedly in Mam's film: in an early scene, Phalla is overwhelmed as she confronts the immense quantities of sand in a Singaporean depot. She muses to the camera: "The size of this country's sand facility is almost like a chunk of Cambodia. They've shipped over all our land" (Mam, 2018). The film allows for paradoxical juxtapositions of ways of seeing and understanding this transnational sand: it is simultaneously raw material and infrastructure, and yet tiny enough to interact with a single body. The provenance of Singapore's ostensibly endless supply of sand is thus excavated in this film and shown to be a both an intimate and a gargantuan affair.

The film lingers upon Phalla's petite frame, dwarfed by dunes upon dunes of the seemingly anonymous, granular material that is essential for Singapore's twin obsessions of land reclamation and building construction. Phalla's own river estuary, where she and her family eke out a modest existence through fishing and foraging in and around the mangroves, has been irrevocably damaged by sand dredgers whose ultimate destination is, we must assume, Singapore. Mam's film makes this transnational, interregional connection explicit. In her accompanying essay, she notes how, since 2007, Singapore "has imported over 80 million tons of sand, worth more than $740 million, from Cambodia [...] for pure unadulterated entertainment" (2018). Imposing feats of (post)colonial infrastructure have been made possible by this sand, not least the aforementioned Gardens by the Bay. By repeatedly placing the central protagonist of her 2018 film face to face with the inconceivable amounts of sand that Singapore has amassed, stockpiled, turned into land and cement, planted on, and built on, Mam's documentary enables us to read material scale through the body of her protagonist.

Parsing how infrastructures produce varying scales, Penny Harvey, Casper Bruun Jensen, and Atsuro Morita propose that "it is not so much that infrastructures have a scale, but rather that scales are generated through the work of configuring, extending, maintaining, or disrupting infrastructure" (2016, 16–17). Singapore may be "small" in a narrow geographical sense, but an excavatory perspective of its materiality shows how it has an outsized impact on the region's ecosystems and bioregions through its relentless importation of sand. In *Lost World*, Mam makes Singapore's invisible scale clearer by using drone footage taken from Lim's *SEA STATE*. Mam's visual vocabulary of a small-scale, independent documentary enters into conversation with Lim's aerial views of the slow and colossal changes that have been wrought on Singapore's coastlines. For her part, Mam asks, "What kind of world can be built from sterile and lifeless sand and land that has no roots, no history, and no memory, except for the violent extraction from its homeland?" (2018).

Cambodia's people have experienced a long history of territorial displacement, from the Khmer Rouge regime to more recent capitalist developments that have resulted in expropriations for vast fields of sugar cane and cassava, hydro-electric dams, and industrial uses (Mam, 2018). Thus, while works like Lim's show how the shifts of land from one country to another can be registered on geological scales, in Mam's work, they are viewed from a singular, personal perspective. *Lost World* follows Phalla in her everyday life in the mangrove with her family. Mam bears witness to how she and other fisherpeople are living through the steady devastation of their native ecologies. Aside from taking Phalla to the depot to show her where the sand ends up, the film also tracks her visit to the spectacular glass-domed, climate-controlled gardens that have been built on reclaimed land in Singapore. Finally, ending on a somewhat hopeful note, Phalla returns to Cambodia, where she visits an undisturbed sandy island that she hopes will survive.

The film alternates between the impersonal, aerial drone footage of sand dredging and land reclamation and the intimate handheld shots of Phalla Vy, her children, and her extended family as they attempt to continue their mangrove-based subsistence lifestyles – digging clams out of the sand flats, carefully negotiating their way through a thicket of mangroves to harvest snails and clams, living on the estuary, and recalling their ability to catch crabs right on their doorstep. Phalla notes:

> [F]or me and most fisherfolk our identity in this coastal region is dependent upon sand. The ocean needs sand, the mangrove, with its roots, also need land. These identities are interconnected and support one another to be fulfilled. (Mam, 2018)

What Mam has done, then, is to begin her story not with questions of hard evidence, or facts and figures about spectacular growth, but rather from daily life alongside one of the sources of Singapore's sand. This allows her to depict the ecological intimacies between sand and those who dwell in the mangroves and estuaries. Her work challenges sand's status as a granular, anonymous media for transnational infrastructure and painfully reterritorializes it. Through the documentary gaze of Mam's work – its long shots very much akin to the rhythm of Lim's films – we come to comprehend the pace and spaces of the sandy mangrove. This is a landscape that demands careful negotiation. Phalla's children walk and climb through the mangrove swamps and are taught to be watchful and alert if they are to forage successfully to feed their families. In a central sequence, Phalla sings that "the beauty of the mangrove rivals the palace garden," foreshadowing her later visit to Singapore.

Life in the mangrove is sharply contrasted with Singapore, and the documentary culminates in a disorienting trip that Phalla takes there. After the sand depot, she goes to Gardens by the Bay. Built on reclaimed land, the Gardens almost certainly began as sand from one of Singapore's regional neighbors. The extreme artifice of the garden – in particular the Cloud Forest, a cooled conservatory that houses flora imported from mountain regions of Southeast Asia – becomes clear through Phalla's point of view. Cutting from a drone shot of the Gardens, we are immediately thrust into Phalla's auditory and visual experiences, as filmed with a handheld camera. The diegetic sound here gives us a disembodied understanding of the purpose of the Gardens. We hear snatches of words from a recorded tour about the "cloud forest" and "mighty super trees." The camera lingers on signs (in English) that exhort visitors not to touch the flora; signs that Phalla may or may not be able to read. The handheld camera follows her as she disobeys the rules of this hyper-regulated space: plucking camellias, touching the water features, bringing flowers to her face. She attempts to recreate her intimacy with the plants and land even as she notes that "these flowers are really beautiful, except they don't have seeds" (Mam, 2018). She wonders whether medicine can be made from the flowers, while the Gardens' planners see them as mere objects for display. She is surrounded by tourists and Singaporeans who obey the injunctions not to touch the plants, and are taking photographs and selfies with the plants and water features, reveling in the carefully curated botanical spectacle.

Later, as Phalla stands outside the dome on an artificial beachfront constructed with the same sand, she picks up another handful of the material, letting it fall through her fingers. She intones:

> [W]hen I see all the people walking I want to tell them, this land is my land, this land is from my country. But I can't express this, because I don't speak their language and I don't know what to do so that they will understand. I can only grieve for the land. I don't know what else I can do. (Mam, 2018)

Phalla's deep grief here recalls Donna Haraway's injunction to "grieve with" in this era of the Capitalocene. Haraway argues that "grief is the path to understanding entangled shared living and dying; human beings must grieve with, because we are in and of this fabric of undoing. Without sustained remembrance, we cannot learn to live with ghosts and so cannot think" (2016, 39). In direct opposition to the relations that the tourists and Singaporeans are enacting with the Gardens, Phalla excavates and then reterritorializes the sand, the plants, and the land, not as spectacle or distraction, but as deeply embodied loss – a transnational intimacy that is rooted in deep knowledge and memory. Before Mam's documentary, it was impossible to come to a full accounting of the destruction. Phalla's sickened realization of her own intimate connection with this seductively beautiful development is unprecedented.

To excavate these intimacies means to turn away from the image that Singapore has constructed for itself as a glamorous, ahistorical tropical setting for the extremely wealthy and the world's political elite. Instead of the glossy, "green" camouflage of artificial gardens or tree-lined streets, we become cognizant of the regional context of exploitation of both land and labor that makes Singapore's existence possible. Phalla's body is also part of the intimate ruins that have been created by Singapore's extraction and use of sand. The Gardens have ostensibly not been constructed for her or her countrymen even as it is the crowning jewel of Singapore's cultivation and control of its environment and landscaping. Phalla's transgressions of the rules of the garden and her very presence in it suggest an out-of-placeness there because of the history of coding of Cambodian (and other regional) human bodies in Singapore as dispensable labor, whether in construction or caregiving. Indeed, Mam notes that "Since the sand dredging began, every family in Koh Sralau has lost a family member, each one forced to migrate to other places and other countries for work" (2018).

In Mam's film, Phalla is able to translate the semiotics of Gardens by the Bay because of her indigenous and transnational perspective on its role in the ruination of her river estuary. This is a personal, communal, and transborder experience, but also one that is acutely corporeal: visual, olfactory, auditory. In *Lost World*, the fishermen and women, including Phalla, take boat trips out to observe the dredgers at work, noting how the river's color has changed, how "it stinks like mud here" and they feel "poisoned by the smell" (Mam, 2018). The shots of dredging are intercut with the mournful faces of the men and women as the mechanical sound of the dredgers dominates the soundtrack. When she arrives in Singapore, Phalla brings this corporeal experience with her throughout her visits to the stockpiles of sand and to the Gardens. She, more clearly than any of the visitors to the eco-development, is able to truly see what Gardens by the Bay is. Indeed, she observes, "if this was real, imagine how beautiful it would be" (Mam, 2018).

"As humans reshape the landscape," Elaine Gan et al. remind us "we forget what was there before."

> Ecologists call this forgetting the 'shifting baseline syndrome.' Our newly shaped and ruined landscapes become the new reality. Admiring one landscape and its biological entanglements often entails forgetting many others. Forgetting itself, remakes landscapes, as we privilege some assemblages over others. Yet ghosts remind us. Ghosts point to our forgetting showing us how living landscapes are imbued with earlier tracks and traces (2017, G6)

Phalla, with her inability to forget the immediacy of what she has experienced in her homeland, haunts Mam's shots of the dizzyingly verdant Gardens and their lush artificial waterfalls. Taking the sand and plants in her hands, she sees what others cannot as they admire the technological feats of the Gardens and Singapore's ecocidal infrastructural project of reclaimed land: that they are ruins and ruination that extend beyond its own borders and continue to affect ecosystems and communities that have been rendered invisible.

Invisible City: In Preparation for Forgetting (*beiwanglu*, 备忘录)

The excavatory, ecocritical impulses in the works of Charles Lim and Kalyanee Mam find their urbane counterpart in the earlier work of director

Tan Pin Pin.⁵ My first experience of Tan's work was during a screening of her first feature documentary, *Singapore GaGa*. This occurred in a darkened screening room at the Substation, one of the few independently run alternative art venues on the island. As a young journalist working for the national news channel, encountering Tan's art-house sensibilities and idiosyncratic approach to Singapore's spaces was a watershed moment for my conceptions of Singapore's spaces. Through her lens, I saw and heard my island city as embodied onscreen, in art, as an intricate, incomplete web of human relations, histories, false starts, pruned efforts, and deeply personal stakes.

I begin with this autobiographical anecdote in an attempt to elucidate the corporeal experience of watching Tan's films. Tan's focus on the corporeal and the sensory in all her films is what makes them such visceral experiences. The spatial practices of her films are firmly centered on the body, what it can hear, how it experiences space, and what it remembers. The filmic techniques with which Tan chooses to depict the body and its experiences in Singapore emphasize the subtle possibilities of its awareness and ability to subvert the planned spaces of the city.⁶

Watson notes how Tan is profoundly conscious of the "highly formulaic elements [...] the militarized, productivist and multiculturalist logic [...] of

---

5 Tan Pin Pin is arguably one of Singapore's most famous and successful documentary filmmakers. Her films have screened at leading festivals including Berlinale, Hot Docs, Busan, Cinéma du Réel, and SXSW. She has won or been nominated for over 20 awards and has been on numerous film juries. She is also a co-founding member of filmcommunity.sg, a community of independent filmmakers in Singapore. She began her career as an assistant director in local Singaporean television dramas before she won an S. Rajaratnam scholarship to study for an MFA at Northwestern University, USA. While there, she won the Kodak Eastman Scholarship for Cinematography. She was called to the Singapore Bar and she has a law degree from Oxford University. Biographical details from tanpinpin.com.

6 *Singapore GaGa*'s city sounds draw our attention to the marginal and indeterminate. The film played to packed halls and theaters all over the island and is an aural record of the disappearing sounds of the island: busker songs that wind their way around our hearts, the cacophony of footsteps in an underpass, the specific hollow echoes of void decks, and an eclectic range of forgotten songs that reflect the city's polyglot, cosmopolitan, postcolonial nature. The film's focus on the easily ignored diegetic sounds of ordinary spaces, and its tactical overlay of nondiegetic songs with particular spaces, also produce a subtle critique of Singapore's highly regulated spaces. At other times, the most ordinary sounds are given full, almost overwhelming presence in a quotidian space. In the latter instances, Tan's films create alternate spatio-temporalities of Singapore simply by pausing to record the mundane on camera. Arguably, this deliberate slowing down of filmic time, in effect the use of long single shots in the film, alter the viewer's relationship to these spaces. These are often places of transition: walkways, void decks, and underpasses – seemingly inconsequential spaces, unmarked on maps and disregarded daily by most commuters. See Leow (2013).

the most disciplined and value-added workforces in the world" (2016, 547). In contrast, the free associative structures of Tan's films are born out of a desire for the past and an alternate conception of time, one that refuses a totalizing agenda, is not for profit, and refuses to pin Singapore or its inhabitants down. This indeterminacy makes memory open to the possibilities of other histories that challenge the basis of the state's control over space and forms of temporality, leaving the film's viewers open to a whole range of complex and nuanced meanings. Tan's films' polyphonies and digressions are especially powerful for their eschewal of any grand narrative to describe a city-state whose government is singularly obsessed with its teleological progress. Her experimental documentaries and award-winning short films have consistently evinced an awareness of Singapore's cramped and disciplined spatialities. Her first made-for-television documentary, *Moving House* (2001), for instance, chronicles the exhumation of graves in Singapore driven by urban development and features a haunting final image of a columbarium filmed in a manner that produces an undeniable visual echo of Singapore's public housing flats. Her film *In Time to Come* (2017) is a time capsule of the rituals, demolitions, and patterns in everyday Singapore life. The film asks, What is worth preserving in contemporary life? In between these two works, Tan has made over a dozen other documentaries and short films.

By revealing the constructed and conditional aspects of Singapore's history and spaces, Tan's work allows us to depart not just from Singapore as mapped space but from Singapore's official history as mapped time. Tan's directorial vision excavates alternative chronotopes of Singapore that are open-ended, frayed at the edges, and still in the process of becoming. These revelations are often tied to the slow, contemplative pace of her films, her refusal to move quickly over the everyday, and the unpredictable or seemingly random aspects of her filmic space. My analysis of Tan's sophomore film *Invisible City* (2007) focuses on her excavations of histories that have been hidden, forgotten or disregarded. These histories leave the film's viewers open to a whole range of complex and nuanced meanings, hewing to Singaporean journalist and scholar Janadas Devan's earlier exhortation, that

> precisely because our history is a forgetting [...] we must never forget, we must never fail, to remember the past: the actual, real past, the muddle which resists summary. Not to do so, not to remember the muddle – the contradictions unresolved, the alternatives abandoned, the intimations refused – can only mean to give up the past, give it over, to ideologically invested simplifications. (1999, 32–33)

This muddled past is inextricably tied to the present time and space of the city, Tan's "teeming, contested terrain." *Invisible City* and its unofficial sequel *In Time to Come* are an attempt to excavate the truly disjointed, disjunctive, fragmented chronotopes of Singapore. Instead of a historical, linear sense of archaeology, Tan's filmic medium enables excavations into alternate rhythms of spaces. Her documentary films alter conceptions of Singaporean space by focusing on throwaway details and forgotten subjects. They present different ways of living in an overregulated and overdetermined space in order to question and shift spatial practices. Tan has argued that her job as a filmmaker is to "to tell a story ... to keep a record of the present for the future" (Heng, 2012). Her poised summation of what her work does is telling; her films focus on a particular form of narrative: "a story," not "the story," and their interest in the "present," enables them to bypass a future-oriented national teleology where a constructed version of the past is already inscribed in the cumulative power structures of the nation. Tan's films turn the nation's spatial practice just slightly askew by listening to voices that are not quite heard, and excavating the unfamiliar terrain of Singapore's hidden histories.

Invisible City is, in her words, "a documentary about documenteurs," "an ode" to all those who have made Singapore the subject of their work and by doing so underpin Singapore's invisible city. Tan investigates the impulses that drive these chroniclers, while bringing their lost histories to light. The film is a recuperative work, and one of resistant historiography and a meta-excavation – how does one perform the work of artistic excavation by observing other excavators and formally displaying the gaps and traces that are revealed by forms of excavation? The film, more than any other in her oeuvre, troubles the mapped spaces of Singapore by providing a glimpse of the complicated and polysemous times (past, present and future) that are inherent in them.

The film's often languorous pacing, elliptical editing techniques, and almost wholly unknown subjects meant that it was only screened in the small art-house film circuit in Singapore. Through a series of interwoven interviews and archival footage and photographs, the film takes us through a spatio-temporal history of Singapore from the voices and perspectives of young archaeologists, retired photographers and videographers, dissident civilian historians, ex-communist guerrilla fighters, and expatriate ethnographers. The disparate range of subjects and timeframes makes for a challenging filmic experience given its lack of a formal narrative structure. In a 2007 interview with *The Straits Times*, Tan asserted that *Invisible City* "aims to give you a visceral experience of the atrophy of memories, whether through self-censorship, death or decay of artefacts. And it allows the viewers to muse on how their experience of the present is shaped as much by luck as it is by the efforts of a few preservationists" (Tan, 2007b).

The film announces its unconventional form from the start as it begins with rare color footage of Singapore in the 1950s and '60s. The shots seem damaged in some way, they stutter frame by frame with a highly audible sound of machinery and running film reel for their soundtrack. Ordinary portraits of families, fishermen eating a meal and vividly colored street scenes are seductive in depicting a period in Singapore's history with so little footage in color. The images move in a slow, distorted fashion, forcing the viewer to confront the limitations of this archival footage: its incompleteness without an audio track, and its heavy reliance on technological mediation obvious from the stuttering hum of the machine. From the beginning of the film, it is apparent that this venture into the invisible city will be fraught, fragmentary, and necessarily frustrating.

Invisible City's filmic style continues in this idiosyncratic way as it negotiates the forgotten and liminal spaces of the island. From this opening sequence, the film abruptly switches to first-person point-of-view shots of wandering into dense tropical vegetation, as a slightly shaky handheld camera struggles through what our off-camera guide calls "the last really wild areas in Singapore," a small patch of jungle on Sentosa Island.[7] We are off the beaten path here, in an unmapped space, as an archaeological team cuts away at foliage and climbs over fallen logs to reach their site. The film lingers on the difficult and time-consuming process of excavating the past of a country where so much has been erased by development and the construction of a national history and ideology. The team are unearthing the remains of an old fort that was built in the 1940s, and more shots of this process continue to be interspersed with other narrative threads throughout *Invisible City*.[8]

Tan challenges what would be a linear retelling of Singapore's history by complicating the trope of archaeology. These slow meditative shots of tropical junglescapes, of archaeologists sifting through dirt, sorting out fragments, and cataloguing finds could, on the one hand, be seen as a metonymic structure for what Tan does in the film, as she pauses to reflect and brush off layers of forgetting in order to achieve limited, piecemeal truths about Singapore's past. However, Tan admits in the audio commentary on the *Invisible City* DVD that while she had initially intended for the entire film to be based on the conceit of archaeology, this fell through because "it was too cerebral." Tan notes, "what worked best was to use the emotional highs and lows as the structure, as the primary way to interact with viewers – the film is structured by emotion and feeling. Since a film is not logical" (2007a). Indeed, in the vein of John Frow's observation that desire (and not truth) is the organizing logic of memory, *Invisible City* here attempts to bypass a cartographical view of Singapore and even an

---

[7] Sentosa is one of Singapore's largest offshore islands and has long been used as both a tourist destination with accompanying exhibits that represent Singapore's history in wax reproductions of historical scenes, and a long-term detention center for prisoners. Sentosa is an ideal example of how the government has attempted to contain history and culture in a clearly defined geographical space that even has the ability to hide a political prisoner with subversive potential. The island's so-called historical exhibits resurrect token memorabilia and scenes from the official history without true engagement with the fullness of that history and an emotional investment in the loss embedded in it.

[8] Crucially, all of the "characters" featured in Tan's film are interested in periods of the past before Singapore's official independence in 1965, another eschewal of a state-imposed grand narrative.

Fig. 13 Film still from *Invisible City* (2007). Archaeologists sifting through their excavated findings, Sentosa Island. Credit: Tan Pin Pin. Used with permission.

archaeological one by turning to the mutability of human emotion. In its artistic excavations, *Invisible City* eschews traditional narrative structures, a geological chronology that is so evident in archaeological work. In its place, it develops a meandering focus that relies on its audience's emotional response to grapple and wrestle with the often disjunctive and thwarted attempts of meaning-making.

The film's sequencing is thus organized by the intense passion and inquisitiveness of its filmmaker and by its "characters" like the archaeologist Lim Chen Sian, the leader of the featured expedition, who, in his own words wants to make an "inventory" and "survey" of what is in the fort to better understand the people who were there before. His desire produces this hidden space, as he excavates the fragments and artifacts in the site. It is not the literal action of archaeology that is privileged in the film, although it is important, but rather the desire behind that action, and the steadfast earnestness of the young archaeologists themselves. Their laborious work produces only an incomplete understanding of the past, but Lim suggests that just being able to hold on to physical remnants of this history, the only history that he can relate to, is worth it because it allows him to experience his country's spaces anew.

The film's central notion of our limited ability to recapture the past finds a resonance with one of the most compelling figures in *Invisible City*: the aging videographer Ivan Polunin. There is, of course, something fitting about the fact that Tan has chosen another filmmaker as one of the central figures in her film. The first glimpse of Polunin is of a young documentary maker who has an eye for both natural landscape and the everyday pleasures of his subjects.

From a sun-dappled shot of a group of Indigenous Orang Asli boys playing with tree branches to the intimate close-ups of weather-beaten middle-aged Chinese fishermen eating a meal of watery rice and small fish, Tan judiciously

Fig. 14 Film still from *Invisible City* (2007). Ivan Polunin's footage of street life in Singapore in the 1950s. Credit: Tan Pin Pin. Used with permission.

presents Polunin's footage of the most mundane, the most quotidian. Watching Polunin's footage within Tan's film adds another layer of meaning to the footage itself; here we do not just get Polunin's empathetic eye to the past, we are also watching what Tan has chosen to incorporate into her film. Tan curates everyday life to humanize the abstraction of the past for the viewer. This is not what Chua Beng Huat notes to be the "abstract sentiments" of "kampung life" (1994, 27); watching Polunin's footage, we are struck by the immediacy of the early color film that augments the reality of this life from the barely accessible mangrove swamps, the meager food of the people, and the busy, bewildering markets where produce is sold off the curb.

These long-forgotten scenes, markers of ordinary life, act as imperfect artifacts of the film's excavations of the past. Tan notes in her audio commentary on the *Invisible City* DVD that she was "mesmerized" by this footage precisely because she was "trying to identify places she could possibly recognize" – excavating the city through its lost and forgotten inhabitants, and long-demolished buildings and road intersections.

Tan's frustrating interviews with Polunin do not attempt to construct an overarching narrative that links together these disparate scenes of Singapore. In fact, one could say that they make a show out of failing to do so, with Polunin often interrupting himself mid-thought or mid-sentence as he struggles to formulate his explanations. We later discover that he is recovering from brain surgery, a fitting physical corollary to the film's awareness of the fragile nature of memory.

Polunin is mostly unable to properly articulate why he found it so important to record and preserve his archive of Singapore in the 1950s. *Invisible City* brings this incoherence and its fragmentary results to the forefront when at a crucial juncture the film lets Polunin's confused voice-overs play over a black screen. Again, as with the repeated shots of the archaeologists' labor,

Fig. 15 Film still from *Invisible City* (2007). An aged Ivan Polunin being interviewed by Tan Pin Pin. Credit: Tan Pin Pin. Used with permission.

Polunin's rather poignant musings on the significance of his work and even his frequent inability to provide geographical and historical details are testament to the impossibility of a perfect record of memory and history, of the risks of excavation and archiving in this indeterminate space. Tan emphasizes the fragility of Polunin's collection, when she shows how his reels are kept in antiquated tin cases on a rickety looking shelf, with an ominous reminder of their flammability represented by a shot of the small fire extinguisher that is mounted next to them.[9]

As the film progresses, it becomes apparent that it is interested in a specific period of Singapore's history: the years just before the nation achieved independence. In one scene, Chan Cheow Thia, an academic interviewed by Tan, says that he wants to look beyond the artificial marker of 1965, the year of Singapore's independence, because seeing it as the beginning of Singapore's modern history means that the years just before 1965 will be neglected. The fifties and early sixties were part of a period of transition and upheaval for Singapore, and as the journalist and the film both suggest, one of forgetting. A great deal of the official history written of this period has been constructed with the intention of bolstering a triumphant account of a vulnerable new nation. The period saw rapid spatial changes in the city, and the documentary wrestles with the continued legacy of the British Empire in the spaces it discovers. Where this is most obvious is *Invisible City*'s portrayal of the photographer and activist Marjorie Doggett and her book *Characters of Light*. Tan's film intersperses interview sequences with the very frail, bedridden

---

9 It is worth noting that after Tan's documentary was screened, Polunin and his work enjoyed newfound fame that resulted in a television special, a museum exhibition, and requests by the National Archives of Singapore for access to his film reels.

Doggett with her black-and-white photographs of colonial-era buildings, many of which have since been demolished. This is an empire of failing expatriate memories and crumbling syncretic architecture.[10] In her audio commentary track, Tan notes that Doggett's book includes a map of these old buildings to show their place in the colonial parts of the city. One might read the book as a preemptive act of colonial mourning, evidenced by her choice of epigraph: an 1823 imperial apologia from Sir Stamford Raffles, where the aforementioned "characters of light" are in fact a metaphor for the buildings of the British Empire, inscribed onto and defining Singapore's spatial reality.[11]

Doggett's book is nostalgic for a certain colonial past, even as it anticipates a postcolonial era in which she notes how "masses of colonial buildings were demolished." Paradoxically, her now obsolete literal and figurative mapping of the old colonial landmarks, her "characters of light" present a way beyond the colonial map. The hand-drawn map in the book (not shown in the film), which Doggett calls a "Sketch Map," is arguably a counter-cartographical document in and of itself. It maps what is no longer there, or what was about to destroyed at the point of its creation. Unlike other colonial maps that I have discussed above, this map does not plan or zone. Turning to moments of great intimacy, it plots an emotional and spectral geography of a Singapore in great upheaval, in the years between the end of the Second World War and its 1965 independence. Tan's inclusion of Doggett's photographs of demolished buildings, the obvious specters of this map, reorients them as a critique of Singapore's current urban space. As with her directorial decision to focus on the quotidian scenes in Polunin's footage, Tan's reanimation of Doggett's work through a late interview with her speaks to the photograph's relation to the contemporary spaces of Singapore. The film's excavatory portrayal of Doggett's work traces a genealogy of material and psycho-geographical loss in Singapore's physical landscape, and serves as a kind of anterior warning of the hubris and fragility of empires. *Invisible City*'s depiction of Singapore's colonial past does not shy away from its complex, fraught complicity. Tan embodies it in Doggett herself, her voice slow, measured, and barely audible, her age and infirmity tenderly documented. *Invisible City* shows us that this seemingly monolithic colonial history is undercut or shot through with individual agency

---

10 This is not to say that all colonial architecture has vanished, of course. As I noted in the Introduction, the Singaporean government retained much of the colonial government architecture almost as a perpetuation of its own power (see Bishop, Phillips, and Yeo, 2003).

11 The full epigraph reads: "Let it still be the boast of Britain / to write her name in characters of light; / let her not be remembered as the tempest / whose course was desolation, / but as the gale of spring reviving / the slumbering seeds of mind and / calling them to life / from the winter of ignorance and oppression. / If the time shall come / when her empire shall have passed away, / these monuments will endure when her triumphs / shall have become an empty name" (Doggett, 1957, v).

and experience. Personal memories and, crucially, idiosyncratic spatialities can reclaim human agency even in the remembrance of colonial architecture.

In other moments of the film, the camera follows its subjects as they are brought back to the exact geographical places where social spaces of civil society and community had been created in earlier times. The camera lingers on nondescript streets, storefronts, school grounds where attempts at civil society, at community organizing were made. Central to the stories of one of the film's key interlocuters, Han Tan Juan, is the vilification of the Chinese student protest movement in the 1950s and '60s in approved history textbooks. As Hong Lysa posits, Han seeks to rehabilitate them, seeing them as colonial fighters rather than violent communist agitators (2008). Han's vivid recounting of the use of tear gas in the school grounds that seem idyllic in contemporary times, and his photographs of police violence against the students, represent some of *Invisible City*'s most overtly political moments. Repeatedly, the film returns to seemingly ordinary spaces to excavate their significance for individuals and communities who do not fit into Singapore's spatial and historical ideologies.

While Charles Lim's work, with its lack of overt commentary and non-narrative modes, may sometimes seem detached and aloof in its observations of Singapore's developmental politics, *Invisible City* (2007) is an example of how desire, nostalgia, and affect come into play in a praxis of excavation. Texts that are invested in desire to excavate the past with its contradictory details, conflicting agendas, and complex human intentions, instead of authoritarian forms of "truths," provide counterpoints to the abstract spaces of the late capitalist city. As Frow puts it, the past and "its meaning and its truth are constituted retroactively and repeatedly" (1997, 229). In effect, these works make us aware of the instability of temporal progression in space, as the past is created and recreated continually, and our present is made and remade. The scale of Lim's work gives an inkling of how one might need to engage with Singapore as a space relentlessly planned and perpetually altered by the state. Tan's work choreographs a poignant dance involving excavation, desire, and memory, and in doing so unmoors a singular, official history. *Invisible City* reminds us of the mutability of the past itself, how it cannot be preserved in any fixed form as it is so easily lost to us and, further, open to the interpretations of every new generation. Memory, these artists remind us, can never be complete, thorough, or exhaustive.[12] Indeed, therein lies its power in an overmapped space and time.

---

12 Indeed, *Invisible City* provides only an inkling of the scale of historical reclamation that needs to occur to fully counter the dominant cartographical views of Singapore. Hong Lysa points out that Tan's film is still an exercise of privilege in the production of spatio-temporalities in Singapore. She notes how many of the people featured in *Invisible City* have simply "gathered sufficient social capital to have a sense of the limits that they can go" or that their stories are now "useful to state discourses" (Hong, 2008). In Singapore, much remains to be excavated.

"A Fluid and Borderless Past"

This chapter has explored the political and ecological implications of artistic excavations without yet considering the issues of indigeneity, deterritorialization, and dispossession in Singapore. These ideas are fraught and contested in the Singaporean context, and are underlying complications to how the state sees itself as exceptional for its Chinese-majority population in the region. This is particularly with regard to its histories of union and separation with Malaysia, and its post-independence conflict with Indonesia. For ideological and geopolitical reasons, the state would rather not recall its complex pasts as they are profoundly situated in the Malay World or Nusantara (the Indonesian term for Maritime Southeast Asia; see Evers, 2016). It is beyond the scope of this study to undertake any definitive stance on the concept of indigeneity. But it is necessary to include, in our consideration of excavatory art practices, the invisible histories of the indigenous peoples who were displaced for Singapore's development. Excavating Singapore inevitably returns to its mutable coastlines, revealing that some of this land used to be sea and is bound to the larger archipelago that surrounds it.

In what follows, my examination of the visual and performance artist ila's transmedial work "A Fluid Borderless Past," does not seek a full accounting of these histories – fragmented and buried as they are. Working against the idea of completeness, ila's art, through its the multiple modalities of photography, memoir, ethnography, dance, and video installation, creates an excavatory practice that recalls the archipelagic relations and intimacies that predate the colonization of Singapore and its surrounding islands.[13] Published on the dissident website *Singapore Unbound*, edited by the Singaporean-American poet-activist Jee Leong Koh, ila's piece traces the relationship between a fishing village in Batam, Indonesia, and Singapore's intensive development of its coastlines. Through oral interviews with the fishermen, first-person reportage, and historical research, ila depicts the communal and personal effects of Singapore's complete alterations of its shores and offshore islands. She reflects on her own Javanese and Bugis ancestry, and reminds us of the indigenous Orang Laut communities who were displaced and dispossessed. She returns to Punggol Beach in Singapore and remembers its violent history as the site of the Sook Ching Massacre during the Japanese occupation of Singapore in the Second World War. Paired with her writing are her evocative

---

13 ila is a visual and performance artist who works with found objects, moving images, and live performance. Her main themes include gender and identity, peripheral communities, and history. Her work has been presented in the exhibition "Arus Balik – From Below the Wind to Above the Wind and Back Again" (2019) at the NTU Centre for Contemporary Art Singapore and in other international and national exhibitions. In 2022, her collaborative video work *Suap Lidah* produced with her partner Bani Haykal was commissioned by the 5th Singapore Literature Festival in New York City.

photographs of the fishermen in Batam, their boats, the shoreline, the sea, and the industrial infrastructure in the intertidal zones. The piece ends with a poetic description of her performative video installation, *bekas*, which was shown at the NTU Centre for Contemporary Arts in March 2019. The accompanying video trailer features her nude body, covered in black inked words from conversations about ancestral lineage, and what it means to be Javanese, Boyanese, or Malay.

In ila's work, as in Lim's and Tan's, we see how multiple modes and genres are necessary to excavate the mapped spaces of Singapore. Where Lim uses documentary film, installation art, remedial cartography, and so on, Tan's *Invisible City* curates the efforts of ethnographers, anthropologists, archaeologists, photographers, historians, journalists, and ordinary Singaporeans whose multiple and affective modes of engaging with the city reveal its hidden contours. Similarly, ila's hybrid piece "A Fluid Borderless Past" moves between autobiography, historical research, site specific performance, interviews, and photography as a multimodal way to excavate the complex ecological, communal, and familial histories that lie beneath the surface of Singapore's intensive development of reclaimed coastal land – in effect the most highly planned spaces on the island.

Fixed temporalities and spatialities are elusive in ila's work, even as she marks the piece with date and location markers that ostensibly place them in time and space. For instance, the opening spatio-temporality is: "2:15 pm, 2nd February 2019, Tuas, Singapore," yet the piece is also marked by a timeless personification of the weather:

> The air was salt and brine and it billowed; bulged in and out; but the sea was nowhere in sight, no matter how far into the distance one tried to look. How did the sea, in all its vastness disappear completely? I stood amidst the metal beams, gazing around the barren land, looking up at the towering cranes catching the glint of the shifting midday sun. The winds were relentless; like restless spirits that danced on lands but were hungry for their sea. They forgot that waves could not form on land but they could not stop themselves from trying.
>
> The sea, even if it was buried by all these rocks and cement merging into the soft red soil and even if all the life that thrived inside it was drained out, could never disappear completely. My ears caught echoes of the waves. *It is common for sea breezes to penetrate 40 to 80 km inland.* How far was 40 km and how did one measure it in relation to an absence? (ila, 2019)

ila's text achieves a magical realist quality here as she blends the descriptions of Singapore's developmental landscape with it "towering cranes" and "metal beams" with her characterization of the winds as "restless spirits that danced on lands but were hungry for their sea." Even as the very weather has been altered by coastal development, ila's text points to this liminal space as one where the air continues to be "salt and brine" recalling that this land used to be the sea. The sea itself, even as it "buried by all these rocks and cement merging into the soft red soil [...] could never disappear completely." Her vision of the sea still beneath the reclaimed land and the sea breezes as "hungry for their sea" are in direct contrast to the quantitative fact that sea breezes "*penetrate 40 to 80 km inland*" since, as she puts it, one cannot measure it "in relation to an absence."

The discombobulation that the narrator faces in this moment continues through the piece as she attempts but fails to visit Tuas, which houses heavy industry, incinerators, an immigration checkpoint to Malaysia, and is in the process of becoming a mega-port, the largest in the world. The area in question is "completely off limits, barricaded and heavily protected with signs and security posts" (ila, 2019). She is similarly unable to see Jurong Island, an artificial island which used to be a collection of seven offshore islands whose residents were resettled on the mainland in the 1980s. ila imagines "my home disappearing into a giant landfill bearing no traces of my past" (2019) and includes a map showing exactly where these islands were, superimposed with the new Jurong Island developments.

This excavation goes beyond Singapore's shores and across its southernmost tip to a fishing village in Batam, Indonesia, where ila interviews Pak Ramlan, a fisherman from Tanjung Uma, one of the oldest villages on the island. He enumerates the ecological changes that have taken place since Singapore's independence, which have resulted in a loss of fishing waters for the community. He notes, too, that he and ila "are from the same place, the same sea. We always feel that the sea divides us. We forget that the lands divide us but the sea connects us. *Kita serumpun*" (qtd. in ila, 2019). ila translates the Malay word *serumpun* as "a group sharing the same language and culture from the same origins" (2019), while the word *kita* means "we" or "us." By shifting our understanding of borders and situating Singapore in the larger Riau Archipelago, ila's text shows us the lost possibilities of the island state's maritime contexts. In a later part of the text, she further complicates the monolithic idea of Malay identity by musing on the difference between being Bugis and Javanese.

As with the work of Lim and Tan, the bodies that exist within the borders and infrastructure that mark Singapore's seascapes and landscapes evince an uneasiness when confronted with the buried past. Pak Ramlan can no longer go to either Singapore or Malaysia because of the mapped waterways of these sovereign nations. In a conversation with ila, he notes the incommensurability between his body that knows the waters so keenly and the national borders that portend violence and exclusion:

> "How do you know where the borders are? Are they marked?"
> "Yes, in the coordinates."
> "Does your boat show these coordinates, Pak?"
> "No, but my body remembers it for me."
> "Do you want to go Singapore again, Pak?"
> "Even if I want to, I have no passport." (ila, 2019)

In her conversations with him, ila is performing an excavation of Singapore's transnational, fluid, and borderless histories. Ones that are not easily apparent from its identity as one of the world's busiest container ports. Where the port city is usually defined by its crucial position as an important node in global supply chains, here its watery identity is all about relation, kinship, indigeneity, and loss.

"A Fluid Borderless Past" further evinces a sharp awareness of the haunted landscapes on Singapore's beaches. ila's visit to Punggol Beach turns up the "bones, teeth, and other human remains" (ila, 2019) uncovered as the sand was washed to be used in the construction of Singapore's public housing. The state's removal of sand from the beach exposes the history of the Sook Ching Massacre, where large numbers of Chinese men were shot dead by the Japanese, their corpses left on the shore. She notes as well the "scattered shrines of discolored sun-beaten deities underneath the trees, probably there to appease the restless spirits" (ila, 2019). The idea of the very matter of the country, its land, consistently in flux and ecologically compromised, is tied intimately to the spiritual and spectral beliefs of its communities. ila notes that she thinks "of the bones buried in the sand, bodiless and silenced, and the sand used to extend borders" (2019).

Repeatedly, the text explores the connections between land and body, finding in its excavations an intimate and visceral connection. In the final part of ila's text, she describes *bekas*, the Malay word for "used." It is a performative video installation that arose out of conversations with several people about "what it means to identify oneself with one's ancestral lineage and what it means to be, for example, Javanese, Boyanese, or Malay" (ila, 2019). In the video, parts of these conversations are written in black ink on ila's naked body as she performs dance-like movements on the lands in Singapore that were taken from the sea in Punggol, Tuas, and East Coast:

> My hands pressed against the ground as I tried to push myself up, before my entire body collapsed back into itself. My movements were limited. I could see the arch of my right shoulder, both my arms, the back of my hip. I could see my breath dancing against the dust and small stones. I could not see anything beyond this. I did not know where I was. All I could feel was the heat of the sun against my body and a slow throbbing coming from underneath me. I tried to push myself up again, this time shifting my hands from the front to my sides. I collapsed once more, from the same invisible current and the weight of the throbbing. There were markings, writings that I could not read, all over my body. These markings were disintegrating like wet earth after rain, paving meridians and parallels across my skin. I embodied what I had forgotten.
>
> My body refuses to forget. (ila, 2019)

This artistic intervention into a state-sanctioned homogeneous "Malay" identity depicts the heterogeneous and contested ways of understanding indigenous cultures in the Malay Archipelago. ila's performance excavates the body that is in tension with the colonized land. Her dance signals the impossibility of return coupled with the intense longing for unity. The markings on

Fig. 16 Film still from *bekas* (2019). Credit: ila. Used with permission.

her body "disintegrating like wet earth after rain" convey the aphasia and limitations of language itself to convey the deep grief of being deterritorialized. The abstraction of the performance placed at the end of her prose nonfiction text provides an alternate, affective representation of the buried layers and weight of the land itself.

Preceding this description is a poem in Malay and translated into English:

bekas:

1 tanda yang tertinggal atau tersisa (sesudah dipegang, diinjak, dilalui, dsb);

2 sesuatu yang tertinggal sebagai sisa (yg telah rusak, terbakar, tidak dipakai lagi, dsb):

3 pernah menjabat atau menjadi, tetapi sekarang tidak lagi;

4 sudah pernah dipakai

5 berkesan; memberikan kesan:

6 tempat menaruh sesuatu.

1 residual marks

2 abandoned and not used anymore

3 used to be but not anymore

4 have been used before

5 to affect/to create affect

6 a receptacle. (ila, 2019)

It is impossible not to read this an oblique critique of the colonial and (post) colonial ecological devastation that has been wrought on Singapore's seas and coastlines. These bodies of land and water have, as the untranslated portions of the work suggest, been stepped on, passed, damaged, burned, and used. The grief and powerlessness that ila's work suggests is itself an important testament to the harm that is revealed through these excavations. "A Fluid Borderless Past," read alongside the work of Lim, Mam, and Tan, provides a necessary indigenous perspective on the changes wrought to Singapore's landscapes and seascapes. All four works trace the disintegrating ruins of a constant and amnesiac pace of change. These artistic excavations of Singapore's development are also remedial histories – ones that make visible how the state has hidden its reliance on vast quantities of raw materials, indentured labor, indigenous dispossession, and political repression.

Community Excavations

In half a century or so of independence and development, actual archaeology in Singapore has, for the most part, received little or no governmental funding or support. One might speculate that there is a kind of fear of what might be discovered about Singapore's precolonial, pre-independence history that might disrupt the narrative of the farsighted British colonialists and Singapore's subsequent (post)colonial government. Writing about the work of the archaeologist John N. Miksic, Iskander Mydin posits that "the singular contribution of archaeology in the Singapore context has been to establish the fact that Singapore's history does not begin with the arrival of the British in 1819; it was preceded by a precolonial past" (2013, vii). Miksic, after 28 years of archaeological excavations in Singapore, asserts that far from being a "recent historical accident," "Singapore is one of the oldest capital cities of Southeast Asia: older than Jakarta, older than Ayutthaya, older than Manila or Yangon" (2013, 23). The threat or distraction of a longer, more complex history beneath the mapped spaces of (post)colonial Singapore, and the potential contestations to the state's control over space, made archaeology a methodology *non grata* in Singapore.

But beyond academic interest in an archaeological knowledge of Singapore, community-driven excavations of the mapped and planned spaces of the island point to the ways in which affect and spatial practice are intertwined in these counter-cartographical gestures. In 2011, there began a revival of interest in the centrally located Bukit Brown cemetery after plans to construct a road through the site were announced, requiring the exhumation and destruction of 5,000 graves. Nature conservation groups pointed out that this rare, undisturbed pocket of the island was the habitat of near-extinct flora and fauna. In describing the site, the United Nations Special Rapporteur in the field of cultural rights noted that the cemetery, which is unique to the region, enables people to trace their family trees by providing otherwise unavailable information, to learn about their past including the history of Singapore and its regional linkages, thus contributing to building a sense of identity and belonging to the region; it also provides a valuable database for researchers and scholars. The value of the Bukit Brown cemetery is reflected in the living practices of people who continue to pay their respects to their ancestors in the form of ceremonial rites, offerings, as well as in highly personalized ways in continuity of living cultural practices. (Shaheed, 2012)

As with its mistrust of archaeological practices, the cosmopolitan, multicultural, and regional histories that the cemetery evinced were at odds with the state's construction of a national identity based on racial differentiation and exceptionalism in the region. Further, the state viewed this rare grassroots desire for conservation as an inconvenient hindrance to its desire to construct an eight-lane expressway across the site and eventually an entirely new housing estate. The resulting furor among concerned citizenry and academics was notable for being an unprecedented response to developmental policy in the country's contemporary history.

The grassroots movement was ultimately unsuccessful in its bid to preserve Bukit Brown intact. However, the seemingly irrational, not-for-profit driven impetus behind the drive to document, record, and counter-map the space points to the upswell of emotion and desire for a historical accounting that valorizes the ordinary and the everyday. Even though eminent figures of Singapore's colonial history were buried at the site, there was a lot of concern for the tombs of ordinary people. Engaging with this social history, community-based excavations of the site involved, among other activist actions, independently organized guided tours and storytelling sessions. These were distinctly not part of any tourism guide, nor did the centuries-old cemetery figure as part of the state's policy of marketing Singapore as either a leisure or a business destination. What these gestures of excavation suggest is that in spite of the overzoned and overdetermined nature of Singapore's urban spaces, there remains an inherent desire to transcend their cartographic silences.

CHAPTER 2

Circumventions

Circumscribed Realities

Tan Pin Pin's film *To Singapore, With Love* opens with an exterior shot of a modest townhouse in London and cuts to a man frying noodles in a wok. The man, Ho Juan Thai, has been exiled from Singapore for over three decades. He is making *char kway teow*, a soy sauce and chili-infused dish of rice noodles and seafood beloved of overseas Singaporeans and one that is difficult to obtain outside the country. As the film cuts from a close-up on Ho Juan Thai, he quips that this is "quite different from the Singapore way of doing it." He adds, "Although you can't buy it here, but you can cook it yourself. It's partly how you cope when you are abroad, not to feel defeated you still try to cook your own Singapore food" (Tan, 2015). Ho's simple act of cooking in exile is one of a series of quiet, defiant circumventions that are documented in Tan's film. In the previous chapter, I discussed how her film *Invisible City* performs a quiet excavation of the city-state's seemingly inconsequential, ordinary, and forgotten histories. *To Singapore, With Love* moves quite differently in or, rather, around Singapore's spaces. In this chapter, I begin with this film as I move away from the spatialities of excavation and its emphasis on complicated verticalities and mingled horizontalities. As I turn to centripetal movements, I consider Tan's 2015 film in tandem with Jeremy Tiang's short story "National Day," and Tania De Rozario's poetic memoir and political commentary *And the Walls Come Crumbling Down*. The latter two texts are focalized through minority perspectives: those of migrant construction workers and the LGBTQ community in Singapore.

In the Singaporean context, the existence of these circumventory texts is not self-evident. Growing up in Singapore during the 1980s and '90s meant reading history textbooks and attending state-sanctioned "National Education" programs that were invested in producing a story of a nationalist, one-party-dominated, heteronormative Singaporean state. This narrative begins with the city-state's colonial founding in 1819 and in the post-independence period, proceeds apace through the principles of free trade, its official version of multiracial and multi-religious equality, and meritocracy under the uninterrupted rule of the People's Action Party (PAP). Yet there were strange lacunae in the high-school history curriculum regarding the time after the Japanese occupation of Singapore (post-1945). This tumultuous period includes: the Malayan Emergency or the Anti-British National Liberation War – a war between colonial forces and communist guerrilla fighters (1948–1960), decolonization (1963), a failed merger with present-day Malaysia (1963–1965), a declaration of independence through separation (1965), and the consolidation of the ruling party's power. These events were glossed over in our history textbooks. Looking back, it is impossible to see this as anything other than a strategic amnesia and state-sanctioned forgetting which served a young nation-state eager to bolster sanitized narratives of nation building. Only in recent years have more concerted efforts been made to understand and reflect upon the violence in the period of decolonization and its intimate connections to political repression in the 1970s and '80s. These latter decades saw a rise in activism around migrant and local workers' rights and the ruling PAP used colonial-era emergency legislation to suppress this nascent activism along with its political opponents, often by accusing them of being communists. There were mass detentions without trial, alongside numerous politically motivated exiles and arrests. As legal scholar Jothie Rajah (2012) has elucidated, the laws that were used to justify these repressive actions were direct legacies of colonial laws now used in the service of power consolidation in this single-party state.

    Unhampered access to the state archives of this period and regarding these events is critical yet impossible given the restrictions on this sensitive information. In recent times, historians, scholars, and artists have relied on the testimony of witnesses and former political detainees which notably diverge from the official narratives of these events. Activist historians have filled in some of these gaps by combing the archives in and outside of Singapore. The urgency of this project has increased due to the aging and deaths of many witnesses and dissidents. This is a significant development for a country has no Freedom of Information Act or equivalent of a declassification rule. Gareth Curless notes that "material relating to foreign affairs, defence, and internal security is generally unavailable, while other records require permission from the relevant ministry and may be subject to strict conditions of use, such as no transcription or citation" (2014). Scholars have found it frustrating when authorities deny even requests concerning the most banal of subjects, such as trade, work, and housing, and have turned to oral histories and records outside Singapore in American, Chinese, Japanese, and British colonial archives. These attempts to use foreign archives or rely on oral histories have their limitations: the historian Loh Kah Seng points out that "as the 'moving wall' of historical research progresses into Singapore's more recent postcolonial period," foreign diplomats and analysts have had less access to the inner workings of the Singapore government (2010, 17–18). Oral histories, on the other hand, are subject to the vagaries of official historiographic methods, informants' continued fear of consequences and reprisals, or the internalization of the state's perspectives (Loh, 2010, 20–21).

In tandem with this historiographical and historical approach is the production of a range of nonfictional and fictional texts like podcasts, plays, musicals, documentaries, eyewitness accounts, graphic novels, and literary fiction. Indeed, twenty-first-century Singapore is seeing a renaissance of political and historical writing about this period. Notable examples include Boo Junfeng's film *Sandcastle* (2010), Jeremy Tiang's novel *State of Emergency* (2017), and photographer-artist Sim Chiyin's ongoing transmedial project on the Malayan Emergency. The Singaporean playwright Tan Tarn How has called this the "scar literature" of Singapore, a term originally used of works about China's Cultural revolution but which Tan has deemed to be cultural texts that "deal directly or indirectly with […] the time up till the late 1980s, during which the government locked up without trial politicians, social activists, and playwrights, journalists and other intellectuals" (2017). As Tan points out, the government has admitted that between 1959 and 1990, 2,460 people were detained without trial, albeit not all for political reasons. Chia Thye Poh, the prisoner who was held the longest, was imprisoned for 32 years (nine of which were under house arrest). "Scar literature" retells these histories from non-dominant (non-state) perspectives and is a form of justice that corrects the profound belatedness and non-recognition of detentions that preceded independence and continued long after.

The powerful resurgence of these narratives against centrally directed acts of censorship and suppression speaks to distinct spatial realities. Aside from the physical inaccessibility of the archives, the bodies of exiled Singaporean dissidents have been literally barred from entering the country. The exclusion of its citizens by a nation-state is only one end of the spectrum of spatially restrictive powers in Singapore. The country has a series of legal statutes that prevent bodies from assembling in space, "(a) to demonstrate support for or opposition to the views or actions of any person, group of persons or any government; (b) to publicize a cause or campaign; or (c) to mark or commemorate any event, and includes a demonstration by a person alone for any such purpose referred to in paragraph (a), (b) or (c)" (Public Order Act Chapter 257A, Section 5, Part 1). This piece of legislation regulates the use of all public space in the country: there can be no assembly without a permit from the police. An "assembly" is so broadly defined that in 2018, the artist Seelan Palay was arrested and charged for being a "procession of one" as he held a mirror in front of Singapore's Parliament House as part of a performance art piece (Guan Zhen Tan, 2017). These laws preclude the possibility of social activism and, by regulating the collective power of assembled bodies, close down the possibilities of the physical environment in Singapore. Assemblies for acts of support, solidarity, and protest are only allowed in one downtown park and one must still apply for a license to gather in that space. Singapore, then, is a policed and disciplined state where bodies are physically regulated through the exercise of specific, spatialized laws regarding who can be in the country and what forms of organized dissent they can express collectively and corporeally. Hong Lim Park, with its special status, has become a circumscribed space, one that contains the threat of corporeal and collective dissent.

In the late twentieth and early twenty-first century, dissident Singaporean movements have also been organized around a series of key issues: equality for lesbian, gay, bisexual, transgender, and queer people through the repeal of a colonial era law that criminalizes homosexual sex, the abolition of the death penalty, improving migrant workers' rights, granting amnesty to exiled dissidents, and a reduction of the censorship of artistic expression. The most well-known and influential of these is the annual Pink Dot gathering in Hong Lim Park, which since 2009 has witnessed an ever-growing crowd (peaking at 28,000 in 2015) gathering to support the organization's call for the "Freedom to Love" and equal rights for LGBTQ people in Singapore (see Lim, 2015). The one-night sit-in protest culminates in participants using pink lights to form a "pink dot."

In 2016, after increasingly high-profile entities like Twitter, Google, and Goldman Sachs began sponsoring the event, the government announced that it was banning foreign companies from supporting the event and even more crucially, only allowing Singaporeans and permanent residents to attend Pink Dot. For the first time, organizers had to erect barriers around the gathering and hire security to perform identity checks prior to entry (Koh, 2017). The circumscribed physical space for this outpouring of personal expression is testimony to the restricted social space for civil society in Singapore and the unequal position of LGBTQ people in Singapore at large. Bolstered by Section 377A, which criminalizes homosexual sex, there are clear rules that prevent positive depictions of LGBTQ relationships in popular culture and the media and efforts to prevent a holistic sex education curriculum from being implemented in the public school system. Further, LGBTQ citizens and residents face significant challenges to access public housing, support for childrearing, and end-of-life rights.

An equally important, if smaller, contemporaneous movement for the rights and voices of migrant workers has also arisen in recent decades. This movement, which in the 1970s and '80s resulted in the imprisonment of activists, has gained more public credibility in recent years through the work of Transient Workers Count Too (TWC2) and the Humanitarian Organization for Migration Economics (HOME). These organizations still exist very much on the fringes of mainstream Singapore and work against the government's refusal to legislate equal workers' rights for migrant workers and Singaporeans' general apathy about the rights of the men who construct their buildings, roads, and subway lines, and the women who care for their elderly and young.¹ In his extensive study of the working conditions of South Asian migrant workers in Singapore, Charan Bal argues that the constant threat of deportation, or "deportability," enables employers to treat these workers as "disposable economic subjects with few or no political rights" (2015, 269, 268). Migrant workers, therefore, bear much of the brunt of Singapore's relentless pursuit of economic growth, as they perform largely unseen and undocumented household labor and childrearing, and underpaid, dangerous, and unprotected construction work. Noorashikin Abdul Rahman argues that there is a "social acceptability" tied to the hiring of domestic workers that is based on "an ingrained patriarchal mindset [...] that sees domestic work as inextricably intertwined with women's roles in society" (2010, 204). This makes it "natural" to "purchase the labor of another woman when the women in the family [a]re unavailable to perform domestic work" (204). Rahman points out the longer history and cultural tradition of middle and elite classes in Singapore relying on paid domestic service (2010, 204).

The draconian and intrusive regulations governing these workers must be noted here: domestic workers are strictly forbidden to overstay their contracts, take on work other than for their employers, or become pregnant. For any of these offenses, they could be sent home and the substantial bond money that their employers pay for them could be forfeited. The security bond and the additional monthly levy that the government requires of employers creates a predisposition to surveillance and mistrust. Migrant construction workers are often victims of their employers' failure to pay their salaries and swift deportations when they fall ill or are injured. In 2013, dissatisfaction with working conditions may have played a role in the eruption of a rare riot (only the second since race riots in 1969) in the Little India district of Singapore sparked by a fatal accident involving a bus and a migrant worker. Some 300 to 400 workers were involved in violence that saw the destruction of symbols of the state: police cars and paramedic vehicles. A committee of inquiry that was set up to investigate the causes of the riot opined that alcohol

---

1 The Foreign Maids Scheme was introduced by the government in 1978 to allow for larger numbers of Singaporean women to enter the workforce. One in five Singaporean households employ a foreign domestic worker. Rapid economic development and the influx of women into Singapore's workforce since the 1980s means that domestic workers, mainly from the Philippines, Indonesia, Myanmar, and India, are funneled through profit-minded employment agencies before being hired for childcare, housework, and eldercare by families ranging from the middle-class to the affluent. In 2015, some 227,100 women from neighboring countries in Southeast Asia were working as foreign domestic workers in Singapore. Many left behind their own families to care for their employers' progeny. They have no access to the labor rights given to most Singaporean workers: an ugly reality exemplified by the fact that the government only legislated a day off for them in 2013 after a decade of campaigning by activists.

was a "major contributory factor" in the escalation of the night's violence and yet failed to address the structural and systemic discrimination that these workers face (see "Little India," 2014). As a result, the district, which has a long history of providing a space with amenities for South Asian migrant workers to relax, shop for groceries, and connect with their peers, was subject to even more surveillance and restrictions (see "Riot," 2013; Jaensubhakij, 2017). Workers are discouraged from visiting the downtown space on the weekends through restrictions on transportation, severe penalties for the consumption of alcohol within the zone, and auxiliary police forces who regularly stop them for random checks. Taken together, the system of legal and spatial controls signals that the bodies of migrant workers are both essential and disposable in Singapore's neoliberal economy – one that uses them to ensure full economic productivity from its own citizens.[2]

Artistic attempts to represent the complex and unjust contexts of foreign domestic workers in Singapore have historically met with disproportionate state intervention. One of the first artistic representations of a foreign domestic worker in a Singapore text was Third Stage's 1986 play *Esperanza*. In the mid-1980s, there were close to 40,000 foreign domestic workers in Singapore and the play depicted a Singaporean employer abusing her Filipino worker. The play became a part of a noteworthy episode of government repression in the arts scene when, along with the company's other politically relevant work, it was used in 1987 to justify their arrests as part of Operation Spectrum. William Peterson notes that because of this arrest, no other theater company took up what was called a "maid's play" (2001, 108) for a decade, since in the 1980s and early 1990s, "*Esperanza* served as a flash point for work that strays too far into the realm of politics to be politically acceptable to the

---

2 Indeed, the fact that foreign domestic workers are deeply involved in the familial lives of Singaporeans, both in real life and in fiction, complicates conventional ideas of family and its "values." Teo You Yenn argues in *Neoliberal Morality in Singapore* (2011) that the assumptions and common sense of neoliberalism as an ideology has taken on some very specific forms that reaffirm the importance of nationalist identity and certain mutual obligations between state and society (116). Teo posits that this "neoliberal morality" has "the capacity to check a state's pursuit of neoliberalist policies" and thus combines "intense individualism and competition" and "a peculiar manifestation of collective well-being" (119). Yet Teo's theory only holds true for citizens of Singapore's neoliberal state. Foreign domestic workers as non-citizens, marginalized and disenfranchised in all the ways detailed above, seem less-than-human components of the Singaporean economy. Even as Teo argues that neoliberal morality "tolerates inequality but also holds accountable the state as upholders of some moral good beyond fundamentalism" (119), the kind of "inequality" in the working conditions of migrant workers in general appears simply to reinforce the workings of the neoliberal economy in the country. Indeed, one might argue that Teo's discussion of neoliberal morality is predicated on the exclusion and subservient status of migrant workers since it is a morality that is certainly not concerned for their well-being.

state" (108). For their critical representation of foreign domestic labor and other politically minded theater, the playwrights Wong Souk Yee and Chng Suan Tze were charged with Marxist conspiracy against the state. Thus, from the first instance, literary and dramatic representations of foreign domestic workers in Singapore had immediate political consequences and implications. While, as Terence Chong notes, English-language theater in Singapore began in the mid-1980s to become "a truly local form of cultural-political expression" and a "site for expression of political critique and marginal identities" (2010, 91), the subject of foreign domestic labor continued to be taboo.[3] While these restrictions have loosened in the intervening years, with works like Anthony Chen's award-winning film *Ilo Ilo* (2013) and Haresh Sharma's play *Model Citizens* (2012) enjoying commercial and critical success, this episode remains an important historical and political precedent.[4]

This chapter thinks through how the centralized conception of Singaporean space is predicated on the exclusions of bodies, citizen, migrant, and minoritized. I will examine artistic and literary interventions that mirror the circumscribed and circumventing movements that these subjects are compelled to make when confronted with Singapore's pervasive system of discipline and surveillance. While I am not holding the positions of each of these subjects as coeval, it is important to note crucial solidarities between the various minoritized communities within Singaporean's authoritarian, neoliberal, and heteronormative state. In the context of a hidden and inaccessible archive, the enforced exile of multiple generations, and the physical and psychological disciplining of minority populations, the three contemporary texts that I examine in this chapter are representative of a shadow body of literary and

---

[3] In the first years of the new millennium, a resurgence in semi-independent Singaporean filmmaking saw works that took up the issue of foreign domestic labor. This was due in no small part to the fact that from 1978 to 2005, the number of foreign domestic workers in Singapore had tripled to 150,000 – representing employment in one in seven households. Kenneth Chan posits that films like Kelvin Tong's horror *The Maid* (2005) and Eric Khoo's activist short *No Day Off* (2006) treat the marginalized figure of the foreign domestic worker as "metonymic of an emerging racialized (and even racist) class system produced by Singapore's embrace of global capitalism and its often exploitative strategies," even as they critique the system. He points out, however, that both films still risk "unwitting complicity" (2010, 57) with the system since they were both made from the perspective of Singaporean filmmakers. Both films, Chan argues, risk using the figure of the foreign domestic worker as a culturally essentialized way of critiquing contemporary Singaporean society.

[4] There have been attempts to support a nascent foreign construction worker literary scene. Since 2014, volunteers and Singapore writers have organized a migrant workers poetry contest that has led to the visibility and publication of migrant worker writers. The independent publisher Ethos Books has since published Md Mukul Hossine's *Me Migrant* (2016) and Landmark Books has put out MD Sharif Uddin's *Stranger to Myself* (2017).

artistic texts that have arisen in the past two decades despite and in response to these realities.

In addition to the acts of excavation that I theorize in the previous chapter, I contend that the act of circumvention might provide a new theoretical lens through which to consider how art functions in the face of repressive historical and political practices of the state. While in Chapter 1 I argued for the excavatory function of my own critique, in this chapter, my praxis traces the centripetal routes that Singaporean writers and filmmakers take to tell stories that have been banned, suppressed, and ignored. The texts I examine function within and despite the larger structures of spatialized power that are produced by access to government funding, availability of physical spaces for artistic works, censorship, and access to archival resources. Each of these elements is directly affected by mapped and planned spaces of the Singaporean state as in many other nationalist, (post)colonial spaces. In my analysis of authoritarian Singapore, specifically, given its long history of censorship of art, this produces an opaque, powerful centralized bureaucracy and political power that controls mobility, freedom of speech and expression, and living conditions.

In *To Singapore, With Love*, Tan produces heteroglossic counter-histories in her numerous interviews with political dissidents and her film circles the island's maritime borders to produce a lived experience of exile outside Singapore. Tiang's "National Day" is a first-person plural account of migrant workers who take a day off on Singapore's independence day only to find themselves unwelcome on an offshore island where they have come to allow for a different perspective of the country. De Rozario's memoir *And the Walls Come Crumbling Down* depicts a queer minority subject who through her peripatetic movements around the island circumvents the dominant modes of capital, circulation, globalization, and citizenship that direct Singapore's planned speculations. De Rozario's text spatializes queer desire – giving us a lens through which to view the material, symbolic, and textual spaces of Singapore that are wholly unplanned, not profit-driven or planned-for. With excavation, the debris of suppressed histories and materialities is unearthed. With circumvention, the routes and trajectories of the marginalized make visible the calibrated and ever-shifting contours of authoritarian power in Singapore's efficient, gleaming cityscapes.

My analysis traces an incomplete inventory of a sidestepping of these mapped and disciplined spaces, whether they are the country's political and geographical borders, its surveilled and surveyed streets, or its regulated public housing. In all these texts, acts of physical circumvention are both literal and metaphorical ways of inhabiting Singapore's spaces in ways they were not planned for. Circumvention dwells in liminal and marginal spaces, those that are unmapped and unmappable. By evading or finding a way around, it calls into question borders that seem fixed and outlines the contours of spatialized power that may have been invisible. It overreaches and outwits, it is a transgressive, subversive inhabitation of space. My own reading of texts on the margins of the planned city, whether banned or marginalized, is itself a circumvention of the canon of narratives of authoritarian forms of nation-building, postcolonial progress, and economic success.

To Singapore, With Love

Banned by the Singaporean state, *To Singapore, With Love* enables us to reconsider the spaces of an authoritarian state from outside its borders. The film's preoccupation with spatial journeying and movement contrasts the fixed position of the nation, suggesting that different forms of Singaporean nationalism have been and are being cultivated outside the country's borders, in centripetal motion. By focusing on the quotidian textures of exiled life, the filmic text contests the celebratory global and transnational aspects of the city-state and its supposedly 'mobile' subjects. Tan's film circles the island's maritime borders to produce a lived experience of exile outside Singapore. Indeed, *To Singapore, With Love* shows how the bodies of the men and women banned from entering Singapore are themselves living, forgotten archives of a complex moment in the nation's history. Instead of attempting to produce new narratives from hitherto closed or unavailable archives, Tan relies on the complexities and nuances of her form to challenge the orderly, teleological production of Singapore as a successful postcolony, a global city.

Despite being banned in Singapore, Tan's film galvanized the overseas and diasporic Singaporean community in an unprecedented show of support, with screenings organized by ordinary citizens in Europe, the United States, Canada, and other parts of Asia. In September 2014, Singaporeans unable to watch the film in Singapore queued to take buses to neighboring Malaysia for screenings (see "To Johor Bahru," 2014). The enthusiastic overseas reception of Tan's film was fitting for a work that was filmed entirely outside of Singapore. Perspectives from a community of political exiles in London, Malaysia, and Thailand provided a seldom-seen view of the island state. The film's geographical circling of the island acts as a structure for its attempts to retrieve exiled narratives and records. Further, the film's attention to the politics of sensation in documenting the everyday lives of exiles enables it to bypass the state's literal refusal to admit them within its borders. This focus on the affective and corporeal is also apparent in the film's recuperation of fragments of Singaporean political protest music – a tradition that has no extant archive in Singapore due to political suppression.

Tan's circuitous film structure switches between a series of Singaporean exiles whose time away began in a series of expulsions and escapes 30 to 50 years ago. Her style is what Bill Nichols might classify as "poetic documentary" which in nonlinear ways opens up "the possibility of alternative forms of knowledge to the straightforward transfer of information" (2001, 103). The film

Fig. 17 Film poster of *To Singapore, With Love* (2013) showing Singapore exile Ho Juan Thai looking at the Singapore coastline from Johore Bahru, Malaysia. Credit: Tan Pin Pin. Used with permission.

begins with Ho Juan Thai, who left Singapore to escape detention without trial in 1977, and eschews a linear chronology of these exiles, moving rapidly back and forth from Ho to Ang Swee Chai, her deceased husband Francis Khoo, Barisan Socialis members in Thailand, Tan Wah Piow, Said Zahari, and Tan Jing Quee. The film's free associative structure reveals the unexplored connections between the exiles, and narrates fragmentary tales of loss, separation, and longing. The documenter's interest in the human aspects of this history are apparent from the film's meandering structure and its long sequences of road travel through Malaysia and Thailand. The film's repeated journeys to Thailand and Malaysia, circumventions of Singapore's laws banning the exiles, resituate the country in the context of the larger Southeast Asian region. Commemorations, memorials, funerals, and talks held in neighboring Malaysia and Thailand further recall the complicated and fraught decolonial and postcolonial histories of the region in the aftermath of the Second World War. The scenes in London with Tan Wah Piow and his personal archive of hitherto unseen photographs and newspaper clippings recall an active student and dissident network that was paradoxically possible in the metropole but not in the former colony.

Ultimately, *To Singapore, With Love*'s preoccupation with spatial journeying and movement is in direct contrast to the fixed position of a physical archive, suggesting that different forms of Singaporean identity have been and are being cultivated outside the country's borders, in motion. This motion is ultimately circular or, more precisely, centripetal. As the film's title suggests a postcard from abroad, so the exiles' interviews continually return to the object of their longing. We listen to Ang Swee Chai's gut-wrenching observation that she spent 35 years away before she was able to bring her husband's ashes back on a single visit. We watch the elderly men and women who attempt to keep up with the political news from the country, hoping one day to return. We are witness to an emotional recitation of a patriotic and nostalgic poem. The closest the film gets to a Singaporean location is Changi Airport, where the film lingers on the emotional reunion between Ho's mother and his wife and children even as he cannot be there himself. This centripetal force brings us, at the end of the film, to the unremarkable environs of coastal Johore Bahru, the Malaysian city across the straits from Singapore where Ho "attends" his mother's birthday via a Skype connection. Some of the film's final scenes linger on these views of the country from just outside its borders, focusing on the distant public housing towers and construction sites.

Intimate domestic and interior scenes persistently interrupt these sequences of motion and of the contemplation of landscapes. These are seemingly banal sequences: a close-up of a wok of *char kway teow* or fried rice noodles (a Singaporean dish that evokes the gustatory and corporeal pleasures of a home unavailable to the exiles); small children wandering around a cramped London house; the peeling of a mangosteen; a shed full of dusty memorabilia; or the everyday work of a noodle factory. To understand these seemingly quotidian scenes, it useful to turn to Davide Panagia's theory of the politics of sensation.[5] Panagia argues that "moments of sensation punctuate our everyday existence, and in doing so, they puncture our received wisdoms and common modes of sensing" (2009, 2). In their circumventions of an inaccessible nation-state, the repeated spatial practice of the exiles in Tan's film seem to extend the boundaries of Singapore. These moments of sensation become powerful symbols of longing and memory that supplement the moving interviews conducted by Tan. In effect, by focusing on the commonplace textures of exiled life, Tan's film enables its audience to perceive exile in a way that transcends the limitations of written texts or histories. Sensation, what Panagia defines as entering "a world of contours, resonances, vibrations, attunements, syntonizations, hapticities, and impulses" (2009, 9), interrupts our conventional ways of understanding the world and in doing so becomes a political act. Tan's film, through its exploration of the combinations of the sensory realities of being outside of Singapore, enables us to reconfigure our

---

5 For this connection, I am indebted to Victor Li, who first mentioned Panagia's work in relation to Tan's film at a post-film screening panel at the University of Toronto.

understanding of the costs of exile. The long, drawn-out shots of the stooped, aging bodies of the exiles shuffling away suggest that they themselves are the living archives that have been discarded and banned by the state. Dissident filmmakers, as Tan points out in a conversation with another colleague, Martyn See, become "archivists in the best sense of the word" (Loh, 2010, 282), eschewing neutrality to balance the views of state-commissioned political documentaries.

Adding to this combination of traveling sequences, interior scenes, and a series of affecting interviews, the film's only use of nondiegetic music provides an unavailable aural archive of protest movements in Singapore. Tan uses two rare tracks of protest music by the late Francis Khoo, a lawyer who died in political exile. The first, "Fifteenth of February," is an account of his escape from arrest in Singapore and the second, "Anak Pulau Singapura," or "Child of Singapore Island," is an English- and Malay-language song of exile. These songs, resonances, vibrations, and attunements in and of themselves, must be understood in the context of the Singaporean state's long history of propagandistic songs. Commissioned since the 1980s, state songs often resembled advertising jingles at first (the first few songs were written by a Canadian jazz pianist who worked for the firm McCann-Erickson), even as their goal was to instill values of patriotism, and to produce an affective response in its citizenry. The archive of these state songs, sung in the weeks leading up to the country's national day celebrations, are designed to "inculcate a civil religion that directs favor and fervor towards the nation" (Kong, 1995, 447). They stress such themes as "love, belonging, pride, attaining excellence, unity, commitment to Singapore, productivity, hard work, and teamwork" (Ortmann, 2009, 33). The creation of this ideological repertoire of songs produced a centrally controlled aural and musical space of state-dictated patriotism. That its production coincides with a period of heightened repression, detentions without trial, and a consolidation of power is particularly chilling. Studying the cultural texts like the official *Sing Singapore* songbook, Lily Kong notes how "the ultimate concern is to develop in Singaporeans a love for their country, a sense of patriotism and a willingness to support the ruling elite who have led the country through the short years since independence" (1995, 451). These songs provided a carefully curated soundtrack to a (post)colonial state that was creating an echo chamber for itself by exiling and detaining dissident voices.

This is not to say that there was not an underground countercultural music scene in the 1970s and '80s, yet Khoo's songs provide a wholly distinctive, and circumventory perspective on "loving" Singapore through music. In the context of a state-controlled and commissioned body of patriotic music, "Fifteenth of February" gives us an alternate date in Singapore's history to 9 August, which is the day the nation commemorates its independence and separation from Malaysia. The song is an account of illicit nighttime escape from the authorities who "at dead of the night / [...] kept knocking /

and banging [the] door." These distressing lyrics are sung over a simple and memorable tune. The history of nighttime raids on dissidents is told in a song that has been effectively banned for distribution in Singapore along with its dissident songwriter. Khoo's guilt at his escape when "the others could not" is compounded by the fact that he knows that he would "see them no more." The song makes starkly clear the reality of exile from a country that has been touted as a global hub and a transnational success. What Khoo's circumventory song gives us is the reality of the contours of power that shape Singapore's spaces. Khoo lists the names of his friends who have been arrested and notes that they are "once more / behind Changi wall." Changi is the historic prison that saw the detentions of numerous dissidents but also POWs in the Japanese occupation – a space of incarceration during the war that would resonate with British veterans in the country of Khoo's exile. Khoo sees his departure from Singapore as a journey into the unknown, where he never knows "what lies ahead," and he strikes a defiant tone even as he speaks of "the darkness" that surrounds him. The moving last lines of the song hint at the impossibility of return, and are addressed to the country's people:

> O my people,
> my homeland,
> the ones that I love,
> I will never see you again,
> till the storm clouds gather
> at break of the dawn
> and *bunga raya*[6]
> shall bloom in the rain.

Khoo's song is one that is resolutely in exile, despite his love for the people. In Tan's film this part of the song plays over a shot of a motorcycle headlight and an ensuing lens flare in the dim tropical twilight of a Malaysian country road, an artistic gesture recalling Khoo's own hasty departure from Singapore.

More hauntingly, the film's credits end with Khoo singing "Anak Pulau Singapura":

> so as a child of my island
> I know the ink is not dry
> our story's still yet unwritten
> today I'll join my people's cry.

While "Fifteenth of February" speaks of the pain of departure and exile, "Anak Pulau Singapura" or "Child of Singapore," describes an ineffable bond to the country born out of a history of immigration and collective nation-building. In the final lines, Khoo equates these transnational movements and material

---

6 *Bunga raya* is the Malay name for the hibiscus, which is the national flower of Malaysia. Khoo's reference to this may also evoke Singapore's longer history as part of Malaya. Singapore's national flower is the hybrid orchid Vanda Miss Joaquim.

efforts with the writing of a story – one that is incomplete in the context of official narratives of the dominant political party and (post)coloniality. Singing from outside Singapore and yet still of Singapore, "Anak Pulau Singapura" "joins" in a "people's cry" that resonates beyond state-imposed borders. Its lyrics here suggest that the power of circumvention may lie in writing a counter-history, one that may only be fully legible outside of Singapore's borders, away from the censorious regime.[7]

Tan's films, both *To Singapore, With Love* and *Invisible City*, are testimony to how the political is the personal, that the illogical, emotional, affective component so often missing in the government's teleological view of material progress, is precisely the space of quiet dissent in its population. This is a government that has tried repeatedly to engineer national feeling through parades, patriotic songwriting competitions, and the invention of pseudo-mythical icons like the Merlion. Tan's films rely on unexpected and idiosyncratic emotions, and their prima facie refusal of heavy-handed propaganda presents circumventory and excavatory ways of producing identity beyond both an engineered patriotism and an oppositional politics.

"National Day"

While the subjects of Tan's film are prevented from entering Singapore, the migrant workers in Jeremy Tiang's short story "National Day" from his 2015 collection *It Never Rains on National Day* are subjected to spatial controls that prevent their mobility within its borders.[8] The text is told through first-person plural narration, in the collective voices of temporary migrant workers in Singapore. These men perform the manual labor that paradoxically produces the material spaces that they are so constrained in. Tiang's text is aware of this paradox and his story references the glittering skyline made possible by the back-breaking work and millions of man hours of land reclamation, construction, and tunneling that produce Singapore's much-vaunted infrastructure. The short story uses the first-person plural narrative to respect the men's collectivity and to refuse the presumption that a Singaporean author might be able to assume an individual's interiority

---

7 When I screened the film to a full house in Toronto in 2014, Tan's only set of explicit instructions were to not switch on the houselights until the end of the credits, to enable the audience to listen to this song in its entirety.

8 Jeremy Tiang is a novelist, playwright, and literary translator. They have translated over twenty books from across the Chinese-speaking world, including novels by Yeng Pway Ngon, Yan Ge, Lo Yi-Chin, Liu Xinwu, and Zhang Yueran, and plays by Chen Si'an and Wei Yu-Chia. Their plays include *Salesman* 之死 and *A Dream of Red Pavilions*. Their novel *State of Emergency* won the Singapore Literature Prize in 2018, and their short story collection *It Never Rains on National Day* was shortlisted for the same prize.

from his privileged position. In his acknowledgments, Tiang notes that the material for this story came from interviews conducted with migrant workers at the non-profit organization Transient Workers Count Too (TWC2). These firsthand accounts are woven into this unusual short fiction where the lines of power and privilege are illuminated through the workers' attempts to watch the country's National Day Parade from an offshore island, away from the mainland of Singapore.

This literary evocation of the sharply drawn lines of class, race, and nationality in Singapore is reinforced by the story's position in Tiang's collection. "National Day" is the penultimate story and is followed by "Sophia's Party," a gently satirical account of a group of Singaporeans celebrating the country's national day by watching the annual parade on television. The latter story depicts the banal and unquestioning celebrations through the slightly skeptical perspective of a Singaporean woman's (Sophia) white British husband. When Nicholas protests Sophia's elaborate preparations for her national day party, she "claim[s] it was all ironic, but he found himself wondering whether Singapore's famously monolithic education system hadn't left its mark on her after all" (Tiang, 2015, 150). Tiang's choice to place this story after "National Day" illuminates the cultural and material structures that regulate and shape the city-state. Nicholas is a foreigner like the migrant workers in "National Day," however his race, class, and nationality mean that he has a very different socio-economic and spatial position in the country. Still, his outsider status means that he is able in some ways to provide an outsider's view in the story. The story, in its third-person limited perspective, allows cynical and skeptical asides as Nicholas observes Sophia and her friends watching the parade on television. This is the center of power, comfort, spectacle, and complacency that the foreign workers in "National Day" must circumvent:

> the broadcast is handsomely produced, stirring images of young people rehearsing dance steps against the setting sun, of an old man correcting his granddaughter's fingering on the sitar.
>
> And in between, the camera pulls back to the seating stand, where rows of people wave balloons, oddly blank-faced but apparently determined to have a good time. Tickets are free, but must be balloted for months in advance, and every year there are rumors of them changing hands on gumtree or craigslist for hundreds of dollars. Can this really be? But people will buy anything these days. (Tiang, 2015, 171)

Tiang's story carefully documents what has become an annual extravaganza of nation building and the stoking of patriotic fervor. Each image in the "handsomely produced" broadcast is designed to evoke youth, plenty, tradition, and racial diversity. Yet the story also subtly hints at the manufactured nature of this spectacle, how its audience is "oddly blank-faced but apparently determined to have a good time" and even free tickets to the event are mired in pragmatic and transactional politics.

The minority subjects in Tiang's text are unable to move freely, or even circumvent how their lives are mapped out in Singapore. Sara Ahmed enumerates the numerous meanings of "to stop" in the context of black and queer activism: "to cease, to end, and also to cut off, to arrest, to check, to prevent, to block, to obstruct, or to close" (2006, 139). She argues that "some bodies more than others are 'stopped' by being the subject of the policeman's address" (2006, 139). The artistic texts themselves attempt to circumvent ways of seeing and treating queer, minority, imprisoned, migrant, and laboring bodies in Singapore. These bodies are part of the state's plan for maximum value extraction from the land – through their labor or their elimination from the efficient state machinery. Close reading of a text like "National Day" reveals how the stories circumvent official constructions and barriers to these bodies by critiquing their usual depictions in the national discourse. What circumventions are possible in reality? These are the troubling questions that are raised by the depiction of race- and class-based discrimination against South Asian migrant workers by Singaporeans.

"National Day" begins by situating us outside this hypnotic splendor of the National Day Parade and plunging directly into the collectivity of the workers on a rare day off:

> So we take a boat to St. John's Island because where else can we go, every other place will be crowded and just for one night we want to leave the dormitories, the noise and stink of eight bodies pressed into each small room, just for a few hours we want to escape. Tomorrow is a public holiday so we will start work later than usual, not for our sakes but because the residents complain if construction starts too early while they are still asleep, and the foreman will not say anything if we are back at the site before ten. (Tiang, 2015, 151)

In this opening paragraph, Tiang plays with the notion that Singaporeans see these migrant workers as an amorphous, unidentifiable mass of people. They have no names, and appear to all have similar desires and routines. In effect, the story's opening performs a subtle critique of ways of seeing the men even as it documents their abysmal living and working conditions. *Where* to house the migrant worker population and *how* to accommodate their leisure time has been a constant source of tension in Singapore. Residents consistently refuse to have dormitories situated near public housing estates or private condominium developments.[9] On 8 December 2013, a rare riot broke out in Little India, a shopping and dining enclave that has historically catered to South Asian migrants in Singapore. An inebriated worker was run over by a bus that was supposed to take him back to his dormitory and this sparked the worst riot in Singapore since independence where 300 workers took to the

---

9 See Sorluan (2008) for a range of resident interviews that cover their often xenophobic views on the "threat" of foreign workers.

streets for about two hours, setting emergency vehicles on fire and injuring a number of police officers and first responders. The government blamed the incident on alcoholism among the workers and instituted draconian laws that conceived of the ethnic neighborhood as a regulated, disciplined, and controlled space with strict laws governing alcohol consumption (see Goh, 2004).[10] Members of organizations that have been working for the welfare and rights of foreign workers pointed out that the riot had also to be read in the context of systems of severe spatial discipline, low wages, and lack of recourse to a full set of labor rights. As Daniel P.S. Goh puts it, "For the masses of low-skilled foreign workers in Singapore, the issues of tenancy, housing and the commons manifest themselves acutely in the denial of access to the global city they are helping to build" (2014). In the Singaporean context, foreign workers are fundamentally spatially and legally marginalized.

While the Little India riot occurred after the writing of the story, the desperation and claustrophobia in the opening paragraph of Tiang's story seem to be a precursor to this rare episode of unrest. The men take a small boat to an offshore island as they are literally and figuratively pushed to the margins of Singaporean society, their labor seen as expendable and disposable, even as it is essential to Singapore's material construction. The men's bodies are coded in Singapore's built landscape as less than human and invisible. They ask, "where else can we go" if they want to "escape," "just for one night." Even though the next day is a public holiday celebrating Singapore's independence, the men will not partake in this time and space of rest, only starting work a little later to avoid noise complaints from residents. Their decision to go to the offshore island and to observe the country's independence day celebrations from a remove can be read then as an embodied form of protest, a form of political expression that would be illegal in the country.

After this opening paragraph, even as the story continues in the first-person plural, it begins to introduce these men, naming them, distinguishing their bodies from each other even as they move together: Arul, Neelish, Mohan, Antony, Jairam, Feroz, and an unnamed narrator. The narrator describes the contact zone that they find themselves in, "leaning across each other to talk in our mixture of languages, fractured English and Tamil and Bengali, reaching for whatever words we can find to make ourselves understood" (Tiang, 2015, 152). The men's names signal their arrival from various parts of South Asia, a continent of languages between them as they form a new community even as "few heads turn to look at us, no one cares what we have to say" (Tiang, 2015, 152). The men carry a kind of exclusion zone with them as they move through Singaporean space. Jairam has been injured at work, his leg amputated at the knee, and his body stands as a metonym for their collective vulnerability.

---

10 Goh's analysis of the Little India Riot explains its spatial origins and consequences. Kaur, Tan, and Dutta (2016) provide an account of how the media covered the incident.

Others like Neelish are battling alcoholism because of the hard labor. They settle on a beach and turn to face the skyline that they have built but where they are not welcome:

> The sun is not setting yet but the shadows are long, and the tall buildings of the city are at their most attractive, glittering as brightly as the water. They look like beautiful toys, like we could reach out and pluck them from where they stand, the great wheel of the flyer, the three reaching fingers of the casino, the hard-angled glass and steel of the CBD.
>   We gape and take pictures if we have cameras on our phones. Mohan points at the lotus flower museum and shouts, *Look, I built that. Ah*, we laugh at him, *but have you ever been inside*, knowing he hasn't, because who could afford that admission fee, and just to look at old porcelain or some foreign painting? Still, we cannot resist doing it too, calling out what we've made, office building, skyscraping banks, the Gardens by the Bay with their giant metal trees. *That's mine, I built that*. Despite ourselves, we feel a flicker of something at being a part of this machine, and having operated the cranes and laid the bricks that brought the great city into being. (Tiang, 2015, 153)

In the story's descriptions, Singapore's coastal skyline, its markers of success and globalization are reduced to "beautiful toys," as the workers' offshore perspectives hint at the inconsequential and transient nature of the city's material wealth as represented by the spectacular skyline. In circumventing the mainland, the workers' vision echoes the model-like nature of the city as it is reproduced in the City Gallery's scale model of Singapore, revealing its mapped artifice. The text reveals the spatial inequalities through this liminal view even as the workers "lay claim" to the fruits of their material labor. The city is a model and a machine, sprung into being through human labor that has been shunted out off-site. If excavation reverses state-enforced amnesia, circumvention and the circumventory movements of texts by Tiang and Tan give us new spatial perspectives that allow us to understand the contours and boundaries of power and planning. It is no surprise, then, that the workers astutely parse the acute paradox that they are unable to enter the very buildings they have built.

As the story progresses, "National Day" gives us an outside view of the annual national day celebrations from a vantage point that "is still Singapore, and yet […] is not" (Tiang, 2015, 154), being undeveloped compared to the mainland. Still, there are reminders that this is still the regulated, disciplined space of the Singaporean state:

> There are signboards all along the path, green and white and yellow, and Feroz snorts, *These people don't know what to do unless there are black and white words to instruct them, they don't dare wipe their own backsides without government approval*. We stare at the different-sized rectangles, making out the words do not pluck flowers no fishing beyond this point warning no lifeguard on duty. (Tiang, 2015, 155)

The textuality of this liminal space, its admonishments and warnings, serves as a foreshadowing of how the men will be treated by Singaporeans on the offshore island. As Feroz notes, they are visual symbols of how the local population has been conditioned by the state and its spatialized power. Here is where they talk about the unproven rumor that gives Tiang's collection its title, *It Never Rains on National Day*, they "have heard that they seed the clouds a week before to dry them out" (Tiang 2015, 156). While the Singapore government has denied this, the rumor's persistence in the national imaginary is testimony to the fact that most citizens would not see an attempt by the state to micromanage the weather as something extraordinary.

The men settle onto a beach to observe the celebrations, and feel "a hum of thirty thousand people's excitement [...] from here" (Tiang, 2015, 157). The text details elements of the parade that would be familiar to a Singaporean audience in their yearly repetitions.[11] From this distance, "gouts of music come to us, distorted by the wind [...] Guns are fired in quick sequence, pop pop pop pop, and there is more cheering" (2015, 197). The distortions and disembodied sounds highlight the workers' displacement from the center, as do their meagre rations (leftovers from the home of a Singaporean family who employ a domestic worker who is romantically involved with one of the men), which they eat around a fire that they have built to keep warm. As the men continue to watch and listen to the "leftovers" of the National Day Parade from afar, the scene takes on an incongruous nature with "choreographed [...] tightly managed" sequences of "lasers flicking across neighboring buildings, helicopters hovering, speedboats churning by close to shore after finishing their turns by the floating platform" (2015, 159). From this remove, the text alters these sensory perceptions in uncanny ways:

> Even with the neon lines of the city back the way we came, there is something primal in the air, as if the noises on the mainland are the crashes and screams of war and we are the only ones who made it out, refugees crouched around the campfire as dark shadows approach. (2015, 159)

In critiquing its displays of military prowess and technological capabilities, "National Day" may be recalling historical traumas both in the Singaporean context and in the transnational memories of the South Asian workers. While these are never specified, the haunting of this celebratory, nativist space is made apparent by the story's sudden turn to dystopian imaginings. These fantasies recall Singapore's wartime history, when it was the site of a Japanese invasion and occupation in the mid-century but further cleverly reverses its contemporary status as a so-called exception of postcolonial

---

11 For a capsule view of the yearly event, see Tan Pin Pin's seven-minute avant-garde film *9th August* (2006), which splices together 40 years of Singapore's National Day parades in a repetitive sequence of jump-cuts that make it clear how formulaic and unchanging the displays of military might, racial harmony, and patriotic fervor have been. Available at: https://vimeo.com/43513408.

success. The workers are glad to be off of the island while it is "telling some version of a story that doesn't include us" (Tiang, 2015, 161), intuiting and embodying the suffering that makes its success possible. While the nation-state is the most prosperous in the region, Singapore consistently refuses to take in refugees, citing a lack of physical space even as its policy documents are planning for a population growth of 1.5 million by 2030.[12] This ironic extrapolation of the sounds of the country's celebration speak to both the fragility of its existence but also to its highly racist and profit-driven regime.

This underlying and systemic inequality comes to a climax as the story depicts the only interaction between Singaporeans (a group of evangelical Christians) and the migrant workers. The Singaporeans accuse the workers of being on the island illegally, of not being able to understand the sign that regulates their behavior and bans the lighting of fires on the beach. They equate the workers' presence with danger and the Singaporean man confronting them, Wilson, declares their rights to the beach in financial terms: "*we shouldn't have to put up with this after paying for the use of our campsite, all your illegal activity*" (2015, 161). Wilson further threatens the workers with the police and the loss of their work permit – highlighting their tenuous position in the country and encapsulating their minoritarian status. One of the workers replies, "*This isn't your island*" (2015, 161), challenging the man's authority and recalling Singapore's migrant and colonial histories. To his insults equating them with dirt and noise, one of the workers responds:

> *You think you're so clean, we're the ones who clean up after you*, sneers Neelish, and we all nod because it is true, we have seen how dirty the streets are each day, how the troops of sweepers clean them just before dawn. We see this and think we are lucky to at least be doing our work, making something that will last, not vanishing unremarked with the sunlight.
>
> We are all motionless now, we have faced people like this before, whenever we try to rest in a park or under a block of flats they come and tell us to leave, not to make the place untidy, not to sit so close to their children. (Tiang, 2015, 163)

Reminding us of the labor that makes the buildings and clean public spaces possible in Singapore, Tiang's fiction repeatedly recalibrates what it means to inhabit and know Singapore. In this space just off the mainland, a circumventory space that the workers have created for kinship and rest, Tiang's fiction makes these epiphanies possible. The workers' confrontation with the Singaporeans echoes and reenacts the entirety of their experiences in the city-state – their movements and behavior constantly under surveillance and scrutiny, their bodies marked out as threats.

---

12 See Jones (2018) and the Ministry of Trade and Industry's population white paper "A Sustainable Population for a Dynamic Singapore," https://www.strategygroup.gov.sg/images/chart7.png.pdf.

After this confrontation, the workers are left alone again to observe what Singaporeans usually see as the highlight and climax of the annual parade: a fireworks show which culminates in the recitation of the pledge and the second rendition of the national anthem. These are the oral rituals that open every school day for every child in Singapore – thus, their repetition at the end of the parade with fireworks is meant to aurally and visually cement a specific form of disciplinary patriotism. Indeed, in the next story, "Sophia's Party," it is clearly crucial that the middle-class Singaporean guests of the titular party are "childishly excited" by "the climax of the pyrotechnics" (Tiang, 2015, 181, 182):

> *Fireworks!* she cries, and sure enough they are bursting ripely over the night sky, pink chalky streaks, green whirligigs and yellow stars, fizzling on the TV screen at the same time as the emcee shouts *Happy Birthday, Singapore!* and the spectators wave the giant inflatable lions they've been given. (2015, 181)

The comfort and complacency of this annual spectacle has already been disrupted by our first view of it in "National Day," coming on the heels of the argument between the workers and the Singaporeans. The men view the same fireworks from a completely different vantage point:

> There is a streak of stark white light over the city that turns into starburst of magenta, and then one of green and yellow. *It's started*, says Feroz without enthusiasm. We sit and watch the fireworks as they spiral and dance in the sky, the reason Neelish persuaded us to come to this island, and the view is as impressive as he promised, but they are not for us, and we see now that we were mistaken in thinking we would be able to enjoy them, they are as foreign and untouchable as the gleaming buildings across the bay, as the teenagers now securely behind the fence of their campsite.
> The display goes on for about ten minutes, zigzags and circles and arcs. When the last spray has fizzled away, they play more music. At the parade, people will already be starting to leave in order to beat the crowds and on TV the hosts will be screaming, *Happy birthday, Singapore!* We stay where we are still sitting, looking at the sky where afterimages linger. (Tiang, 2015, 164–65)

By changing the semiotics of the National Day fireworks through a spatially and socially altered vantage point, "National Day" critiques the empty and exploitative success that is repeated *ad nauseum* each year. Where the Singaporeans see some sort of catharsis, the workers regard the spectacle as "foreign and untouchable," much like their own status in the country. The contours of power here are given actual material form as the "gleaming buildings across the bay," buildings that they paradoxically helped to construct even as their inhabitants need to "fence" them out. The illusory idea of national progress and Singaporeans' famous fear of losing (they start to leave to "beat the crowds") are contrasted with the workers' stubborn desire to stay where they are, simply "looking at the sky where afterimages linger." This circumvention is both spatial and temporal, a way for the men to step out of the calculations of industrial time and endless labor.

Tiang's story ends on an ambiguous moment that while filled with a sense of openness and possibility, is tempered with despair. The ending of "National Day" suggests that for some minoritized persons, circumvention means doing things that seem to make no sense in the disciplined, centralized, rule-bound space of Singapore. The story asks but does not answer the question of what it might mean to survive transnational exploitation. One of the workers, Neelish, peels off from the group who have ended up sleeping on the beach:

> Neelish takes careful steps towards the water, leaving his slippers neatly on a rock before he steps into it, still warm even this late at night. He feels coarse sand and pebbles beneath his feet and the greasy sheen of dirty water against his skin but continues, his trousers wet and then his shirt, kicking his legs when they no longer reach the bottom.
>
> When Neelish reaches the floating barrier he ducks under it and then is in the open sea, slight current pulling him this way and that, the rolling black surface just visible. From this angle the city buildings seem even higher, even further, but he continues striking out towards them, not looking back, his face tight and angry as if the water has offended him. Now he thrashes his arms and legs in an inexpert way, his energy pouring into the ocean, propelling him forward a few inches at a time. The waves swell and tumble, but he keeps his head above them. It is just under a mile to the mainland. Perhaps he makes it. (Tiang, 2015, 166)

Neelish's body, vulnerable and alone on the maritime outskirts of mainland Singapore, provides a sharp scalar contrast to the city buildings that loom ahead of him. His perspective is just out of the bounds of the city even as his body sinks into the dirty coastal waters, polluted by the oil refineries that surround the main island. The city is seemingly unattainable, even though it is so close geographically. Neelish's "inexpert" swimming is a counter-cartographical movement that questions the basis of the state and its carefully regulated exclusions and boundaries. His thrashing and the energy that he dissipates into the water are not directed towards the grand project of building this skyline; his movements reflect the visible and invisible barriers that prevent him from truly arriving and inhabiting Singapore.

And the Walls Come Crumbling Down

Forced to circumvent centers of authoritarian power and inequalities of class and race, Tan's and Tiang's texts give us outsider perspectives of Singapore from the movements of exiles and migrant workers. The last text that I will examine in this chapter explores how it might be possible to imaginatively circumvent the dominant modes of capital, circulation, globalization, and citizenship from within Singapore's material borders. Through memoir and creative nonfiction, the queer Eurasian writer Tania De Rozario's *And the Walls Come Crumbling Down* spatializes queer desire – giving us a lens through which to view the material, symbolic, and textual spaces of Singapore that are wholly unplanned, not profit-driven or planned-for.[13] In a state where homosexual sex between men is still criminalized by a colonial-era law, queer women are doubly effaced, their relationships viewed as transgressive but not even visible enough to warrant a mention in the legal code. In terms of collateral cultural effects, however, one of the law's effects is a distinct lack of positive cultural representations of queer women's bodies. The production of queer spaces in art and everyday life for women, girls, and gender-non-conforming bodies is thus particularly urgent. By directly engaging with the ordinary and everyday lived environment, De Rozario's work queers and circumvents Singapore's disciplined and regulated heteronormative spaces.

In my linking queerness with space-making and its possibilities, I draw from the work done by Sara Ahmed and José Esteban Muñoz. Their theorizations of queerness as phenomenology and ideality that is uniquely spatialized have shaped the ways in which I think through the queering of the specific context of Singapore's carefully planned and policed spaces. Muñoz argues that

> We have never been queer, yet queerness exists for us as an ideality that can be distilled from the past and used to imagine a future. The future is queerness's domain. Queerness is a structuring and educated mode of desiring that allows us to see and feel beyond the quagmire of the present. The here and now is a prison house. We must strive, in the face of the here and now's totalizing rendering of reality, to think and feel a *then and there*. (2009, 1; emphasis original)

In his envisioning of concrete utopias, a queer aesthetic that "contains the blueprints and schemata of a forward-looking futurity," Muñoz gives us a way of considering how queer aesthetics map out future social relations that challenge heteronormative, colonial, and patriarchal spaces of the Singaporean state. His spatial and temporal theorizations of the way queerness might operate focuses on its ability to circulate, to cruise around the pragmatism of mainstream gay politics, to enable the possibility of spontaneity and chance. The Singaporean context is one where homosexual life is constrained by colonial-era laws and further regulated by other laws governing the freedom of assembly and expression. LGBTQ rights events are heavily regulated, even

---

13 Tania De Rozario is a writer and visual artist engaged with issues of gender, sexuality, home, memory, and horror. She is the author of *Tender Delirium* (Math Paper Press, 2013), *And the Walls Come Crumbling Down* (Math Paper Press, 2016; Gaudy Boy, 2020), and *Somewhere Else, Another You* (Math Paper Press, 2018). She was the 2020 winner of the New Ohio Review Nonfiction Contest, the 2021 winner of the Muriel Craft Bailey Memorial Poetry Contest, and the 2011 winner of Singapore's Golden Point Award for English Poetry. She left Singapore and is currently living in Vancouver, Canada.

barricaded in, while positive depictions of queerness are forbidden in the national media. Muñoz's injunctions, when read in these specificities, become even more urgent.

Ahmed's theorization of "queer phenomenology" offers "an approach to sexual orientation by rethinking how the bodily direction 'toward' objects shapes the surfaces of bodily and social space" (2006, 68). Ahmed argues that "to act on lesbian desire is a way of reorienting one's relation not just toward sexual others, but also to a world that has already 'decided' how bodies should be orientated in the first place" (2006, 102). In effect, their "orientations" are not "straight" (in Ahmed's terms) but either driven by queer desires and highly aware of the limits that their movements come up against, what Muñoz deems as "the present's stultifying hold" (2009, 28). Circumvention, when theorized through both Ahmed's and Muñoz's ideas of circulation and orientation, enables a different habitation of Singapore's space. It is one that is at once anti-normative and transgressive, but also highly sensitive to the boundaries of power.

Thus, the central persona in De Rozario's autofiction develops alternate ways of traversing and inhabiting heavily regulated urban sites because of her inability to be accommodated by the gendered and sexual mappings of Singapore. Her itineraries across the city produce textured spaces of desire that elucidate and transcend the ways heteronormative and racist norms map these spaces. Ahmed posits that "'becoming lesbian' [is] a very social experience and allows us to rethink desire as a form of action that shapes bodies and worlds" (2006, 102). Thinking through Ahmed's concept of queer phenomenology enables us to read *And the Walls Come Crumbling Down* as a counter-cartography of Singapore. It attempts, through its spatializations and circumventions, a gesture that Ahmed might see as a "queer commitment" that would "trace the lines for a different genealogy, one that would embrace the failure to inherit the family line as the condition of possibility for another way of dwelling in the world" (2006, 178) – as De Rozario puts it in her book's dedication, "for the families we build from scratch" (2016).

Using the material details of a crumbling house as an extended metaphor for non-normative relationships, *And the Walls Come Crumbling Down* eroticizes and queers the site of the home. De Rozario challenges the heteronormative underpinnings of house, home, property ownership and their links to reproduction and biopolitics in contemporary Singapore. Instead of beginning with an ideal house, De Rozario's text begins in a peripheral crumbling rental, in "a Singapore I had never known buried under the weight of time and concrete" (2016, 10–11), replete with tropical overgrowth and infested with insects:

> The termites had built miniature tunnels all down one wall. Soil and feces like veiny fingers trailed down from the roof, the tunnels providing adequate moisture and shelter for them to conduct their chewing. (2016, 4)

In the face of resplendent representations of Singapore, De Rozario's text reinserts the tropicality, humidity, and decay that circumvent the orderly, the planned, and the pristine. Her circumventions involve more than human figures, and take place within, unseen in the disciplined space of Singapore.

Her depiction of this space does not produce a tidy binary; her conflation of the body of her lover and the built environment signals a more complex set of spatialities: "Everything about you leads to home. Veins visible like tributaries running up your forearms. Skin mapping scars, creases, bends, and beyond the armour of your teeth, visceral constellations" (De Rozario, 2016, 5). Her evasions of Singaporean space in the built environment are superimposed onto her lover's body – itself a queer geography of desire and pain. The metaphor of mapping here is disrupted with references to pain and desire, "armour," "scars," and "constellations," testament to the multiple scales of spatial understanding.

And the Walls Come Crumbling Down is divided into three sections that explicitly commingle this corporeal grounding one with narratives that have both large and small implications. These range from the themes of escape, improvisation, decay, and travel in "Holes in the Wall," to the stories of demolition and rejection in "Tear Down the House" and then reconstruction in "From the Ground Up." The central narrative of the text is that of a failed queer relationship, challenging the larger notions of success, wholeness, and reproductive imperatives that dominate the Singaporean setting of the text – De Rozario addresses her lover, "Everything about you leads home. And my house is falling apart" (2016, 9).

In "Holes in the Wall," a series of smaller chapters, "expel," "pack," "vacate," and "fly," are so titled to animate and complicate the fixed abode of a house in the face of a relationship that is ending between Singapore and Amsterdam. The fragmentary and achronological aspects of this section enable a portrait of a queer relationship to emerge that is the antithesis of a teleological, heterosexual "happy ending" with reproduction as its state-encouraged goal. In the text, the relationship is depicted in complex temporal parameters as one that has failed, is failing, and will fail. It is a love that is not visible in the conventional mappings of space by a patriarchal city-state. The holes in the wall are ruptures in this state-mandated reality, epistemological and ontological "holes" that suggest voyeurism, furtiveness, decay, violence, and unplanned space. The text interrupts a description of a lovers' fight with a description of a circumvention of a progress-driven industrial and neoliberal time:

> *Rewind.*
> But that is yet to come. In this undefined space where we will fly circles around each other. In this uncharted territory where we will kiss so tenderly that our insides feel as though they might spill out of our mouths. Where we will hold each other so tightly that we will forget whose limbs are whose. (De Rozario, 2016, 21)

The lovers' bodies are precisely in an undefined space, an uncharted territory, because there is no sanctioned space for their queerness to exist. Muñoz argues that "the present is not enough. It is impoverished and toxic for queers and other people who do not feel the privilege of majoritarian belonging, normative tastes, and 'rational' expectations. Let me be clear that the idea is not simply to turn away from the present" (2009, 27). De Rozario's text refuses to turn away from this painful present, but spatializes her desire by circling the hidden and transgressive queer spaces repeatedly through narrative strategies of repetition, recursion, and fragmentation: holes in the wall.

The text's second section, "Tear Down the House," reinforces this free associative and disorienting structure with a series of nonlinear, autobiographical snippets that provide glimpses of the difficulties of growing up queer in religious and state-controlled spaces. De Rozario's conservative, religious, and heteronormative upbringing causes her to run away from home. The smaller chapters in this section have parts of the house as their titles: "windows," "stairs," "drawers," "bed," "doors," "roofs," "walls." In each instance, the spatial form of each object or physical construction is inextricably linked to sexual violence, abandon, and other subversive uses of the everyday spaces of a house. Each space is inscribed with queer desire and familial dysfunction, all conscious of the history of housing policy in Singapore. The text refers to this history of urban development through quantitative metrics where "almost 240,000 flats had been built [in the 1980s] and soon the entire nation would be living in the sky" (De Rozario, 2016, 40). The narrator moves again and again, circling the acceptable spaces of the nation, at the mercy of the vagaries of a housing system that privileges heteronormative families and capitalist accumulation. The text declares, "housing on your own terms requires either money or moving. I had no money, so I moved. And each time I added keys to my collection" (De Rozario, 2016, 78). These are keys that are obsolete since they will not open the "doors, gates, mailboxes, bedrooms, storerooms, drawers" of her previous dwellings but serve to track her circumventions, the auditory "jingle-jangle of nomadic history" which begins to ring "a little too loud" (De Rozario, 2016, 78). Ahmed points out how "Lesbian desires create spaces, often temporary spaces that come and go with the coming and going of the bodies that inhabit them" (2006, 106). These keys, then, like letters, markings on beds, and so on, function as a set of ruins, the remains of tearing a house down.

In the final section of the text, "From the Ground Up," De Rozario turns from confessional memoir to political commentary, musing about the effects of Singapore's housing policies and its intolerance of deviance from the norm. In the subsection entitled "Blueprints," she notes:

> We needed to be organized. Separated. Resettled. Squatting was a sure sign of trouble. So we built. And we built. And we never quite stopped. By the sixties, one in ten lived in public housing. By the mid-eighties, eight in ten. The government had done it. Housing for the masses. When we ran out of land, we stole it from the sea. And once we ran out of that, we tore it down again so that we could start over. Put the people in their flats, the leaders said. All that is wild, must be contained. (2016, 101)

This metafictional section of the text can also be read as a guide to the rest of *And the Walls Come Crumbling Down*. Moving away from a strictly autobiographical lens, the text takes on the perspectives of the bureaucrat and the subaltern, the unfeeling elitist politician, the evicted pig farmer, and the abused foreign construction worker. Through these multiplicities, it narrates an incomplete history of displacement and dispossession.

The sections "blueprints" and "home" in "From the Ground Up" seem incomplete and provisional, recalling the spirit of Muñoz's injunction that "queerness is not yet here" (2009, 1) or that, as Ahmed reckons, we need to find "other ways of gathering in time and space" (2006, 179). De Rozario's queer and racialized gaze of Singapore's heteronormative state housing policy allows for an intersectional understanding of how spatial control functions in the country. In an intersectional manner, she further notes the struggles of the underclass of migrant workers who are fastidiously kept separate from Singaporeans as another aspect of this spatial control. Their living quarters are cramped and dismal. While preliminary and brief, these insights of the intertwined abuses of minorities and the most vulnerable begin to build hitherto unconceived solidarities based on Singapore's unequal spatialities.

In a context where LGBTQ activism has only really come into the mainstream in the past two decades or so, it is fitting that De Rozario's text ends with a hopeful if desperate call to her lover as she moves into another house in Singapore – in the final subsection called "home":

> Come home to me, lover. The door is open. The bed is made. Of my flesh, make a dwelling, to my voice, fall asleep.
> Open the door. Break down the walls. Take off your shoes.
> Choose *me*.

The conflation of the speaker's body and the dwelling itself here reveal and unsettle the connections between bodies and buildings in planned Singapore. It circumvents the bureaucracies, strict quotas, and restrictive rules that have been imposed. Through messiness and desire, the text finds the intimate, material connections that have been excised from conceptions of home.

CHAPTER 3

Wayfinding

Grandma Positioning System

In Kelvin Tong's short film *Grandma Positioning System* (2015), a family cross over into Malaysia to find and pay respects to the grave of their family's patriarch. In a tragi-comic moment, their car's GPS fails and leads them into a continual loop in the cemetery. They must rely on the spatial memory of the grandmother, the dead man's wife, to find the site. Once at the grave, amidst the Sinitic rituals of tomb cleaning and the burning of paper offerings, the woman begins a one-sided dialogue with her deceased husband. Crucially, she speaks in Hokkien, a sinophone language that was outlawed for many years in the state media as an impediment to the nation's progress in both English and Mandarin.

At first, it seems that she is merely updating him on the gossip in the neighborhood, but it soon becomes clear that the lengthy discourse that she offers to his tombstone is an extremely detailed route of the journey from his grave to the family's current address. Her account is full of news of who has moved, who has passed away, which food stalls are still in operation, and whether the roads have changed or the buildings have been demolished and replaced. There is then an ellipsis, and the film depicts the family again lost in the cemetery, only this time on foot and without the grandmother. The grave numbering does not appear to follow a sequence and the family seem hopelessly lost until their daughter remembers a distinctive tree that indicates that they should turn.

At the grave, we notice that the grandmother has now also been interred with the grandfather, and their progeny are now attempting to continue the tradition of visiting their graves. We sense the parents' impatience as they hurry their children through the rituals and return to the car. Once in the car, they are unable to leave the cemetery, losing their way yet again. At this point, their son bolts from the car, running back to his grandparents' graves. The family follows suit and witness him, on his knees, taking up his grandmother's lengthy monologue as he instructs his grandparents on the exact route that they must take to leave the graveyard in Malaysia to journey across the Johor Straits to visit them in Singapore. One by one each family member drops to their knees and continues the detailed description of the route, enumerating its many changes and carefully directing the ghosts on their journey.

Part of the filmic omnibus *7 Letters* which was commissioned by the government for Singapore's jubilee celebrations, *Grandma Positioning System* is mired in nostalgia and determined to tug on its audience's heartstrings. Tong is an award-winning Singaporean film director who has had both art-house and commercial success.[1] His contribution to this state-sanctioned omnibus, while adhering to "traditional" values like filial piety and Chinese heteronormativity, still performs a gentle critique of Singapore's rapid and disorienting urban development. In an idealist counter to the developmental impulses of the (post)colonial city-state, the film proposes solace rooted in traditional Chinese ancestor worship to cope with the irreversible changes that have reshaped the urban landscape. In an email interview I conducted with him in 2018, Tong pointed out that his short film purposefully links the negotiation of Singapore's urban spatiality with temporality and mortality:

> As Singapore is in a constant state of topographical flux, part of that defiance of death and search for immortality involves the dead needing to be updated on street and landscape changes. By doing this, we conjure the dead into the present. We make them come alive in our memories.

In effect, Tong's film produces a chronotope, "the intrinsic connectedness of temporal and spatial relationships that are artistically expressed in literature" (Bakhtin, 1981, 84). In the final sequences of Tong's film, the dead are literally conjured with their ongoing and eternal relationships to the spaces they once traversed as we watch the ghosts of the elderly couple slowly walking along defunct train tracks between Singapore and Malaysia to visit their living family. In this haunting, as Bakhtin would have it, "Time, as it were, thickens, takes on flesh, becomes artistically visible; likewise, space becomes charged and responsive to the movements of time, plot and history" (1981, 84). It is not just that the ghosts represent the past made visible in these spaces, but that the everyday routes and itineraries that are described in the film take on additional significance in the present.

Tong's film actively thinks through the material minutiae of these haunted routes and the actual practicalities of this journey. As he put it,

> Ghosts walk old roads. That is why in ghost stories, we have incidents of ghosts walking through walls. Before their deaths, the wall didn't exist.

---

1 Kelvin Tong is a celebrated writer, producer, and film director in Singapore. Trained as a lawyer, he worked as a film journalist for the *Straits Times* from 1995 to 1999. His first feature-length was *Eating Air* (1999), and his work has spanned multiple genres including horror, thriller, and musical comedy. One of his most successful films is *The Maid* (2014), which broke the box-office record in Singapore at the time for a local film.

And hence, the ghosts of the grandfather and grandmother in GPS walked the sole route they knew – way before modernisation and urban planning erected walls. (Interview, 2018)

In order to counter the ghosts' inevitable confusion at the ever-changing urban spaces of Singapore, the family must continue to "update" their positioning systems as it were, in a strange combination of the supernatural and the technological. This magical realist conflation of the hyper-modern and the dead, the contemporary and the mortal, complicates the narrative of Singapore's sleek and teleological modernity. Like many other films in the omnibus that treat specters and monsters as part of everyday life, Tong's film evinces the return of older forms of understanding, inhabiting, and moving through space. The film produces chronotopic forms of Singapore that are thick with ghosts, past selves, and demolished buildings, and often not even physically in the country. Tong's film and many others in the omnibus were filmed entirely or partly in Malaysia, recalling its past political union with Singapore but also simply for the practicality of filming sites and buildings of a certain vintage that have already been demolished in the city-state.

What Tong's characters are doing in the film is creating intergenerational spaces through the process of wayfinding. To wayfind, as Timothy Ingold puts it,

> differs fundamentally from navigation, just as mapping differs from map-using. For when navigating in a strange country by means of a topographic map, the relation between one's position on the ground and one's location in space, as defined by particular map coordinates, is strictly synchronic, and divorced from any narrative context. It is possible to specify where one is – one's current location – without regard to where one has been, or where one is going. In ordinary wayfinding, by contrast, every place holds within it memories of previous arrivals and departures, as well as expectations of how one may reach it, or reach other places from it. (2000, 237)

As Tong's film suggests, the graveyard is not navigable by GPS, nor by any system that would set it apart from the spatial stories and the memories that the family carry with them and, by implication, remember their forebears. As the father figure in the film finally falls to his knees in front of his parents' graves, he ends the description of the route home with a tearful recollection of his mother's favorite food stall, which is in a market that has so far escaped the planned demolitions of the Singaporean state. His final words to her tomb are a rhetorical question to her ghost: does she recall the many family trips to the food stall when he was a child?

Fredric Jameson, writing about Kevin Lynch's exploration of the production of mental urban maps in *The Image of the City* (1960), argues that,

> Lynch's subjects are rather clearly involved in pre-cartographic operations whose results traditionally are described as itineraries rather than as maps: diagrams organized around the still subject-centered or existential journey of the traveler, along which various significant key features are marked – oases, mountain ranges, rivers, monuments, and the like. (1991, 51–52)

Jameson calls for a social cartography that arises from these pre-cartographic itineraries, "cognitive maps" that "enable a situational representation on the part of the individual subject to that vaster and properly unrepresentable totality which is the ensemble of society's structures as a whole" (1991, 51). What would these "cognitive maps" look like? Even as Lynch understood it, ordinary maps were an insufficient means of engaging with the urban, since

> At every instant, there is more than the eye can see, more than the ear can hear, a setting or a view waiting to be explored. Nothing is experienced by itself, but always in relation to its surroundings, the sequences of events leading up to it, the memory of past experiences. (1960, 1)

Given the multi-temporality and affective nature of actual urban space, the contemplation of personal history, governmental history, and close attentive journeying are needed to negotiate the complexity of lived space in Singapore. While this may be true for any human environment, to live in Singapore, as Tong and many others have put it, is to experience so much topographical flux that ordinary wayfinding may be difficult and at times perplexing. It is not an overstatement to argue that most Singaporeans have borne witness to the wholesale destruction of the plain, ordinary, and run-down, under the aegis of modernist and authoritarian city planning, and the demands of a globalizing capital-driven economy. How then can collective memory, as represented and enabled by communally available older architecture and spaces, continue to function? And, as importantly, how can a culture that has been divested of its organic urban diversity create the possibilities for new ideas and art that are not deracinated and disoriented by the rapid urban renewal that has taken place in the past half century?

Wayfinding through literary and artistic texts enacts a recovery of spatial memory and attempts to function in the literal and figurative voids that have been left in the wake of aggressive urban redevelopment. Artistic artifacts such as Tong's film seek to act as proximate landmarks, *lieux de memoire* for wayfinding the city without maps. In this chapter, I read Tong's populist film in concert with creative nonfiction by Tan Shzr Ee and flash fiction by Alfian Sa'at as counter-cartographies of Singapore's relentless demolition and reconstruction. These artistic and literary works might be what Pierre Nora would call *lieux de mémoire*. They exist because, as Nora notes, "there are no longer any *milieux de mémoire*, settings in which memory is a real part of everyday experience" (1996, 1). In the wake of Singapore's *tabula rasa*, it might be possible to consider artistic and literary interventions as ways to create an imagined space that is an "interaction between memory and history," where the poet or artist is able to "inhibit forgetting [...] immortalize death and [...] materialize the immaterial – all in order to capture the maximum possible meaning with the fewest possible signs" (Nora, 1996, 14, 15). Nora argues that these *lieux* must have a "capacity for change [...] to resurrect old meanings and generate new ones along with new and unforeseeable connections (that is what makes them exciting)" (1996, 15). Literary and filmic texts that wayfind through this wholly changed and continually changing history, as dynamic *lieux de mémoire*, enable us to find new routes and trajectories through the mapped city.

Grandma Positioning System's humorous and poignant depiction of one family's extended struggle with the ongoing and disruptive changes to their version of Singapore is clearly an act of wayfinding beyond the planned and overdetermined spaces of the city-state's development. Unlike in my previous chapters, this spatial and artistic gesture is neither what I call excavation (the artistic unearthing of suppressed histories) nor circumvention (the careful negotiation around amorphous and dynamic forms of authoritarian power). Like these earlier tactics, wayfinding brings us up against the colonial and (post)colonial cartography of Singapore as an endlessly hyperlinked and zoned space but in ways that emphasize the ongoing, processual, and contemporary efforts to inhabit and traverse it. Wayfinding, as practiced by Tong's film and the other texts examined in this chapter, produces alternate chronotopes of space. Similarly, the latter part of this chapter will consider the unmapped traversals and journeys that Tan Shzr Ee's *Lost Roads: Singapore* and Alfian Sa'at's *Malay Sketches* make across the island.

Tong ends his film with a superimposed text, "Home is the road travelled together," casting his film as one such road from Malaysia to Singapore, from the living to the dead and back again. This is not mapping or mapmaking but instead what Ingold might call the process of wayfinding, since

> To find one's way is to advance along a line of growth, in a world which is never quite the same from one moment to the next, and whose future configuration can never be fully known. Ways of life are not therefore determined in advance, as routes to be followed, but have continually to be worked out anew. And these ways, far from being inscribed upon the surface of an inanimate world, are the very threads from which the living world is woven. (2000, 242)

In Tong's film, however, it is the ways of life and the ways of death that are entwined as the film's family wayfind in the mapped space together, evincing a deeper spatio-temporal understanding of Singapore. The other texts that I read in this chapter similarly attempt to draw our awareness to the unmappable, the "ways of life" that depend on corporeal and affective modes of being. Whether creative nonfiction, flash fiction, or mural, they find their way around urban spaces by focusing on the details that push them along their trajectories. Where a cartographer feels the need to do away with a "fog of detail" since a map is not processual, a wayfinder is not troubled by this detail since, "the richer and more varied the texture of the environment, the easier it is to find one's way around" (Ingold, 2000, 242). Ironically, it is easier to know where one is without a map, since a map provides only the abstract coordinates of a homogenized landscape. This "fog of detail," its seemingly throwaway details and memories of favorite food stalls, the ruins of demolished buildings, small road realignments, and so forth, is the power of wayfinding. Literary wayfinding as an act of both writing and reading gives us what can be seen and what can no longer be seen, what can be heard and what can no longer be heard, the story that is coming into being and changing even as it is being narrated. These are not just confined to loss or death in the city, they are processual, ongoing, and ever-evolving.

Lost Roads: Singapore

In her experimental memoir, Tan Shzr Ee's semi-autobiographical first-person narrator declares herself unwilling to rely on maps. The protagonist actively seeks out where this fixed way of navigating space fails: where roads and infrastructure stop, where blankness indicates unimportance or uselessness of space to the government mapmakers.[2] *Lost Roads* looks for "white ribbons that nudged themselves into green patches on paper" and the narrator relies on "postmen and dispatch riders for secrets" or on "family and friends to drive me into the furthest corners of Singapore" (Tan, 2006, 10). The text, in its wayfinding beyond the mapped, gives us the ever-changing, fragmented glimpses of an unmappable city. This eschewal of the quantifiable and the exact is a deliberate departure from the colonial and neocolonial planned city. Wayfinding in Tan's text gives us a method to perform an idiosyncratic counter-cartography of planned space, to focus on liminal spaces: coastal areas, intertidal zones, offshore islands, cemeteries, traffic crossings, and abandoned ruins. The texts themselves become alternate landmarks, marks on the land that eschew mapped views of the city. A collection of anecdotes, lists, verbatim reportage, first-person accounts, and autobiography, *Lost Roads* revels in what Doreen Massey calls, "the disruptions of space, the coming upon difference. On the road map you won't drive off the edge of your known world. In space as I want to imagine it, you just might" (2005, 111). Tan's text provides us an actual model of what it means to challenge the map-like view of Singapore by literally driving and walking beyond the map, falling off the edge of a flat, two-dimensional world. By doing so, the text defamiliarizes the planned space, revealing its artificiality.

The genesis for Tan's book *Lost Roads: Singapore* was her bi-weekly column for Singapore's national newspaper *The Straits Times*, "Accidental Tourist."[3] The text comes at a threshold moment in Singapore's developmental history.

---

2 Tan Shzr Ee worked as an arts correspondent for the main English-language newspaper in Singapore, *The Straits Times*. She is a musician and an ethnomusicologist at Royal Holloway, University of London. *Lost Roads: Singapore* is her only non-academic publication.

3 Tan's text was commissioned by SNP Editions, a subsidiary of the government-owned Singapore National Printers Ltd. The book was originally inspired by a series of columns called "Accidental Tourist," which ran in the national newspaper *The Straits Times*. The book, however, is substantially different in style and content from the more superficial explorations of the newspaper columns.

At this point in the mid-2000s, Singapore's planned spatial politics are well-established. The country has enjoyed numerous economic booms since independence but also weathered the Asian financial crisis in the late 1990s. Land reclamation and development are accepted facts of life, but the country has not broken ground on its most ambitious project of building an entirely new downtown. Work is ongoing for the new subway lines on the island, but they are not complete. The 2008 Master Plan, with its projections of a population of 6.9 million in 2030, has not yet come into existence. All these impending developments loom over Tan's highly self-conscious text, even as it details the as yet undeveloped spaces of the island with its semi-fictive inventories.

Tan sees her book as a pastiche, a variety of genres that have come together to make:

> a scrapbook – of real and imagined experiences; of half-remembered stories from family, friends and strangers; of interrupted memories; of anecdotes disengaging and dysfunctional; of rabidly untrue rumours; of bizarre signs and notices spotted in unremarkable corners; of overheard conversations and useless laundry lists ... throwaway epiphanies that have presented themselves in the course of my travels through *ulu* Singapore. (2006, 10)

Tan journeys to the *ulu* or out of the way parts of Singapore to create this unpredictable inventory of unverified stories, truncated memories, and minute throwaway details. The text produces spaces through wayfinding, whether they are sacred, natural, domestic, fictional, or an unwieldy combination of the above. The unsettled, polyphonic style of Tan's prose reflects its engagement with a city where land reclamation has left its inhabitants unsure where the island will begin or end, where incessant development alters landscapes overnight, where certain parts of the island are privileged over others, and where others have been left to neglect, waiting the next developer's excavator. *Lost Roads* encounters these unmappable anxieties and instabilities, and internalizes them in its form and content.

With its prefatory material, *Lost Roads* immediately shows that it is aware of the planned and zoned nature of Singapore's urban spaces. Indeed, there is an official map of the island in the first section of the book, with boxed insets of areas that the book will focus on – an orienting guide of sorts that is carefully labelled with the names of each general region. Using the accepted vocabulary of maps, there is even a legend that denotes the usual multicultural religious sites, transport lines, terminals, and "Places of Interest." Superficially, the overall structure of the text is seemingly map-like as it geographically stakes out its objects of explorations in the east, north, west, central, and offshore areas of Singapore: Loyang/Changi, Sungei Punggol/Buangkok, Sembawang, Lim Chu Kang, Jalan Bahar/Jurong Road, Central Singapore, Southern Islands, Pulau Ubin, and Mount Sophia. Nonetheless, even as the text consults a street directory and takes this accepted conception and experience of Singapore as its point of departure, it seeks to unsettle this view of Singapore.

The initial framework of the formal maps and geographical organization makes the text's wayfinding desires visible. From unusual grammatical tenses and shifting narrative perspectives to unconventional historiography and experimental prose forms, Tan uses a range of formal tactics. One of the most significant things that the text does almost immediately, though, is to warn us not to "believe everything you read in this book" (2006, 9). The narrator suggests that what she is trying to document in this work is "an empty category, a genus of an extinct species, a barely there slip of air between two dog-eared cardboard dividers in a filing cabinet" (2006, 9). The planned and zoned landscape that Tan's text pushes against is the product of an endlessly mapped city-state – one where spaces conceived by government urban planners and property developers turn rapidly into a physical reality. This is a spatial practice that is wholly dominated by representations of space. In the face of this, Tan muses on the impossibility of her quest for "lost roads" since,

> if a road is well and truly lost, you wouldn't be able to find it anymore, would you? You scour old naval base maps, 1950s street directories and ancient bungalow blueprints, only to find that the assam tree which guarded a shrine marking the start of a squiggly path in Pulau Ubin has since been uprooted, its surrounds flattened into would-be army land.
>
> A once straight thoroughfare in Boon Lay has been chopped into limbs by urban development, its surviving appendages rewired into large ringlets of HDB satellite towns.
>
> The school where you were detained over three afternoons gardening (as punishment for eating Mamee in class) has been transplanted elsewhere and far away, even as it continues to bear the name of the road where it was first built.[4] Are there really lost roads in Singapore, this proverbial air-conditioned city? (2006, 9)

Tan's search for the "lost" or the "absent" produces literary urbanisms beyond the reach of maps. The text sees the archive, the "old naval base maps" and so forth, as wholly inadequate to its task. Indeed, while portions of the rest of the text have carefully researched historical anecdotes, these are only secondary to the lived experiences of the spaces that Tan explores. In this case, maps are unable to provide the minutiae of the natural and emotional spaces that are bracketed by the ever-changing roads and paths. Roads themselves are "chopped into limbs" with their "surviving appendages rewired" in a disturbing

---

4 Mamee is a snack only found in Malaysia and Singapore that is a packet of uncooked instant noodles, seasoned with a condiment pack that is included. It comes in distinctive plastic yellow packaging with a blue monster logo. The use of the brand name here localizes this memory and imbues it with a nostalgia that Tan's Singaporean readers would immediately understand.

combination of the mechanical and the corporeal. The text's surreptitious addition of an autobiographical, throwaway anecdote is crucial here, and part of Tan's tactics of the everyday. What would have been an anonymous school, just another victim of a bureaucratic displacement, becomes an intimately remembered place through a series of intensely personal chronotopes, the recollection of "three afternoons gardening (as punishment for eating Mamee in class)." In referring to these "unimportant" afternoons, Tan raises the personal stakes of lost spatio-temporalities.

Her methodology in the book is summed up as a corporeal practice: "I walked and walked" (Tan, 2006, 10) – a reminder of de Certeau's *Wandersmänner*, whose walking "creates within the planned city a 'metaphorical' or mobile city" (2002, 110). With these unplanned trajectories, *Lost Roads* produces new ways of inhabiting space, a wayfinding that challenges the totalizing confines of Singapore's urban planning. By this wayfinding, the text rhizomatically restores the unexpected and unpredictable in Singapore's spaces. This is emphatically not a comprehensive act of preservation – the text "isn't meant to champion the valiant cause of conservation" (Tan, 2006, 9) – but an act of resistance, as *Lost Roads* refuses to mold itself to fit into any one genre (whether fiction or nonfiction, historical narrative or contemporary account, autobiography or polyphony). It provides us with ever-changing, fragmented glimpses of an unmappable city.

The text's improvisations are not just a semi-fictional record of a moment of Singaporean life, they are also a recuperative move for the consciousness of the population. Its detours allow for a different mode of existing in an urban space that only allows for fixed destinations. The affective and social life of a city's inhabitants is at stake here, one that is intimately entwined with a visceral particularity of living in Singapore – a point made clear as the text's introduction localizes the cliché "Stop and smell the roses":

> I'd like to suggest, "Stop and smell the grass." Inhale the heaviness of a sky crying to rain, the oily odours of towkays who sit by cracked parlour floors looking for old faces reincarnated in the Maybelline rouge of China girls. Breathe in the colours and fumes of ICI Dulux over dead leaves accidentally memorialised on a dirty wall given a quick paint job. (Tan, 2006, 11)

What the narrator calls for here is a wayfinding that is necessarily constrained by the rapid and totalizing changes in Singapore's urban landscape. The text revels in the excess of everyday detail, and a sensorial surrender to the unexpected, unmappable spaces of the city. These are spaces of untold stories, continual migration, and transnationality, and the often uncanny juxtapositions of the natural world and urban development. The text's observations on the fringes of the planned spatial reality of contemporary Singapore are crucial because these possible alternative trajectories around and through Singapore's overdetermined urban spaces represent an important resistance to the abstraction of lived space emotionally, intellectually, and corporeally. Tan's inventory of these "lost roads" is intentionally neither comprehensive nor infallible. This eschewal of the quantifiable and the exact is a deliberate departure from the colonial and neocolonial planned city. This idiosyncratic counter-cartography of Singapore is necessarily a liminal one, one involving neglected spaces.

We begin with Changi/Loyang, an eastern area of Singapore known primarily for its proximity to the country's international airport – an award-winning, much-lauded symbol of international connectivity and gleaming modernity. The airport is the point of departure for most journeys away from the island and is strictly policed by the country's immigration authorities and auxiliary police forces. Crucially, the text bypasses this "important" space in its journey eastward, "your car takes you past the airport (which is as far as you usually go)" (Tan, 2006, 15):

> You glide through an endless stretch of highwayesque tarmac, a zoom of streamlined expanse fringed by the Changi Meteorological Station, a noisy, incense-steeped Chinese temple, a landfill, liver-red brick apartments (where, incidentally, Singapore's only professional Baroque fiddler and harpsichordist allegedly lives) and rows of short, ugly buildings.
>
> The newer buildings – assemblages of glass-pretending-to-be-plastic, and plastic pretending to be steel, or possibly the other way round – beam at you with the brand-newness of their constructions. They scream efficiency and air-conditioning.
>
> The older ones – chalky walls, algae-seeped paint, exposed ceilings – resist you with decrepitude and the judder of a potential live-in ghost (surely these buildings must look quite different, disused, at night?). The windows are black and silent, hiding empty rooms on a Saturday afternoon. (Tan, 2006, 16)

The deployment of the second-person narrative here and in a great deal of the text has the effect of inserting the reader into the text in an immediate, physical way. The attention to detail in this passage is not just an attempt to make sense of the uneven modernity of Singapore; the text's inventory of the random, insignificant details and sights provides a textured, heterogeneous view of this urban space, even of its "short ugly buildings." The coded representations of modernity and the past are made clear, and yet both are imbued with a sense of instability – where even the raw materials are of an unknown provenance. In particular, the uncertain possibilities of the older spaces are emphasized. In this first extended description of space, we get a "throwntogetherness," what Massey argues is "the unavoidable challenge of negotiating a here-and-now (itself drawing on a history and a geography of thens and theres); and a negotiation which much must take place within and between both human and nonhuman" (2005, 140). This haphazard, chance-filled interaction with space is what the text privileges above all else. The level of detail and overwhelming specificity that we are given in the text is what enables it to move beyond the abstraction of planned Singaporean space.

The text continues to wander off the map by following a nondescript path that borders a field, all while continuing to inventory the flotsam and jetsam that lines the path. It reaches a green space that it deems "not quite an oasis. It's really a ditch" (Tan, 2006, 17), reminding us of the tenuous boundaries between the urban and the natural in Singapore. The next section of the text makes clear the disingenuous role that confabulation will play in the text's evocation of space:

> The tide is rising, and you can make out shadows in the water. Perhaps they are fish, or mudskippers. Man-made as it comes, there is still something rugged and charming about this band of channelled water – or so you want to believe [...] As you inch along the canal, the flattened grass grows thick and sinks into a marsh of last night's rainfall. It cushions your slippered feet with the taunt of invisible insects that will surely crawl in between your toes and mince on the debris under your nails. (Tan, 2006, 17)

In particular, the phrase "or so you want to believe" implicates the reader in the creative renaturalization of this environment. As the text slips a little further into its reverie, its language takes a pastoral turn: the "flattened grass grow thick," as it "cushions" one's footsteps. Nature threatens to overwhelm the bodies in this space, as it manifests as "the debris under your nails." The texture of this space is palpable and there is a fragile romanticization of the landscape. The prelude ends as the text speaks self-reflexively: "you tell yourself that you'll take all the ugly, beautiful, insipid and magnificent surprises which throw themselves upon you literally, in stride" (Tan, 2006, 18). And, again, the idea of chance here becomes paramount, opening up the possibility of the unforeseen in a city where almost everything has been relentlessly foreseen.

Repeatedly, *Lost Roads* comes up against geographies of power that it attempts to challenge. In one instance, it does this by revealing the contrived nature of state narratives that have been imposed on a historical site. In this case, the text embeds unpredictability and chance in the formal elements of its account of the Johore Battery, a little-known British ammunition store in tunnels near the Changi Prison. In a quietly satirical way, the descriptions of the site send up textbook and guidebook accounts of Singaporean history. The section on the Johore Battery begins with the polyphonic, free-associative comments left in a guestbook at the site. Almost immediately the text produces a contemporary, almost postmodernist experience of this historical site. The brief, tangential comments by Singaporeans, and tourists in a variety of languages and tones, in disjointed, epigrammatic phrases provide polyphonic, fragmented perspectives that undercut the totalizing official history of the space.

What is clear from the account of the Johore Battery and in other sections of the text is that the unseen geographies of power in Singapore are numerous and multifarious. Aside from the parodic and meta-textual critiques that are performed on stereotypical representations of Singapore space, the narrative also finds itself literally up against physical manifestations of these forms of power and governmentality. In most of *Lost Roads*, there is an underlying consciousness of the ephemeral nature of places in Singapore; at one point in a seemingly deserted space, Tan encounters a large construction site and remarks, "even in the last stretches of green and uncombed Singapore, the tractors are advancing, advancing" (2006, 77). There are clear limits set on the text's ability to cross boundaries around military installations, live-firing grounds, radio transmission towers, and elitist local and expatriate communities. In each of these encounters, the map and its set lines appear to be entrenched in military power, elite privilege, and private property, and the text appears to retreat defensively when faced with these aspects of Singaporean space. While it may be possible to read these instances as failures of Tan's counter-cartography, I see the text's attempts to inventory these spaces and to acknowledge its real fears regarding the latent militarization or gentrification of certain areas in Singapore as highly significant. These unsettling moments in the text provide ways in which to confront the spatial dynamics of power in the island state.

These geographies of power are enmeshed in complex spatio-temporalities that make explicit links between colonial military power, whose remnants remain in the bungalows, chalets, and barracks and "the squirm of roads with fancy English names" (Tan, 2006, 25), and the current militarization of the island.[5] Again and again, the text's encounter with the ostensible history of the place is reinforced by a run-in with contemporary militarized spaces. In one episode, the narrative sets up the possibility of a haunted space of the tropics, imbued with colonial history and historicity. Tan plays with the established tropes of entering a seemingly (postcolonial) Gothic space, with the tunnel-like row of trees, the ruins of the buildings with their trappings of decay:

> The trees close in to form a green-black jigsaw of the sky, the roads wind into gray slabs of crumbling shortcake. And then, you see it. Or, rather, them: a cluster of magnificent, multi-storey buildings with the requisite paint-peeled walls and ambitious gardens of dead leaves.
>
> Ooh. Let's investigate.
>
> You inch your car slowly past a State Land signpost and get out to walk.
>
> Who lived here? British army officers? Who died here? More British army officers?
>
> When were they built? What will happen to the buildings?
>
> Half a century ago, some 50,000 Allied POWs were housed in the Selarang and Roberts Barracks of the era before they were decamped to the too-small Changi Prison to live in huts outside the walls.
>
> Perhaps they were –

---

5 Singapore's defense budget was reported to be $12.3 billion in 2013, the largest in Southeast Asia. It has one of the highest per capita expenditures on defense in the world. See Choong (2013).

But curiosity is killed by a man in a Number Four uniform toting a weapon.[6]

He looms out of nowhere, wearing a crown of green leaves and glaring at you. No apparition this is. [...] And before you open your mouth to speak, you see the signboard depicting one falling stickman being shot by another rifle-toting stickman.

"No Trespassing", it proclaims.

Not quite a ghost, but Number Four is serious enough to make you turn your heel and exit politely. (2006, 26)

In this instance, *Lost Roads* rapidly shifts registers and consistently foils our genre-specific expectations. The text speculates on the unknowability of the past, opening up the possibility of this space to its colonial and wartime history. The series of open-ended questions here point to the forgetting that has taken place, an amnesiac neglect of the colonial traces in Singapore's landscape. These musings are interrupted self-consciously, mid-sentence by the intrusion of a present-day soldier – possibilities and curiosities are "killed" by an armed man. Singapore is haunted not just by the architectural ghosts of its colonial and wartime past, but by the quiet and unseen militarization of its green spaces. The narrative here is anchored firmly in the present, showing how straying off the beaten path in Singapore may set you up against numerous military zones on the island since they make up 19 percent of the island's 71,000 hectares, representing the single largest percentage of land use in the country (see Ministry of National Development Singapore, 2013).

The examples that I have provided from the first few sections of *Lost Roads* are exemplary of the range of literary techniques and tactics with which the text uses to approach Singapore's spaces, and give an idea of the range of the text's foci. In the sections that I have not analyzed in detail, the text goes on to explore neglected colonial-era buildings, and other pockets of colonial architecture that have been turned into expatriate communities in a unsurprising perpetuation of European privilege in Singapore. The text encounters spaces of elite privilege for both rich Singaporeans and foreigners. In its exploration of central Singapore, the text describes a golf course as "the sacred portal where men in soft-soled shoes who whip long sticks that push little white balls with millions of tiny dimples on their surfaces into perfect-fit holes eventually retire to hide from the midday sun (or their wives) and sip ice-cold drinks" (Tan, 2006, 99). The tone of the language here mocks and defamiliarizes the space favored by the Singapore elite. Indeed, the text continues by exposing the hidden wealth that is the unseen power and reward of an authoritarian regime.

---

6 This is the combat-ready uniform of the Singaporean army consisting of green camouflage fatigues. Note that the system of numbered military uniforms is also a British legacy.

In resistance to these mapped boundaries and abstract spaces of privilege and power, Tan's *Lost Roads* seeks out individuals and communities who have taken the time to cultivate emotional and social bonds to the natural world or rare undeveloped spaces. The text fixates on seemingly anomalous spaces like the last *kampong* or village, an old community mosque, and offshore island communities who resist the seemingly endless developmental policies of the Singaporean government. These pockets of heterogeneity humanize the island, imbuing spatial practice with a sociality that is organic, rooted, and complex – in opposition to a manufactured nationalism. Other alternate modes of spatial practice are evident in the motif of subsistence fishing that runs through the text, recalling Singapore's earlier iteration as a fishing village. While I am wary of suggesting this is anything like a 'primal' connection to the island, there is perhaps a way of seeing these sequences in the text as a glimpse of an indigenous, sustainable relationship with the environment. Occurring in the intertidal or coastal areas of the island, the literal edge of Singapore's development, the fishing described is done by itinerant groups or migrant workers, usually foreigners who have a tenuous connection to the developmental state. In one encounter, Thai migrant workers who are catching catfish in the marshy river are taciturn about their haul, suggesting that the narrator has no access to their knowledge of the land or its possibilities. Indeed, these figures appear to understand the island's native ecologies better than the Singaporean narrator.

Lost Roads opens up the possibilities of space on many textual levels – those of narrative structure, genre, perspectival changes, and even in its use of grammatical tense. The bulk of *Lost Roads* is written in the second person, a formal choice that imbues the temporality of the text with an involving immediacy. In the final section, the narrative turns into a first-person narrative in the present tense as it explores the spaces of Tan's own familial history. This shift is not only spatial but temporal as the narrative turns to the spaces of familial memory that resonate in risky, intimate ways. By offering up a form of autobiography in the final section of the text, Tan raises the stakes of what it means to dwell in Singapore's urban spaces. Embedding the complex spatio-temporal trajectories of her own grandmother and family here prevents the narrative from becoming a detached, anthropological view of the island. This is crucial in the light of the numerous "informants" whose voices recur throughout the rest of the book. One informant, Mr. Mike Tan, first credited only as an "early Sembawang resident" (Tan, 2006, 57), is only explicitly revealed to be Tan's father in the last section of the text as he describes the history of the narrator's grandmother's flat.

The text belatedly reveals its autobiographical qualities, making it more than just a set of trajectories traversing the island. The final section, "The Heart of Things," with its disjointed narratives and multiple genres (lists, first-person narratives, third-person narratives, interviews), searches for multiple modes of remembering the narrator's grandmother's apartment that has been lost to the family because of the government's decision to raise the rent to its market value. Each part of this section is a new wayfinding through the slightly altered chronotopes of apartment 42B, Sophia Flats and its environs. The experimental and non-conventional narrative styles of the rest of the text are amplified as it attempts to resolve familial and spatial loss – discovering new lost roads and routes to the past and present.

Here, the text becomes suffused with a kind of autobiographical desire that is individual and idiosyncratic, an entirely human impetus that has led it through its production of space. Memory is central to this desire in the final section of *Lost Roads* as it functions as a structuring device for the text and its production of space.[7] This complicated process of how memory shapes space can be illustrated by examining how the text introduces us to 42B, Sophia Flats. We first see it through the eyes of the narrator as a little girl, an almost straightforward spatialization of the apartment's context through the patina of the narrator's memories. The attention to the specificities of this space speaks to the embodied, textured experience of living and remembering it. As is Tan's habit in *Lost Roads*, the narrator focuses on the minute, throwaway, quotidian details

there was an unused five-foot way around the building too.[8] It was made

---

7 In thinking through memory this way, I build again on Frow's discussion of the significance of textual memory in Jorge Luis Borges's stories. Frow argues that it is not in fact "retrieval" that is important in the textuality of memory, but "reversibility," since "The time of textuality is not the linear, before-and-after, cause-and-effect time embedded in the logic of the archive but the time of a continuous analeptic and proleptic shaping. Its structure is that of any dynamic but closed system, where all moments of the system are co-present, and the end is given at the same time as the beginning. In such a model the past is a function of the system: rather than having a meaning and a truth determined once and for all by its status as event, its meaning and its truth are constituted retroactively and repeatedly; if time is reversible then alternative stories are always possible [...] Like a well-censored dream, and subject perhaps to similar mechanisms, memory has the orderliness and the teleological drive of narrative. Its relation to the past is not that of truth but of desire" (1997, 229). In this exploration of textual memory and its potentialities, Frow's theories complicate the chronotopic aspects of remembered spaces. His distinction between the archive and the text is particularly helpful here in considering the radical possibilities of how textual memory can alter our production of space, whether past or present. Time is not only *reversible* here but also unpredictable, since "alternative stories are always possible." In theorizing the effect of remembering spatially, we must acknowledge how human desire reshapes temporally complex spaces, precisely because it remembers selectively.
8 A "five-foot way" is the covered sidewalk that is ubiquitous in the shophouses of British colonies in Southeast Asia. Their legacy has been traced to Sir Stamford Raffles, who apparently specified their exact measurements. Another example of the precise colonial legacies on spatiality in the colony. These five-foot ways were

of pale, orange-brown and maroon tiles: each one had a feathery pattern across it. The tiles were almost identical except for that one tiny, almost indiscernible waver in the feather pattern unique to each tile; I always wondered how they mass-produced tiles like that in 1930. (2006, 133)

The attention to localized detail in this passage is again very much akin to Ingold's idea that a wayfinder is never overwhelmed by detail as a cartographer would be, but instead revels in it. The narrator's careful, hyper-attentive gaze noting the "one tiny, almost indiscernible waver" suggests a highly embodied presence in the space. Further, in the context of the rest of the contemporary heterotopias that have been explored in the text, the hyper-memorialization of this childhood space produces a kind of equivalency between past and present temporalities that complicates the idea of a fixed, static, mapped space. This memory space is one that is vividly present, with its smell "of something damp, something sour and decayed" (Tan, 2006, 133). The text continues by chronicling the narrator's repeated climbing of the stairs, and at this point, pausing at the threshold of the apartment itself. The narrator then interjects her father's voice, in italics, providing personal histories of his time in the apartment, and further, the dense social networks of neighbors and old haunts that surrounded his home. Quotations detailing the provenance of the street names in the area are provided from Victor Savage and Brenda S.A. Yeoh's *Singapore Street Names: A Study of Toponymics*. Repeatedly, these "official" records and explications of place are challenged by intensely personal memories and more ordinary details of everyday life.

The text is constantly wary of providing a single perspective through these familial histories and at crucial points in this final section *Lost Roads* makes use of the third person, as a gesture of detachment, both from the author's past as a little girl in her grandmother's apartment and her present state as an interloper who sneaks back into the estate in a belated attempt to relive the intense memories of the space. These revisitings and reworkings of 42B, Sophia Flats recall Massey's conception of space as "always under construction [...] a product of relations-between, relations which are necessarily embedded material practices which have to be carried out" (2005, 9). Space, Massey argues, "is always in the process of being made. It is never finished; never closed. Perhaps we could imagine space as a simultaneity of stories-so-far" (2005, 9). Indeed, imagining just this single apartment and its neighborhood in Singapore as "open, multiple and relational, unfinished and always becoming" is, as Massey puts it, "a prerequisite for history to be open and a prerequisite, too, for the possibility of politics" (2005, 59). Here, then, lies the powerful potential of the spatial politics of *Lost Roads* and in particular in the autobiographical aspects of the text; by opening up this familial space to multiple interpretations, socialities,

---

often taken over by itinerant hawkers or shopkeepers whose wares would spill out onto their shopfronts. They were also incorporated into later public housing designs. See Liu (2001).

and temporalities, the text again points us to the ways in which spaces in the city-state can exist beyond the planned and zoned.

To further illustrate the possibilities of the text's open-ended spatial practice, I return to the motif of the staircase in the narrator's repeated vertical traversals of 42B, Sophia Flats. From the narrator's (and narrator's father's) first memories of the apartment, there are recurring references to climbing the various staircases to the apartment. These are embodied experiences that are moments of wayfinding through various iterations of the apartment building. As a literary trope, it is not a conventional form of movement through the city – unlike de Certeau's idea of the walker, for instance, traversing the city streets. I want to argue for its potential to liberate us from an ordinary palimpsestic view of the space of this apartment building. By making us aware of the repeated upward trajectories that are possible in the apartment, the text draws our attention to the mobility and ongoing potential of the space and its histories. This continual, unceasing movement through the apartment up (always up) the staircase gives us a way to understand this complex production of time and space in 42B. In the narrative, the staircase is altered slightly each time that it is traversed – each time showing us the different trajectories possible through the multiple temporalities contained in a seemingly fixed space.

The text ends with the narrator's final ascent up this staircase, an encounter with 42B that begins as chance transgression. In the third person, the narrator returns to her grandmother's apartment block impulsively, *"just for kicks"* (Tan, 2006, 151). Once again, she traverses the five-foot-way and walks up the staircase where "the steps have been retiled into an ugly flesh-coloured pink" and "a weak florescent light casts flickering shadows" (2006, 151). She is with a lover, and they are trespassing on what is now private property, reveling in "the thrill of sneaking up a building, rediscovering things that were or were not there" (2006, 152). As she ascends the staircase, again and again the narrator dwells on the minor and inconsequential: "a wilting, potted dumbcane plant," "a neighbour's dirty grilled door," "original cold, green-gray cement" (2006, 151). These details reinscribe the power of the quotidian, the everyday, and the subjective. The narrator reaches the rooftop only to be disappointed at the changes that have been wrought on her childhood space: "there is nothing to see" from her past, her grandmother's "orchids are long gone," "everything is ugly, ugly, ugly" (2006, 152). Her desire to seek out this past space, however, transforms at the end of the narrative into a sustained openness to its ongoing possibilities:

> Who lives there? Have they converted the open-air kitchen? What about the toilet – literally an outhouse? What happened to the neighbours? Are the other units, offices like this one, or do people still live in them? How much is the rent? Can we live here someday? Shall we repaint the walls? Do we need a new fan? Can we live without air-conditioning? We could have a dog and an aquarium and grow orchids. (2006, 152)

While unable to repossess this space, the narrator nevertheless takes it over with a series of open-ended questions, ones that she knows are "just a little fantastic and fanciful" (2006, 153). Encountering these possibilities towards the end of a text where so much of the indeterminate and unpredictable nature of space has been driven to the liminal heterotopias of the island provides no small degree of hope. The narrator "tingles in anticipation of something – she doesn't know what" (2006, 153), and for the overdetermined, mapped, and planned spaces of Singapore, it is this unknown that so dramatically acts as an antidote.

Malay Sketches

As she is part of the dominant anglophone Chinese community in Singapore, Tan Shzr Ee's work needs to be read in tandem with other minority accounts of wayfinding in the city-state. Her freedoms and privileges as an English-educated Chinese woman allow for forms of wayfinding that may not be possible for other, racialized subjects of the Singaporean state. To this end, I turn now to Alfian Sa'at's collection of flash fictions, *Malay Sketches*, which grapples with the marginalized experience of the Malay community.[9]

Singapore's Malay population generally adheres to the Muslim faith, which "makes them easily identifiable, reduces their intermarriage with other races, and in the world of post-September 11 fears, makes them particularly vulnerable to stereotyping" (Barr, 2005, 162).[10] This stereotyping of indigenous Malays began with British colonial rule, which viewed Chinese communities as more industrious and entrepreneurial than their Malay counterparts.[11] Hussin Mutalib notes that as recently as 2010, United Nations' Special Rapporteur on Racism and Racial Discrimination Githu Muigai "concluded that Singapore's ethnic Malay minority has been disadvantaged by some aspects of government

---

9 Alfian is a prolific writer, poet, and playwright. Besides his first, award-winning poetry collections poetry, *One Fierce Hour* (1998) and *A History of Amnesia* (2001), and his short story collection *Corridor* (1999), Alfian has gone on to great critical and commercial success as a playwright. In the past 20 years, he has written numerous plays in English and in Malay, and in doing so significantly shaped literary and political discourse in Singapore. Alfian will be referred to by his first name in subsequent mentions because "Sa'at" is a patronym.

10 Indeed, since colonial times, the community has also been subject to racial stereotyping from both the colonial authorities and the Chinese majority, the latter of which attributes their lack of economic and educational success to their "traits of complacency, indolence, apathy, infused with a love of leisure and an absence of motivation and discipline" (Rahim, 1998, 9). Beginning in the 1980s, the increasing number of government policies encouraging the Sinicization of the population, with an emphasis on Confucian values, further marginalized the non-Chinese minorities in the country.

11 See Alatas (1977) for an early but influential study on the effects and legacies of British representations of the Malay community.

policies" (2011, 1156). This disadvantage was particularly evident in the education and employment sectors, but also in the underrepresentation of Malays in senior positions in the army, police, intelligence services, and judiciary, because of historical and contemporary inequalities.

In this fraught and unequal context, Alfian's collection of 48 flash fictions functions as a compendium depicting minority indigenous lives in Singapore, carving out alternate urban spaces for them. In view of the cramped spaces that make up everyday life in Singapore (the public housing flat, the office cubicle, and the subway car), the brevity of the flash fiction genre seems particularly apt. The condensed nature of flash fiction and its ability to imply narrative conventions like plot and characterization in its brief lines (unlike a vignette that depicts a single scene) also speak to the genre's potential to *alter* the spatial limits that it inhabits. Even while constrained both by their own form and by the spatial pragmatism of Singaporean society, these very short fictions produce complex and indeterminate iterations of urban space. My critique builds on the work of Maggie Awadalla and Paul March-Russell, who argue that a critical focus on the postcolonial short story enables us to extend a "critique of centers and margins that underwrites the hierarchical practice of Empire but which, arguably, has been sustained by the neo-colonial activities of globalization"; as they suggest, "the restless fragmentation of the short story has a vital role to play" (2013, 8) in this critique – and it is this fragmentation and multiplicity that allows Alfian's work to unsettle the hierarchical spatial ideologies that dominate Singapore's urban spaces. In this section, I argue that, taken as an assemblage, *Malay Sketches* function as an anti-map of spaces that can only be experienced and not catalogued. Unlike Tong's film and Tan's experimental nonfiction, the wayfinding in Alfian's text must confront the racialization of its subjects and further, the consequent obliteration of their precolonial and (post)colonial life worlds.

Alfian's awareness of this imperial legacy begins with his title, *Malay Sketches*, which is taken from the 1895 colonial text *Malay Sketches* by Sir Frank Swettenham, the then British Resident of Selangor, Malaya. Swettenham's text consists of anthropological musings on the Malays, dominated by the gaze of the colonial expert and the voice of a single authoritative first-person narrator, a map of Malay persons and spaces. As a "writing back," Alfian's work allows Malay voices and conversations to proliferate in their diversity.[12] Layered upon the obvious foci of specific geographies and temporalities in the text, *Malay Sketches* examines how the pressing social issues facing the Malay community

---

12 Further, in the postcolonial Singaporean context, the use of the English language in literary works has been figured spatially by Philip Holden, who argues that "the English language exceeded colonial designs for it: it became a space where educated Asians from different ethnic groups in Singapore might meet and discuss issues to do with politics, cultural belonging, and identity" (2013, 51). It is from this evolving linguistic *space* of possible hybridity and postcolonial subversion that *Malay Sketches* works and expands.

are played out in particularly spatial ways: whether it is state-enforced racialization, disproportionate rates of incarceration, or the legacy of state-dictated evictions. These issues are considered from within the seemingly "minor" spaces of the marital bed, the video editing suite, the public housing flat, or the public campsite. The pieces focus on spatio-temporalities that are momentary and unplanned. Their disparate themes and polyphony produce a multiplicity of spaces that, while refusing an overarching narrative, are still interconnected, recalling Deleuze and Guattari's assertion that an assemblage like "a rhizome or multiplicity never allows itself to be overcoded, never has available a supplementary dimension over and above its number of lines" (1987, 9). Alfian's work here engages with the politics of the everyday, where ordinary, mundane routines have the possibility of producing alternate spaces in the city. These are spatialized (post)colonial flash fictions, where setting and character are central, and where the specificity of being a member of a minority Malay community in a neocolonial, Sino-centric capitalist society is inseparable from each narrative.

In both its form and content, *Malay Sketches* is a dissident text that resists the blueprint of Singapore's global capitalist success by reclaiming the affective, the indeterminate, and the unquantifiable – modes of being in space that resist the planned aspects of the city-state. Alfian's fictions have a broad range of subject matter, narrative voice, and setting. The assemblage of shifting, varying, and indeterminate connections that the text produces among its varied fictional voices enables different spaces to emerge, ones that are not tied to the state's grand narrative of investment, profit, and efficiency. With this polyphonic form, I believe that Alfian is drawing from his work for the stage: *Cooling-Off Day* (2011) and *Cook a Pot of Curry* (performed by Wild Rice Theatre Company in 2013) – plays that rely on the technique of verbatim theater, based on testimonies gathered from a series of personal interviews with a wide range of Singaporean residents. These literary techniques are the logical progression of Alfian's earlier poetic experimentation with dramatic monologues in *One Fierce Hour* (1998) and *A History of Amnesia* (2008), and the different focalizations found in his earlier collection of short fiction *Corridor* (1999). *Malay Sketches*' flash fictions reveal unexpected and invisible links between the private and the political. The fictions move rapidly between marital beds and military camps, execution grounds and public housing estates, and connect campsites to the memories of demolished villages. The text traces the effect of fraught histories of displacement and racialized policies (social, linguistic, economic) on everyday Malay lives.

With its attention to detail in each flash fiction's specific locale, *Malay Sketches* illuminates the relations of power and discipline that produce and regulate the everyday spaces of Singapore's Malay community, and the ways in which their lives are dominated by representations of space created by technocrats and planners. These flash fictions find other modes of inhabiting Singaporean space – whether through the indeterminate spaces of an interracial marriage, the aftermath of a state-imposed death sentence, or the fleeting recreation of rural Malay life at a public campsite. Such material and social spaces are central to Alfian's work, since it is particularly conscious of Singapore's geographies – a densely populated island state which places more than 80 percent of its population, according to a strict racial quota system, in high-rise public housing estates that arose from detailed blueprints.[13]

The flash fictions are as short as two paragraphs and rarely extend beyond four or five pages. They take on the voices of children and adolescents, the middle-aged and the very old. In my reading of the work as a deliberately fragmentary, rhizomatic assemblage, I draw from Deleuze and Guattari's spatial envisioning of a minor literature:

> In a book, as in all things, there are lines of articulation or segmentarity, strata and territories; but also lines of flight, movements of deterritorialization and destratification. Comparative rates of flow on these lines produce phenomena of relative slowness and viscosity, or, on the contrary, of acceleration and rupture. All this, lines and measurable speeds, constitutes an *assemblage*. (1987, 34–35)

Each flash fiction marks a wayfinding trajectory through the island state, and each one varies in its function and intensity. Twelve of the shorter fictions, however, are simply titled with a place name and a time, giving the collection a semblance of spatial rootedness in Singapore and a chronological structure that begins in the small hours of the morning and ends 24 hours later. These can be read as a meta-assemblage of the trajectories that the text makes through Singapore's traditionally Malay neighborhoods like Paya Lebar, Geylang Serai, and Kampung Glam. Other sites that are referred to all have Malay place names which reflect their history as Malay fishing villages (Tanjong Pagar, Bedok), seats of Malay royalty (Kampung Glam), and sites of indigenous peoples like the Orang Laut (Kallang, Geylang Serai).[14] Many of these refer to landscapes, botanical elements, and urban spaces that are no longer in existence: fishing villages, swamps, and squatter districts, and beaches that have been lost to land reclamation and urban development.

---

13 According to Singapore's Ministry of National Development (2019), "The Ethnic Integration Policy (EIP) is implemented to promote racial integration and harmony. The policy also aims to prevent the formation of racial enclaves by ensuring a balanced ethnic mix among the various ethnic communities living in public housing estates" (para. 1). In colonial Singapore, the earliest 1822 Jackson Plan made provision to segregate the indigenous Malay population from the Europeans and immigrant Chinese and Indian communities. While attempting to balance the ethnic ratios in the public housing estates, the Singaporean government still relies on colonial categories of race to formulate its spatial policies.

14 For more on toponyms, see Savage and Yeoh (2013).

These spaces and their place names were chosen for their historical and contemporary significance to the Malay community. *Malay Sketches* does not purport to show the entirety of the island or a totalizing view of a single racialized people; however, through its idiosyncratic meandering through these specific locales at particular times of the day, we are given a series of chronotopes of Malay life that work against Singapore's planned landscape. Through its polyphonic structure and multiple focalizations, *Malay Sketches* wayfinds through a diverse range of Malay perspectives that function as an anti-map of Singapore's highly regulated built environment and racially motivated spatial politics. Set in a regimented cityscape that ultimately marginalizes this population, the flash fictions continually insist on being in space through memory and the body.

We begin with an unknown child performing his ablutions and prayers in the tropical dark of "Paya Lebar, 5 AM," where "God's blessings are received like a spider-filament of light, pouring into the concavity of his palms, visible only to the unseen angels" (Alfian, 2012, 31). The chronotopes that follow are similarly sensory, unmappable instants in the lives of the varied characters. They mark each location with an intensely lived moment, a personal history, and a minority embodiment. These include a food stall worker in "Geylang Serai, 6 AM" feeling her way through a plastic bag of noodles, a Malay language teacher listening to her rebellious class in "Telok Blangah, 8 AM," and a story that tracks an office worker waiting interminably for a cigarette break, only to discover that he does not have a light in "Tanjong Pagar, 12 Noon." The latter is depicted as "a man in search of an oasis, his cigarette quivering like a divining rod, not for water but fire" (Alfian, 2012, 95). The plurality of these flash fictions punctures the orderly space of Singapore with instants of useless waiting, desire, and idiosyncratic behavior.

This polyphony of narratives and their acute familiarity and intimacy suggest different forms of spatial knowledge that are possible through the form of the flash fiction. The text gives us, for instance, the boys in "Bukit Batok, 5 PM" who imagine the formless, void deck of their public housing estate as "an imaginary stadium" (Alfian, 2012, 129) for their game even as they know they will be immediately regulated into a system that values punctuality and cleanliness when they return home. It reveals the interiority of the three women in factory uniforms waiting at the bus stop in "Bedok, 7 PM" who hope that their bodies and complicated lives can be somehow crammed into the crowded bus that approaches. The text reminds of other ways in which Malay men are delimited through compulsory military service, as a group of them smoke a shisha and vent about their experiences in "Kampung Glam, 10 PM," "dreading the next morning, their exit from what they now understood as civilization" (2012, 181). In short, these flash fictions give us a way to find ourselves in a Malay Singapore that cannot be seen or understood by its Master Plans. It is an urban space that finds itself and its histories consistently regulated, whether through education, living environment, work, or military service.

In *Malay Sketches*, there is a sense of a longer and more collective history that transcends this mapped existence. In the final flash fiction of the collection, "Kaki Bukit, 3 AM," a boy wakes from a dream of a rural life where he witnesses a buffalo giving birth. The story tells us that he is dreaming of something he could not have experienced, that it is in effect his mother's memory: "he realized how his existence did not begin only when he was born. He had always existed, in some form, before his time, in his mother's childhood. As she, in turn, would also exist after her own time, her memories indistinguishable from his dreams" (Alfian, 2012, 220). Crucially, the boy's dream is of a space in peninsular Malaysia, in a *kampong* in Rembau, Negeri Sembilan – reflecting the artificiality of Singapore's border with its geographical neighbor, and the cultural and familial ties that still bind Malays in both countries. These connections emerge in the boy's dream in the specific spatio-temporality of "Kaki Bukit, 3 AM," exposing this chronotope to be a far more complex thing than its superficial classification in a planned housing estate regulated by racial quotas and other housing grant systems. It reinforces the kinship links and generational memory that the anonymous boy carries within him which the state might see as liabilities in its quest for an obedient and clearly categorized multiracial citizenry.

Many of the flash fictions return repeatedly to the small, crowded lives that unfold in and around the public housing estate. In some of these stories like "Sacrifice," "Proof," "The Bath," and "Second Take," issues played out in brief instances in these flats include drug offenses among the Malay population, the policy of detention without trial enacted upon local Islamic terrorists, the death rituals for a Muslim AIDS victim, and the cross-cultural effects of poverty. Other stories, like "After Dusk Prayers," suggest ways in which the spatial practices of older social communities in the country are fleetingly present even in the confines of the public housing estate. These spatial practices as resistance find their culmination in the final story of the collection, "Overnight." This fiction moves away from the housing estate to a beach camp site, to offer a brief and fragile moment of respite from controlled living spaces. Set on Changi Beach in a temporary campsite, the fiction begins with a simple premise: Farisha and her family are celebrating her son's birthday by purchasing a tent and going on a camping trip. Farisha's father, we are told, had lived on Pulau Ubin, an offshore island that is still today thought of as one of the last remaining rural spaces in Singapore. Thus, embedded in this narrative from the beginning is the fact of systematic rural–urban displacement that occurred through Singapore's years of development, when the population was moved *en masse* from villages and slum housing to public housing flats.[15]

---

15 Loh Kah Seng's comprehensive study on the widespread clearance of the *kampongs* to build new public housing flats shows that the entire process was mired in

"Overnight" symbolically and literally reproduces the space of the *kampong* or Malay village, as the family assemble the temporary "blue trapezoid structure" in a spot "located along a row of eleven other tents" (Alfian, 2012, 41). When the nine-year-old son, poking fun at the enterprise, asks, "Is this our new house?" (2012, 41), Farisha's husband replies in the affirmative. This act of playing house is not mere child's play. As the two-page fiction progresses, the family find themselves participants in the production of what Michel Foucault (1984) would see as a heterotopian space, since it seeks a counter-existence to a city where all living space is zoned for specific uses.

As the characters wayfind through the campsite, they are immediately immersed in its connections to past spaces of freedom and *kampong* life. Farisha finds herself conversing with the other women in the campsite and they realize they have mutual friends and other connections that stem from their earlier lives in the *kampong*. The story focuses on the lived spaces and corporeal experience of the *kampong* as the women "talked about being woken up by roosters, the rain clattering on zinc roofs, nights scented by the haze from mosquito coils" (Alfian, 2012, 42). The act of camping is ostensibly linked to reliving these experiences; Farisha exclaims: "The government took away our kampong [...] and they gave us camping!" (2012, 42). Camping, for Farisha, produces an alternative community, still bound by spatial memories of the auditory, tactile, and olfactory qualities of *kampong* life. The narrative further posits that "camping" is somehow a surrogate for *kampong* life, with its camaraderie and communality. The story does not just dwell on the memory of the *kampong*, but produces this heterotopia again, a thick chronotope in what it calls Farisha's "makeshift neighbourhood" (2012, 42). Her husband returns to the campsite with large quantities of food, and they proceed to share it with the others. The night passes with a barbeque, group singalongs, and a "seashell-hunting expedition." It ends with Farisha falling asleep to "the sound of the waves, a familiar, regretful lullaby" (2012, 42). These communal gestures and social relations are in effect the spatial practice that reproduces the space of the *kampong*.

If the *kampong* is a space that can be reproduced in the contemporary moment by social relations and spatial practice, this complicates an accepted notion of the village as an abstract site of nostalgia for a pre-capitalist past in the collective Singaporean imaginary. In *That Imagined Space: Nostalgia for the Kampong in Singapore*, Chua argues that while there is a palpable nostalgia for this rural space, this does not mean that it is a longing for an actual historical space but a discursive site for a "resistance of the present" (1994, 20). Chua posits that "invoking the spirit of the *kampong* is a popular, if inarticulate, response to the stresses of living under the 'disciplinary' effects of industrial

---

complex politicking, suspicious cases of possible arson, and the loss of "the semi-autonomous urban *kampong* population," which was "progressively being socialised into becoming citizens of the new nation-state" (2009, 642).

capitalism" (1994, 24), even for Singaporeans who have never had firsthand experience of village life. Chua argues for the *concept* of the *kampong* as "an alternative construction" of life, one that the government cannot afford to allow, since its "claim to legitimacy to rule is based on the ability to improve ceaselessly the material life of the population" (1994, 25), following the logic of global capitalism.

Chua's argument assumes that the *kampong* remains in the realm of an abstract alternative or an idealized past. However, the account of the mythicization of the *kampong* may need to be reexamined considering the way the stories in *Malay Sketches* treat this collective memory. Arguably, the abstraction of the *kampong* in stories like "Overnight" is subtly diminished by the brief but repeated acts of transgression which provide the text with a tangible, albeit fleeting, production of *kampong* life. In "Overnight," the conversations about past *kampong*s, coupled with the altruistic actions of food sharing and play which have no profit motive, point to visceral ways in which social connections persist beyond the loss of the physical structures of the *kampong*. Even without the physical *milieu*, Alfian's story manages to relocate it to the campsite in his story, as it becomes a *lieu de mémoire* that produces a collective memory of a pre-mapped life.

Further, Alfian's flash fiction about the campsite is revelatory because of its simultaneous depiction of a space that is nevertheless highly regulated. Many of the Malay characters at the site are there not for a holiday but because they cannot participate in the contemporary spatio-temporality of Singapore that emphasizes the importance of property ownership. This reverie of the *kampong* is ephemeral and brief in Singapore's current spatial configurations, and the family are woken up by a Park Ranger enforcing its boundaries. We realize that the campsite is only a space of temporary escape: as one Malay woman pleads with the official, "We have nowhere else to go. HDB took back our flat," we realize that the family has been dispossessed, presumably because they could not make their monthly mortgage payments. This authority figure "demands" Farisha's "camping permit" (Alfian, 2012, 43), since there needs to be a legal document to prove that she has the right to camp there. Any imagined public commons have been thoroughly wiped out at this point, as the book details in this closing encounter:

> There was something familiar about the proceedings, but Farisha concentrated on locating her permit. She handed it to the Park Ranger, who reminded her to vacate by noon. Farisha realized that no reminiscence of the kampong was complete without the memory of eviction: a rooster crowing at dusk, a roof collapsing under rain, and the ember of a mosquito coil fading from orange, to grey, to a delicate pellet of dust. (2012, 42–43)

The Park Ranger, here as an agent of the state, literally determines who can be "seen" or who needs to be invisible in this space, as he evicts from the campsite a family who do not possess the proper documentation. The story takes up the issue of homeless families who resort to camping because they unable to continue paying their mortgages.[16] Here, the story implies that this eviction is much like the evictions from earlier Malay *kampongs* in the name of urban development – Farisha understands that there is "something familiar about the proceedings."

The story refuses to idealize the *kampong* as an uncomplicated utopian space. It is a remembered space that is shot through with the pain of "the memory of eviction," a fact of Singapore life that continues. The fiction ends with a reworking of the more idyllic memory of the *kampong*: with a rooster crowing at the wrong time, a roof that collapses in its obsolescence, and a final, haunting image of a mosquito coil disintegrating into nothingness. This final image presents us with a telling paradox, that something approaching nothingness, "a delicate pellet of dust," is nevertheless still materially present, reinforcing the fact that the *kampong* is also a set of ordinary, mundane objects and sounds that continue to persist even as they disintegrate into their constituent elements. This image challenges the fixed spatio-temporalities produced by Singapore's urban planning maps, and explores the intersections of communal memory, space, and sociality.

In "Overnight" and the other flash fictions examined here, Alfian's *Malay Sketches* enables a fragile balance between material objects and their symbolic meanings to produce affective, unquantifiable, and indeterminate spaces in Singapore. The panoply of fictional spaces in this collection, as produced through the social lives of minority Malay characters, resists the planned and zoned maps of the country, producing a way through this city without maps but with memories, bodily sensation, and an awareness of the structures of power that govern their living space. They call attention to ways of living (and dying) in the city that transcend the homogeneity of standardized housing and make visible the state's extreme regulation of its citizens' spaces. Their attention to the ongoing production of lived space reclaims minority Malay agency in Singapore and attempts to remember the complex spatialized histories of colonialism, eviction, development, and racialization on which the city-state is predicated.

"In Our Time"

In July 2018, during a visit to Singapore, I spent some time with a room-sized, 55-foot mural drawn and conceptualized by the illustrator and architect Li Xinli. The exhibit "In Our Time" was part of "Imaginarium: Into the Space of Time" at the Singapore Art Museum, which included other similarly immersive

---

16 There has been some press coverage of Malay families camping and leading nomadic lifestyles because of their inability to meet mortgage payments. See Jiang (2008).

artworks. The mural featured the entirety of the main and offshore islands of the state of Singapore, not to scale, packed to the brim with pop culture references, demolished and existing buildings, nostalgic material icons like toys and other knick-knacks, and, crucially, an outsized military presence. Drawn in a non-threatening, cartoon-like manner, the exhibit was the third version of Li's personal mapping of Singapore augmented with meticulous research from historical blogs, old films, photographs from the national archives, and other academic archives. In an email interview, Li told me that he had also been inspired by conversations with senior citizens, his architecture professors, and social media posts according to their geotags. He began with maps from the National University of Singapore's Geographic Information System unit in the Department of Geography. Li, like Tong, Tan, and Alfian, thus began his artwork with the records of one of the most mapped and planned spaces in the world, with its multiple iterations carefully recorded by generations of surveyors and cartographers for the use of future urban planners.

Li, like the writers in this chapter, comes up against the structures of state and military power that shape his conceptions of space. He explains the entwining of personal and political space as part of his artistic process:

> For military areas, part of it is also related to my personal National Service memories. One thing I realized in retrospect was the prominence of military areas. Many areas in Singapore are somewhat tied to military roots, be it post-independence or during the British rule, such as Seletar, Changi, Tanglin, Portsdown, Chia Keng, Mowbray and Sembawang. Then there were areas that were previously inhabited then turned into military use such as the former villages of Ama Keng, Thong Hoe or the islands of Pulau Sudong and Pulau Tekong. (Interview, 31 July 2018)

Fig. 18 Photography of a detail from *In Our Time* (2018) by Li Xinli. Credit: Joanne Leow.

Like the island state itself, Li's own body has been disciplined and conditioned by the process of military conscription. How might that affect his attempts to understand the spaces of the Singaporean state? During the exhibition he often made visits to his artwork dressed in his air force uniform, posing for photographs with visitors to the museum. What might it mean for the most visible aspect of state power to be reimaged with an aesthetic of defused hostility and childlike whimsy? Could his artwork ever fully escape a militarized understanding of the island, which is always predicated on a defendable space being fully legible?

On first impression, "In Our Time" appears to be a counter-mapping, an idiosyncratic mash-up of multiple personal and collective memories and milestones, full of lost buildings and flights of fancy. In his interview with me, Li remarked on the surfeit of materials to which he had access, suggesting that "the mural is only the tip of the iceberg for what Singapore is," even as he is attempting to "illustrate the rapid development that takes place between the 1960s till today." In attempting a complete wayfinding itinerary for the viewer, Li admits a defeat akin to Eco's "On the Impossibility of Drawing a Map of the Empire on a Scale of 1 to 1," except what "In Our Time" is also attempting ambitiously to portray is the passage of time and the various disparate temporalities that haunt its assiduously planned spaces. In its crowded, over-stuffed style, the artwork attempts to contain multitudes even as it must omit so much in order to be legible.

Li's quest for legibility here is perhaps his artwork's critical undoing. In its attempts to mimic, supplement, and humanize the models of Singapore's planned landscapes, Li's artwork softens the authoritarian mode of Singapore's cartography. His work, in my mind, illustrates the real constraints of alternate cartographies of Singapore. The sort of topophilia or "the soft city ... that to which citizens can emotionally relate and contribute to build" (De Koninck, 2017, 133), which Li's work might purport to depict, merely masks the hard facts of the territorial alienation of its population. His illustrations of the lost buildings and lifeworlds in the colorful mural are mere ciphers in the face of a city where most inhabitants have no control over what is preserved and what is demolished. De Koninck notes how this territorial alienation is a tool of social and political control since while "Individuals can share or attempt to share in the financial 'rewards' of constant redevelopment, [...] they nevertheless are neither invited nor expected to contribute to the decision-making process" (2017, 133).

Unlike the counter-cartographies of Tong, Tan, and Alfian, the charm and delightfulness of Li's caricatures seemed to neutralize the historical and ongoing militarization of the island, the ill-effects of extensive industrialization and land reclamation, and the pain of its inhabitants' repeated dispossessions and dislocations. Its attempt at a familiar aerial view recalls the Urban Redevelopment Authority's scale model of Singapore, even as it attempts to inject eccentricity and fantasy into its renderings. One telling detail is his rendering of the downtown Speaker's Corner, which features a cartoon figure whose speech bubble is simply empty – an indication of what cannot be said in this space.

As I paused in front of the mural, trying to locate my own landmarks and *lieux de mémoire*, I became more and more aware of the distancing effect that it was producing from my own feelings about the island. Contained as it was in the 55-foot-long mural, like the carefully comprehensive Master Plan, Li was attempting to make a version of Singapore legible from an aerial view. Li's other work on botany, food, the military, and architectural icons reflects an impulse to categorize and list, to try to be exhaustive. While pleasing in a categorical sense, this echoes the state's similar impulse to control the island's spatial narrative. What wayfinding and the other modes of counter-cartographies reveal are the insufficiency of these mapping impulses, even when they seem poised towards conservation and preservation. Wayfinding in Singapore is about a particular kind of mobility in the city, a form of critique of the shaping of its spaces. Wayfinding eschews the map or the attempt to categorize and plan, for an encounter with the unknown, to step into the unexpected chance of space, to experience it with the messiness of bodies. In this way it rejects the top-down view or indeed any attempt at totality. Wayfinding, as I have read in the works of Tong, Tan, and Alfian, seeks to narrate trajectories that are unexpected, surprising, and always incomplete and ongoing.

CHAPTER 4

Confabulations

"Past Conditional Temporality"

In the epilogue to his memoir *From Third World to First* (2000), Singapore's first prime minister Lee Kuan Yew reflects on the sweep of history and what he views as Singapore's improbable existence. To follow Lee's account, every decision he made was completely pragmatic, directed towards the goal of Singapore's continued survival. Lee's story, meant to echo the planned success of the city-state, is that of the complete triumph of twentieth-century high modernist ideology coupled with authoritarian determination. He locates Singapore's success as part of the industrial revolution and European colonialism, "their inventions, technology, enterprise … the story of man's search for new fields to increase his wealth and well-being" (Lee, 2000, 689). He begins his story with the usual recourse to British colonialism and then ties Singapore's progress to technological advancements and a calculative investment in human capital. It is a singularly seductive tale of teleological progress that maps out Singapore's past and present in a logical and schematic narrative. In order to justify his party's strict regulation of the country's land and its population, Lee reiterates his government's constant refrain of Singapore's vulnerability. He points out that "the future is as full of promise as it is fraught with uncertainty" (2000, 691). Far from being "uncertain," what Lee implies in the last pages of his memoir is that his handpicked successors, from whom he derives "immense satisfaction" (2000, 690), must abide by his legacy. He makes no attempt to imagine an alternative to this elitist, authoritarian mode of running Singapore in what is essentially a state of constant exception and emergency, a siege mentality.

The single exception to this certainty can be found in the last pages of his book. Here Lee allows himself a brief moment of retro-speculation, as he muses, "would I have been a different person if I had remained a lawyer and not gone into politics?" (2000, 688). He describes "the swirling currents of political changes" (2000, 685) that swept him along and rhetorically asks himself whether he *would have* continued on the path to become Singapore's founding leader if he had known the tribulations that lay ahead of him. This is a strange use of the past conditional tense in a relentless memoir full of confident and fateful anecdotes that purports to be a guide, a book that tells you "how to build a nation" (2000, 3). Indeed, without prior knowledge of what was to come, Lee says that he and his colleagues "pressed on, oblivious of the dangers ahead" (2000, 686). He writes,

> Would my colleagues and I have embarked on our journey had we known the hazards and perils we would face when we formed the People's Action Party in November 1954? Had we known how complex and difficult were the problems that lay ahead, we would never have gone into politics with the high spirits, enthusiasm, and idealism of the 1950s. (2000, 685)

Yet the note of uncertainty that Lee strikes here at the end, his musing about alternate paths, crucially stops short of the alternate histories and futures that Singapore might have had.

Critics of Lee's twining of his autobiography with the story of Singapore's success have often used the same metaphor of the path. For instance, the historians Michael Barr and Carl A. Trocki edited a collection entitled *Paths Not Taken* (2019) which focuses on much of the same postwar history that Lee addresses in his autobiography, albeit with more ambivalence. In their introduction, they posit a different version of this period, seeing it as "a dynamic and idealistic culture of political contestation and pluralism" (2019, 1). They point out that it was because the People's Action Party's hegemony was so complete and its belief in its success so unwavering that it became difficult to conceive of earlier alternatives:

> Public discourse now contemplated with horror the possibility that the nation-building project could have had any form other than that which emerged. Alternatives were seen as options for failure, if not chaos and anarchy. Yet the studies presented here suggest that this was not necessarily true. Alternative outcomes to the current state of affairs used to be well within the imagination of Singaporeans, and some of these alternatives may have even contained viable seeds for a different kind of social development than that which Singapore experienced. The present did not just happen. It was crafted. (Barr and Trocki, 2009, 6–7)

Barr and Trocki's collection contains studies on the social and intellectual atmosphere of early twentieth-century Singapore, the growth of civic consciousness in this period, the implications of the Bandung conference and its Afro-Asian non-aligned movements for the country, the complex multiracial party politics of the mid-century, the untold history of activism, and more. Examining these issues, Barr and Trocki reflect on the "counter-factual" possibilities that might have unfolded in the country if its left-wing opposition had survived.

These suppressed histories are the starting point of the literary texts that I read in this chapter, what Lisa Lowe calls "the *past conditional temporality* of the 'what could have been'" (2015, 40). For the most part, Lee's worldview had no time or space for what Lowe sees as the essential power of this temporality. He was only interested in condemning "what could have been" as potential failure without the strict governance of the ruling party. In Lowe's view, however, the past conditional temporality allows "a different kind of thinking, a space of productive attention to the scene of loss, a thinking with twofold attention that seeks to encompass at once the positive objects and methods of history and social science, and also the matters absent, entangled, and unavailable by its methods" (2015, 40–41). Unlike the myriad catastrophic endings for Singapore that Lee often holds up as warnings, Lowe emphasizes the critical openness of this temporal mode and its important representation in literary fictions. Indeed, she writes, we must turn to what could have been "in order to reckon with the violence of affirmation and forgetting, in order to recognize that this particular violence continues to be reproduced in liberal humanist institutions, discourses, and practices today" (2015, 41). In other words, "what could have been" is singularly crucial for examining the truths and paths *not* taken underpinning our current moment, since understanding them is the key to shaping what might be to come.

In this final chapter, then, I turn to where Lee hesitates to go: both in his unwillingness to countenance a different kind of history and an unmappable city-state, but also his preoccupation with an endlessly dangerous and uncertain future. I turn to the ways in which artists and writers in Singapore might "mislead" us as they have recently become attentive to different modes of understanding history through speculative literary fictions. Their work seeks to challenge the myths of insecurity and structures of power on which Singapore Story is based, and the ways in which the built environment of the city might have been affected. The texts that I examine in this final chapter imagine intimate counterfactual histories, speculate on the unbuilt and alternate present and futures, and engage in fantastical musings that are still anchored in the material spaces of the city. The *Oxford English Dictionary* defines the act of confabulation as one that "fabricates imaginary experiences as compensation for loss of memory." In the Singaporean context, the term takes on a modulated valence: when spatial histories and futures are so tightly regulated, to confabulate here is to fantasize and to be able to imagine otherwise, whether in the amnesiac past or zoned future. What might be the role of counterfactual history and speculative fiction in a country where challenging the accepted account of Singapore's inception is anathema and the Master Plan extends 20 or 30 years ahead into the future? How do speculative literary fictions intervene in the production of imagined and symbolic spaces that coexist with their material counterparts?

Fundamentally, to confabulate means being conscious of the *genre* of a text. Confabulation enables us to see how the texts that practice it are challenging generic boundaries between history and fiction, nonfiction and fiction, realism and fantasy. Here I am indebted to Linda Hutcheon's seminal work on historiographic metafiction, where she argues that the genre simultaneously enshrines and undermines its intertexts of history, literature, and culture. In particular, she notes, "the ontological line between historical past and literature is not effaced, but underlined" and that "the loss of the illusion of transparency in historical writing is a step toward intellectual self-awareness that is matched by metafiction's challenges to the presumed transparency of the language of realist texts" (1989, 10). In effect, the use and "ironic *abuse*" (1989, 12) of the intertexts led to a more profound engagement with history, literature, and popular culture by questioning these received discourses. Literary confabulation, like historiographic metafiction, engages with the intertext of history and troubles its borders. Hutcheon's sense of the writer's agency in destabilizing the ontological boundaries between history and fiction is particularly relevant when one considers how reimagining of contemporary and historic spaces in the (post)colonial city means carefully tracing the oscillations between genres, between the mapped city and its unmapped possibilities. In speculative and historical speculative fiction, the conventions of histories and literatures are, as Hutcheon puts it, "simultaneously used and abused, installed and subverted, asserted and denied" (1989, 5). Confabulatory texts show up the fictiveness, hypocrisy, and limitations of official histories and plans.

A sequence in Sonny Liew's globally successful graphic novel *The Art of Charlie Chan Hock Chye* illustrates this point as it satirizes the typical discourse that the Singaporean state uses in its reiteration of Lee's governing philosophies. The graphic novel tells a story of imaginary comics artist Charlie Chan Hock Chye in tandem with the nation from pre-independence days in 1948 to the contemporary moment. Interspersed with this fictionalized biography are dozens of Charlie's published and unpublished works in a huge range of genres and styles that are also meant to trace the evolution of comic art in the latter half of the twentieth century. In the penultimate chapter of the book, we are presented with one of these humorous asides in the form of a comic that "paid homage to the irreverent, satirical humor of *Mad* magazine" (Liew, 2015, 210) with two characters based on popular local stand-up comedians Wang Sha and Ye Fong. In the satirical sketch, Wang Sha plays a reporter interviewing the Minister of Museums, played by Ye Fong, who wants to show him and his viewers the "Singapore story" through a tour of "state-of-the-art **VISUAL, AUDITORY, TACTILE and OLFACTORY** presentations" (2015, 210; emphasis here and below original). The strip is a hilarious send-up of the Singaporean penchant for dioramas, recreations, and museal narrations of the nation's progress. As with Lee, we start with the usual representation of Raffles before glossing over the racialized colonial regimes with token illustrations of multiracial harmony.

A single panel stands out in this section. It depicts Wang Sha and Ye Fong examining "a **splendid diorama** showing all the **tragic fates** that might have befallen Singapore had the **P.A.P.** not been in power!" (Liew, 2015, 211). As with Li Xinli's work, the diorama in question recalls the scale model of Singapore that dominates the Urban Redevelopment Authority's City Gallery. Where the conventional city model suggests the progress of Singapore's material skyline through its attempts to keep up with its constant changes, Liew's iteration of the scale model is more overtly temporal. The diorama is designed to be read from left to right and begins with a small sign that reads "1963" – the year Singapore gained independence from the British by merging with Malaya. The path then splits into two branches with signs that read: "every other way" and the "PAP way." The former pointing to a burning catastrophe and the latter to a familiar model of towering skyscrapers and verdant landscapes. This incorporation of a physical model to represent Singapore's histories – imagined, alternate, and official – lays bare the propagandistic relation between the representation of Singapore's urban space and the ruling party's political power. Wang Sha attempts to challenge the minister's doublespeak, cutting to the heart of the diorama's fine print, which is illegible to the reader. He asks, "Is it really **fair** to label everyone else '... **Communists, crooks, thieves and opportunists**' ...?" (2015, 210). Ye Fong responds with the sentiment that pervades Lee's memoir, "Those of us who've **lived** through those challenging times can see for ourselves! But the **YOUNGER** generation, they can be so easily **MISLED!**" (2015, 211). Here the spatial metaphor is clear: the material effects of PAP rule are emphasized and alternate paths in the past and future, what could have been and what could be, are reduced to heaps of burning ash.

Texts like Liew's *The Art of Charlie Chan Hock Chye*, Alfian Sa'at and Marcia Vanderstraaten's play *Hotel*, and Clara Chow's hybrid work *Dream Storeys* encounter and depart from historical sources, fill in the gaps in the urban histories and imagine profoundly different alternate worlds: buildings not built, anticolonial rebellions not undertaken, fantastical future trajectories. To do so they necessarily rely on experimental forms like counterfactual historical fiction, a metafictional graphic novel, and a hybrid text of unbuilt architectural plans and dystopian stories. They depict a diverse range of spatio-temporalities from nineteenth-century colonial Singapore to twenty-second-century futures. Confabulation creates a social space in the Lefebvrian sense and compensates for collective loss and suppression of memory in an urban setting through fabrication and imagination. In the specific, mapped context of Singapore's urban spatio-temporalities, what does it mean to speculate in possible utopias, dystopias, or would-be dystopias? If excavation reveals what has been repressed and forgotten, circumvention the contours of power, wayfinding other modes of moving through the city that rely on memory and detail, then confabulation imagines other spatio-temporalities that are wholly not of the map. In other words, counter-cartographical movements encompass not only what has been but what could have been

Fig. 19 Excerpt from *The Art of Charlie Chan Hock Chye* (2015). Credit: Sonny Liew. Used with permission from Epigram Books.

and thus imagine what could be otherwise. By reimagining, fabricating, and fantasizing about the country's past and present, writers and artists show us that it may be possible to dream beyond the master-planned future.

Hotel

Alfian Sa'at and Marcia Vanderstraaten's play *Hotel*, set in a single hotel room, has scenes set a decade apart spanning from 1915 to 2015 as it depicts the often-violent and multiracial history of the island city from the intimate confines of a transient yet private room. Ghostly, multilingual, multi-accented voices are conjured in the theatrical space, with each member of the cast playing multiple characters. The play's unity of space, coupled with its multigenerational timeline, creates a paradoxical effect of mobility through stasis – a temporal and spatial confabulation through its unrelenting focus on a single space. Each scene is a chronotope of Singapore at a crucial juncture in its history, confabulating intimacies that have been reduced to the scale of a hotel room.[1]

The heterotopia of the hotel room mirrors other spaces and other tragedies: wars, massacres, evacuations, political separations, and urban development. Their containment in a single room and in the intimate relations between the characters allows the play to perform political commentary from the relatively "safe" space of the hotel room. Many of the relationships are allegories for larger social and political changes. The text of the play and the movement of its ensemble cast become acts of confabulation of the transnational city,

---

1 The play depicts: an argument between an English plantation owner and his Eurasian wife, and her encounter with the Indian Muslim bellboy; a bittersweet reunion between two diasporic Chinese women, one of whom is being abused by her employer; a Gothic depiction of a spiritualist séance which evokes the memories of the First World War and foreshadows the Japanese invasion of colonial Singapore; the doomed love affair between a Japanese intelligence officer and a Malay woman during the Japanese occupation; a meeting of legendary Malay film star and director P. Ramlee with his multiracial collaborators at the height of Singapore's golden filmmaking era; another doomed love affair between a Eurasian-Malaysian repairman and a Chinese Singaporean hotel manager with Singapore's separation from Malaysia as a backdrop; the drug-fueled hallucinations of a transgender Eurasian woman as she contemplates a one-night stand with an American businessman; the return of the Japanese baby from scene 4 as a grown man who seeks a reunion with his estranged elderly Malay mother; Chinese-Indian wedding preparations that reveal the racial prejudices underpinning contemporary Singaporean society; a Muslim Malaysian businessman and his family harassed by the police in post-9/11 Singapore in a scene that has connections to scene 5; and the final scene which sees a Chinese patriarch on his deathbed surrounded by his family and the multiracial hotel staff as they reflect on the significance of dying in the transient space of the hotel room.

as each line is at once meaningful within the context of the hotel room and beyond its confines, producing new and unplumbed meaning of both the words spoken and the historical events they allude to. The performance and script of *Hotel* reveal untold minor histories and imagine the unspoken lives that constitute the city, the room, and the text.

The play begins in 1915, a date that is deliberately at odds with Singapore's colonial-centric narrative which sees the year 1819 as essential – when Sir Stamford Raffles ostensibly founded modern Singapore as a British entrepôt. *Hotel*, on the other hand, begins with a newly married colonial couple: a racist, disagreeable plantation owner and his mixed-race wife who have come to Singapore for their honeymoon. Their presence is already testimony to Singapore's intimate colonial history with its complex racial mixings and hierarchies. Their arrival coincides with the 1915 Sepoy Mutiny, another rarely mentioned event in Singaporean history where 47 Indian Muslim mutineers were public executed by firing squad, witnessed by 15,000 spectators. The mutiny was tied to the impending conflict between the British and Ottoman empires. This scene reflects Singapore's centrality as an important maritime base for the British Empire. As Farish Noor notes, "it was from Singapore that British colonial troops were regularly sent out to quell disturbances in the Malay Peninsula, Hong Kong and as far as China" (2011, 94). Noor further argues that

> The singular event of the 1915 mutiny therefore exposed the weaknesses and contradictions of an imperial socio-economic-political order that was kept together by force and the threat of violence, and made it obvious that the imperial family of nations was a loose instrumental assembly of peoples, divided between the colonized and the colonizers. (2011, 98)

Indeed, Noor makes the argument that the mutiny had far-ranging effects on legal regulations and sociopolitical policies in newly independent and contemporary Singapore that began as attempts at surveillance and control of the behavior of Indian colonial subjects across the Empire. Here, confabulatory artistic choices reveal the shifting basis of Singapore's legal systems and also the history of violence used to shape its earlier colonial forms. This is directly at odds with the more laudatory official stance of coloniality's benefits to the modern state, one that is revealed by colonial names and monuments that are commonplace in the city's material landscape.

Hotel's confabulation is removed from the actual firing lines of the executions after the Sepoy Mutiny which the newlyweds are invited to spectate. We observe their uneasy interactions as Margaret Ann Comber, the Eurasian wife, refuses to attend what she deems "murder in broad daylight" (Alfian and Vanderstraaten, 2015, sc. 1). Henry William Comber, her English rubber planter husband, whom Margaret has seen "deliver lashings to the men" (sc. 1) on his plantation, relishes the prospect of this colonial violence since it preserves the order of Empire, a regimented space where "every race has its part to play" (sc. 1). The space of the hotel room in this opening scene becomes an intimate depiction of how Singapore is predicated on the imperial: where the categorizations of race and class speak to the organization of the colonial city and militarism underpins its strategic geographical location. However, the play's focus on the imminent sexual intimacy between Margaret and Henry, a Eurasian woman and a white man, speaks to the absurdity of enforcing racial lines and boundaries. Henry repeatedly downplays Margaret's Chinese heritage until he grows frustrated with her refusal to watch the executions, at which point he cuttingly remarks, "I see now how your mixed blood is interfering with your good judgment" (sc. 1). Tellingly, he scales up Margaret's refusal to leave the hotel room to her lack of *spatial* understanding of just how imperial power must persist:

> HENRY: Empires are destroyed from the edges, like a piece of paper consumed by fire. We at the fringes of Empire have a duty to stamp out the flames before they reach the centre. Every mutineer we shoot today is a loud and unmistakable warning to a thousand other would-be mutineers. This is how you rule and there are no two ways about it. So either you come with us and face the reality of war and Empire, or you secret yourself in this room and finger the new trinket I have latched around your neck. (Alfian and Vanderstraaten, 2015, sc. 1)

Henry's diatribe here is emblematic of the first scene's numerous references to and echoes of Singapore's political and spatial histories. Alfian and Vanderstraaten's historical confabulation here does more than allude to a frequently omitted event – it seeks to illuminate how authority over Singapore's space is derived and exercised through this colonial legacy of mapping. Singapore's narratives of siege and precarity are signaled through Henry's speech on the violence and discipline needed at the edges of Empire, a paper reality, specifically where Singapore is located. Imperial rule's need to dissuade would-be dissenters through violence is again prefigured in the execution of the mutineers – a reflection, too, of the illiberal laws of Singapore's contemporary government and its consistent argument for the death penalty for low-ranking drug mules to deter crime.[2] Singapore's mapped spaces are repeatedly refracted and echoed in the opening scene as the play uses the fraught and complicit relationship between Margaret and Henry as the linchpin by which to understand the relational mechanics of imperial rule and collaboration with the members of the local population. The hotel room itself becomes a retreat where Margaret can "secret" herself if she is unwilling to "face the reality of war and Empire." It is also a prison where Henry's necklace becomes a chain that has been "latched around" her neck.

---

2 Singapore had one of the highest per capita execution rates in the 1990s with a mandatory death penalty instituted for drug trafficking. See "Singapore: Executions Continue" (2017).

The play's opening is not unrelentingly bleak in its depiction of the violence and racism of Singapore's colonial history. Despite the dominant structures of power in this historical moment, the scene ends with an unlikely connection being made between Margaret and Dawood, the Indian Muslim bellboy. Despite their linguistic differences, the two forge a precarious understanding against the colonial powers. The scene ends with Dawood confessing, in Urdu, his desire to "turn around and shoot every whiteface in the crowd" (Alfian and Vanderstraaten, 2015, sc. 1) during the public execution. The play here uses Singapore's multilingual nature to dramatic effect: Margaret is unable to literally understand Dawood even as his Urdu is translated into surtitles for the audience. As she points out to him, it is a secret that he can tell and keep at the same time. Dawood, on the other hand, due to the gulf of class and status between them, is unable to relate to Margaret's growing realization that the man she has married is a cruel sadist who beats coolies "not out of duty but pleasure" (sc. 1). The two form an unlikely bond as Margaret gifts him the necklace that Henry has given her, signaling her unwillingness to be bought or controlled. She then calls for transportation to attend the mass execution. As she leaves, Margaret asks how to say "sorry" in Urdu – something she repeats as a farewell to Dawood.

It is this deeply private moment that *Hotel* chooses to use as a prelude to the issues of race, spectacle, punishment, class, labor, and (post)colonial intimacies that will dominate the play's scenes. The hotel itself is already a transient, unequal space, deeply divided by class and by labor. The play repeatedly returns to the staff in the hotel, tracing the routes of labor migration to other parts of Empire from obscure villages in China. Its attention to these histories links them to contemporary labor practices in Singapore, where in 2015 over 200,000 women from Southeast Asia were working as domestic helpers and caregivers (Manpower Ministry, 2015). *Hotel* connects the ancestral histories of modern-day Singaporean citizens with the underclass of domestic workforce they employ who have no access to the labor rights given to most Singaporean workers.[3] These confabulations challenge the

---

3 Rapid economic development and the influx of women into Singapore's workforce since the 1980s has meant that domestic workers, mainly from the Philippines, Indonesia, Myanmar, and India, are funneled through profit-minded employment agencies before being hired for childcare, housework, and eldercare by families ranging from the middle-class to the affluent. In 2015, some 227,100 women from neighboring countries in Southeast Asia were employed as domestic workers in Singapore (Manpower Ministry, 2015). Many leave behind their own families to care for their employers' progeny. They do not benefit from labor protections like most Singaporean workers, an ugly reality exemplified by the fact that the government only legislated a day off for them in 2013 after a decade of campaigning by activist group Transient Workers Count Too (see "Government Making Weekly Rest Day Mandatory," 2012). Domestic workers perform largely unseen and undocumented household labor and childrearing, which enables greater female participation in Singapore's workforce.

arguments for Singaporean superiority in the region. This was most famously characterized by Lee Kuan Yew's statement that ministerial salaries needed to be high since the alternative would be "a dose of incompetent government" resulting in Singaporean women leaving to become "maids in other people's countries" (qtd. in Lim, 2007). In *Hotel*, we are repeatedly reminded of how the room is predicated on class divisions and diasporic labor. Its ability to be an exclusionary space is never in doubt. In the second scene, even as two servants play-act rich women, the first injunction that the younger bondmaid offers in Cantonese to her older cousin is, "You're not supposed to sit on the bed" (sc. 2). Loy Dai's response to Ah Ying's fear demonstrates the paradoxical nature of an exclusionary space that is produced by her own labor as she replies: "What do you mean it's not for us? I've probably washed this bedsheet before. Come" (sc. 2). Ultimately, the temporary fantasy that the two women construct for themselves in the room cannot last, as Ah Ying reveals the bruises all over her back from her abusive employer.

In an unsettling past reminder of a known future, *Hotel* reveals Singapore to be a site for recurrent violence against migrant workers; the marks on Ah Ying echo the present-day maltreatment of domestic workers in Singapore (see Huang and Yeoh, 2007). This abuse, as Shirlena Huang and Brenda Yeoh have pointed out, reworks the home as "a paradoxical space for paid domestic work" which increases the vulnerability of a live-in domestic worker given her liminal status as a member of the household and a paid employee (2007, 197). Huang and Yeoh argue that "larger geographies of the nation (such as transnational labor migration) impact upon the micro-geographies of the home (such as the insertion of a domestic worker into an employer's household) as well as *vice versa*" (2007, 197–98). The space of the hotel room is set apart from the home, and its similar if transient privacy and intimacy allows for the revelation of Ah Ying's abuse to Loy Dai. *Hotel* helps us understand the historic, underlying structures of power, even as the play remains in the room.

By containing the action of the play in the heterotopian and flexible space of the hotel room, the text repeatedly challenges colonial and nationalist historical narratives through intimate scenes of love and loss. What happens in the hotel room is not so much a "behind the scenes" to the larger historical events but rather the smaller scale, often incommensurable or ambiguous moments between seemingly inconsequential figures. For instance, in scenes 4 and 6, we have two pivotal moments of the country's history in 1945 and 1965 reworked as failed love affairs. The former is between a Japanese intelligence officer, Captain Matsuda, and a Malay woman, Sharifah, whom he has rescued from sex work. They have made the hotel room into a transient domestic space and have had a baby together, imagining a future that is in jeopardy due to the impending Japanese surrender. Scene 4 opens at the end of the war, days before the surrender, with Sharifah in a kimono speaking Japanese to her elderly Japanese attendant as they pack to evacuate to Japan. Here, *Hotel* challenges numerous stereotypical tropes of depicting the Japanese occupation of Singapore. The scene is premised on a romantic relationship that crosses the lines of the war. In this scene, *Hotel* dissembles the many narratives that were told about the war – one that the Japanese positioned as anticolonial liberation even as it was an often-brutal occupation. Amidst these horrors, Matsuda is seen as a someone who produces the propaganda of the Japanese military and yet refuses to "turn lies into truths" (sc. 4). Through his relationship with Sharifah, the play arrives at a fraught and complicated rendering of this period of Singapore's history.

As Matsuda and Sharifah sadly reminisce about that time together, now that they will be parted since the Japanese military will evacuate her baby but not her, the hotel room takes on the poignant status of what might once have been an improvised home. The fleeting possibility of the alternate narrative of love and new life with which Matsuda and Sharifah have been "experimenting" (sc. 4), as Matsuda's superior Ichikawa notes, is also a recognition of Matsuda's potential as husband and father, and not just a soldier. As Ichikawa remonstrates Matsuda for his fantasy, the play's confabulations point to an alternate pathway through Matsuda's musings: "We came to this place and everywhere we went we brought death along with us. I wanted to see if I could bring life into the world" (sc. 4). The play does not rewrite this history or gloss over the complexities of this chaotic moment in Singapore's past. It meta-theatrically depicts why its own artistic confabulations are necessary to uncover the potentially lost stories of war and occupations. These minor

Fig. 20 A scene from a staging of the play *Hotel* (2015) showing lovers Sharifah and Matsuda looking at their baby with Matsuda's superior, Ichikawa. Credit: W!LD RICE Singapore. Used with permission.

stories have been hidden or forgotten due to the occupation's central status in the construction of Singapore's perception of itself as a small, vulnerable nation-state that must resort to pragmatism and militarization.

Since it is unthinkable that any postwar narrative would positively depict a love between a Japanese soldier and a Malay woman, Matsuda attempts to protect Sharifah by constructing a new, more palatable story, since "people must never know what happened in this room" (sc. 4):

> MATSUDA: *You shared a bed with their enemy.*
> Sharifah berkongsi katil dengan musuh dia orang.
>
> SHARIFAH: *I shared a bed with someone I loved.*
> Pah berkongsi dengan orang yang Pah kasihi.
>
> MATSUDA: *You're not supposed to love someone like me. The only reason why you should share a bed with me is so that you could wake up in the middle of the night and kill me in my sleep.*
> Sharifah tak sepatutnya berkasih dengan orang seperti abang. Kalau Sharifah berkongsi katil dengan abang sepatutnya Sharifah bangun waktu tengah malam dan bunuh abang semasa abang tidur. (Sc. 4)

Matsuda and Sharifah's real relationship is *anti*-metonymic and inconvenient to Singapore's wartime narrative. Matsuda tries to return Sharifah's narrative to a politically acceptable one to save her from a traitor's fate – as a propaganda officer he is all too aware that the victors write history. He tries to cast Sharifah in the stereotypical role of an alluring counterspy to subsume her into the official narrative and its characterization of the space of the hotel room. The problem of the child they have together remains, and Matsuda notes to Sharifah that "If you hated the Japanese like everyone else, you would have killed the baby in your womb" (sc. 4), to which Sharifah counters, "But how could I kill something which is also a part of me?" (sc. 4). The play here suggests that confabulation never reveals the easily understood or the singular. The messiness and multiperspectival aspects of spatialized history can only be fully explored in these ambiguous artistic moments. In a formal attempt to depict this mingling and overlapping of incommensurable views of the Japanese occupation, the play's multilingual dialogue produces a polyphony of linguistic and cultural connections *and* misunderstandings. While played to comic effect in some of the earlier scenes, in the scenes with Sharifah and Matsuda, their respective fluency in Japanese and Malay allows for an iconoclastic depiction of a Malay woman and a Japanese man in 1940s Singapore. The dialogue between the lovers alternates between Malay and Japanese as they painfully decide to separate for the sake of the child and Sharifah gives up her baby, Natsuo, to be evacuated on a Japanese military ship. When they decide to part, the remaining lines are spoken in alternating Malay by Sharifah and Japanese by Matsuda, where before both languages were interchangeable and signaled a multilingual intimacy between the two.

Through this all too human heartbreak, *Hotel* imagines the more problematic and complex human messiness that has been lost to the instrumentalization of the Japanese occupation as a rallying point for a newly independent nation. It depicts similar anxieties and uncertainties with Singapore's departure from the Malayan federation. However, in scene 8, at the height of Japanese investment in Singapore's economy, the play's technique of revisiting the island every decade enables an increasingly complex depiction of the space of the hotel room itself. Nowhere is this clearer than in scene 8 when we see Matsuda and Sharifah's child Natsuo returning to Singapore as a businessman working for Sony's Walkman division. This role is played by the same actor who played Matsuda in scene 4. The 1980s was a period of heightened Japanese investment in Singapore and this scene quietly reveals the contradictions between the national narrative, which is predicated on a complete vilification of the Japanese, and the rapidity with which Japanese investment comes to be deemed essential for Singapore's economic success.

Natsuo points out that Japanese ignorance of their wartime atrocities is due to incomplete history books and the fact that "Singapore good for business [*sic*]" (sc. 8). His eventual reunion with Sharifah, who visits his room as a wheelchair-bound older woman with her granddaughter Putri, is fraught with the ghosts that now haunt the hotel room. Sharifah observes, "This room is dirty [...] it's dirty. You just don't see the dirt" (sc. 8). Again, the multilingual nature of the script here plays with the characters' various levels of comprehension. Because she does not speak Japanese, Putri does not understand the full extent of Sharifah's relation to Natsuo. Because Natsuo does not speak Malay, he cannot understand Sharifah's sharp comments to Putri about the room. Because Sharifah does not speak English, she cannot make sense of the polite awkwardness between Putri and Natsuo. In revisiting the room with the same characters some 40 years later, the play makes its most powerful statement about how the hotel room reflects and refracts the trauma of the occupation and the doomed relations that it produced. In a climactic moment during scene 8, Sharifah, who has been diagnosed with Alzheimer's, begins blurting out words in Japanese, starting with basic terms like dog, rice, sugar, and water, before taking on the persona of a violent Japanese soldier:

SHARIFAH : *(Japanese)* Bow. *(Pause)* I said bow. *(Pause)* Search the house! *(Pause)* On your knees! *(Pause)* Kneel, you Chinese bastard! Kneel! Kneel! Kneel! You Chinese pig! I'll skewer you! Die! Die! Die!
お辞儀。*(Pause)* お辞儀しろ。*(Pause)* 家の中を捜索しろ！*(Pause)* ひざまずけ！*(Pause)* ひざまずけといったんだ、支那人め！ひざまずけ、ひざまずけ、ひざまずくんだ！支那の豚！串刺しにしてやる！死ね、死ね、死ね！
Ojigi. *(Pause)* Ojigi Shiro. *(Pause)* Ieno Nakao Sôsakushiro! *(Pause)* Hizamazuke! *(Pause)* Hizamazuketo Ittanda, Shinajinme! Hizamazuke, Hizamazuke, Hizamazukunda!! Shinano Buta! Kushizashini Shiteyaru! Shine, Shine, Shine!

Confabulations

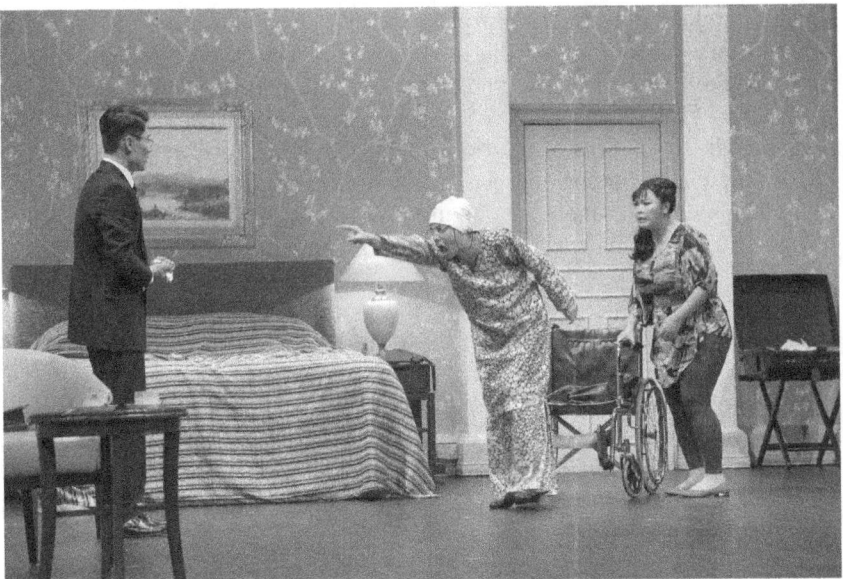

Fig. 21 A scene from a staging of the play *Hotel* (2015) showing an older Sharifah confronting her son Natsuo as her granddaughter Putri looks on. Credit: W!LD RICE Singapore. Used with permission.

In this outburst, the effects of *Hotel*'s confabulation of this troubled period of history come to the surface, bringing to the fore the contradictions and incommensurabilities of the various assignations for the Japanese in Singapore's history: enemy, torturer, lover, investor, amnesiac, and offspring. While the play may have only shown the final stage of the Japanese occupation as the bittersweet end to a doomed romance, Sharifah's outburst here, seemingly possessed by the ghost of a dead Japanese soldier, also reminds us of the terrible violence of the period. Her outburst begins with simple words, possibly the first nouns that Sharifah learnt as a young Malay woman seeking to speak to her Japanese lover. Her haunted ventriloquizing of the Japanese soldier also bears witness to her other, terrible memories of the occupation. These uncomfortable and irreconcilable truths accrete outsized significance because of *Hotel*'s dramatic strategies: both in the script (unity of setting) and in its staging (the use of the same actor to play Matsuda and Natsuo, for instance). This dramatic spectrality is thus a metatheatrical device that is also used in an earlier scene that depicts the possession of various members of a spiritualist scene by a dead soldier from the First World War. The hotel room in Singapore is haunted by the specters of transnational violence that have shaped the country's history. These confabulations are repeated in other contexts in the play, contrasting the age of multiracial cinema production in scene 5 with the racial disharmony of a mixed-race wedding in scene 9 and the racial profiling of Muslim Malaysians post-September 11 in scene 10.

The hotel room provides a private space for the revelation of views and secrets that would not be possible in other spaces. The play represents a retreat into a single, comprehensible, and comparatively unchanged space amidst the bewildering pace of material change in Singapore between 1915 and 2015. *Hotel* plumbs the depths of the transient space of the hotel room, noting the echoes of subaltern labor, colonial racism and sexism, and economic exigency. It confabulates an intimate, sedimented portrait of the country that is full of collisions of desire, hatred, failure, hauntings, and unexpected solidarities.

The Art of Charlie Chan Hock Chye

While *Hotel* focuses both on the *longue durée* of Singapore's colonial and (post) colonial history with the hotel room as a centrifugal space, Sonny Liew's celebrated metafictional graphic novel *The Art of Charlie Chan Hock Chye* uses biography as a counter-national genre.[4] Arguably, it is an attempt by Liew to write *the* Singapore novel where a *bildungsroman* is interwoven with the story of nation-state. Historically in Singapore, political comics and caricatures were deemed too controversial and crucially, accessible, for the authoritarian Singaporean government. The development of this artistic form was stymied by both overt and self-censorship. Lim Cheng Tju calls the political cartooning that was permitted in Singapore a "consensus-shaping tradition" (1997, 144), unlike its more widespread use for satire and political critique. Liew's graphic novel builds on the possibilities of political cartooning in a regulated space like Singapore, and expands on its ability to mock, satirize, parody, and question authority. *The Art of Charlie Chan Hock Chye* is presented as a personal archive of published and unpublished comics, portraits, newspaper clippings, satirical poster art, artifacts, and photographs telling the fictional story of "Singapore's greatest comics artist," Charlie Chan Hock Chye.

The text features an additional layer of commentary by the comic version of the author Sonny Liew, who is "presenting" this archive that begins in 1948 and ends in 2014.[5] As we have a closing-off and policing of public space in Singapore, the domain of political comics, caricatures, visual depictions is also

---

4 Sonny Liew is a Malaysian-born comic artist, illustrator, and author who was educated in the UK and the USA. *The Art of Charlie Hock Chye* has won numerous awards in and out of Singapore, including the Singapore Literature Prize and four Eisner Awards. Aside from these successes, the text has been translated into numerous languages and had its English print run sell out a few times – testimony to its wide appeal. Liew has also worked on other graphic novels, such as *The Shadow Hero* (with Gene Luen Yang), *Doctor Fate* (with Paul Levitz) and *Malinky Robot*, as well as titles for Marvel, DC, DC Vertigo, First Second Books, Boom Studios, Disney Press, and Image Comics.

5 The literary ruse was so successful that some believed that Charlie was a real person. See Holden (2016).

a policed public space. Liew's text acknowledges this history of censorship and suppression with a counter-archive of Charlie's unpublished and unpublishable works (alongside ones that have been published in this fictionalized version of Singapore). Spanning a diverse range of comic book genres and styles, the graphic novel traces a series of colonial and postcolonial suppressions, and urban developments that have shaped Singapore's contemporary spaces. These include the unrest and police violence of Chinese school students in the 1950s, the decolonization process and separation from Malaya in the 1960s, the vilification and elimination of the leftist movement in Singapore in the 1960s and '70s, and the consolidation of PAP power and the suppression of the media in the 1980s and '90s. Charlie's final, unfinished comic in the text appears to be a meditation on the role of Singapore in regional and international money laundering through its *laissez-faire* financial structures. In each of these cases, Liew uses various graphic comic styles that reflect the ongoing evolution of the medium (and realistically, Charlie's budgetary constraints) and provide a wholly alternate view of the politics of the time.

To this metafictional narrative, the graphic novel adds competing visions for Singapore, most clearly represented by Lee Kuan Yew and his rival, and erstwhile political partner, Lim Chin Siong. The latter was imprisoned without trial for his alleged communism, his party the Barisan Sosialis dissolved, and its members detained. Lim died in exile at the age of 63 after having worked as a fruit seller in the United Kingdom. Charlie's lack of success in comics is entwined with Lim's abrupt fall from power – the authoritarian state that Lee produced is seen as intolerant of satirical or political cartoons, and to other political paths for Singapore. Liew implicates the artist and writer in the process of historiography and storytelling, deconstructing the visual impact of the political elite and imagining various alternate histories.

Deeply concerned with the intertextual possibilities between history and fiction, *The Art of Charlie Chan Hock Chye* is extensively supplemented with historical material. Yet, instead of relying on these sources, Liew's graphic novel reworks the very genre of these histories. The text interprets and explores the contested political history of postcolonial Singapore through diverse forms such as war comics, parodic modes, children's comics with anthropomorphized animals, superhero comics, science fiction epics, and Disneyesque capers. Through each form, familiar political figures such as Lee Kuan Yew and Lim Chin Siong shapeshift from science fiction heroes and villains to, among other iterations, cunning mousedeer, superheroes, and unreasonable bosses of printing presses. Throughout, the work evinces a keen metafictional awareness of its own craft and the ongoing construction of Singapore's history. At one turning point in Charlie's unconventional career, as he is creating science fiction epics in the midst of the tumultuous 1950s, he remarks that those days were so "electrifying [...] it seemed to us that during such times, no fiction could be stranger, or more exciting, than the truth" (Liew, 2015, 117–18).

This oscillation between truth and fiction holds Chan's archive of "historical" comic strips in a mesmerizing coevality with the records of actual historical events. For instance, the part of the text that provides excerpts of Charlie Chan's comic "Invasion" superimposes boxes with Charlie's voice over sepia-tinted panels of the imagined comic. Charlie, drawn wearing a costume from the comic, points out that the stories are based on the actual political landscape of the time and a critique of the British and their allies. In this complex and shifting way, the text provides multiple layers and perspectives in viewing this historical moment. In lieu of providing a static document or a single interpretation of this fraught political moment prior to Singapore's independence, the text offers us multiple readings of each historical incident. The expansive and plural medium of the graphic novel allows for a layering of histories, perspectives, and fictionalizations. As Philip Holden puts it, this bricolage means that "Charlie, as author, and Liew as 'presenter' are embodied in the text, and questions of multiple layers of authorship, partiality and perspective cannot thus be read out of it" (2016, 517). Writing about the text's convoluted structure, Jini Kim Watson further notes that "Liew's intricate narrative and visual folding signify the graphic novel's potential in reimagining those *other* futures of decolonization that were discarded in the nation's race to success and prosperity at the same time that it gestures toward the very difficulty of doing so" (2018, 182).

In the book, colonialism and authoritarian regimes are depicted as dystopian cities, alien invasions, pulpy superhero narratives, and alternative futures where there is still a possibility of redress for political detainees. Detentions without trial are depicted as office politics that culminate in petty punishments in the janitor's closet – referencing the detainees' solitary confinement. At many points in the text, its deep explorations of Singapore's history are made explicit in ways that mimic a textbook or museum exhibition: comic strips are placed on a page as if they were taped into a scrapbook and accompanied by historical commentary explicating their relevance and meaning. The text's use of pointed, satirical humor is also effective: the 1987 Marxist Conspiracy that led to the detentions of social workers is transformed into the Richard Marx Conspiracy, whose goal is to "replace all its music with the music of our beloved Richard Marx" (Liew, 2015, 252). The absurdity of this confabulatory gesture mirrors and mocks the heavy-handedness of Operation Spectrum, which detained over 20 social workers and members of the Catholic Church and accused them of plotting to overthrow the government to establish a Marxist state.[6]

Additionally, through its meta-confabulation of Charlie as a bystander and observer of these events, the graphic novel employs his mode of drawing

---

[6] The result, carefully calculated, as I have mentioned in my introduction, was to continue to suppress the country's nascent civil society and to deter it through the politics of fear.

as studying and seeing as new and immediate ways of reexamining these histories. The text, among the other genres it performs, is a *künstlerroman* – one that sees its artist protagonist move through the history of comics from the 1950s to the present day – asserting that "drawing is in fact a kind of studying, to draw is to see and discover" (Liew, 2015, 19). Early in the text, Charlie acknowledges the "manipulative" potential of the medium, but emphasizes that this is beside the point since "that's how you tell stories" (2015, 53). *The Art of Charlie Chan Hock Chye* is thus a historiographic metafiction, but one in which Holden has argued the artist himself "does not stand outside history but is woven into its fabric" (2016, 522). Holden posits that the text understands that alternative histories "are provisional" and the "awareness of the pleasures of historical telling and retelling, of identification with and of separation from larger found narratives" offer "genuine possibilities of agency for social change" (2016, 522). This element of meta-confabulation, confabulation that draws attention to itself as it invents what has been forgotten or lost in a nation's collective memory, is ultimately what gives *The Art of Charlie Chan Hock Chye* its power and prevents it from becoming overly didactic. Because we become emotionally invested in Charlie as a character, we are willing to excuse his flights of fancy and delusions of grandeur. As a character, his body and his commentary (along with an illustrated Sonny Liew) are embodied in the text simultaneously as an elderly man reminiscing about his life to Liew (who acts as an interviewer) and in the ways in which he draws himself throughout his life. The final, metafictional images of the novel embed that act of art-making within history-making – depicting the tools of the cartoonist, and the onomatopoeic sound of knocking off the excess ink from a brush. A gesture that echoes Francis Khoo's songs of resistance, pointing out that when it comes to Singapore's histories and futures, the ink is not yet dry.

Taken *in toto*, *The Art of Charlie Chan Hock Chye* offers us a confabulated city that is still being contested, that is temporally and spatially unsettled. Unlike the Master Plan, the text revels in complex, variegated depictions of urban spaces in Singapore and produces an alternate spatial poetics. This begins with the nostalgic look at Charlie's childhood and the scalar alterations of "geylang hill" – apparently a "small mound a few inches tall" (Liew, 2015, 24–25) where Charlie used to play with his childhood friends. Three panels on the page illustrate three different lenses through which to view Singapore's spaces. The first has the movement and color of memory, the lines here serve to illustrate sound, excitement, dynamism. The perspective makes the mound seem enormous, having it dominate half the panel. The next panel is a static black-and-white photo with quiet subjects lined up in a row, a memory that seems distant and receding. The largest panel on the page gives us an abrupt shift in temporalities, while retaining the black-and-white tones of the photograph panel. Overlaying an aerial view of a contemporary Housing Development Board heartland are text boxes arranged in poetic lines: "And if you went back to the place itself today / There would be no way of knowing

/ if it was a trick of the light / how things really were / in those days of being wild" (2015, 25). The superimposition of the text boxes on the banal, almost architectural rendering of the slab and tower blocks of public housing infuses the drawing with longing and loss.

Yet the graphic novel refuses to stay mired in nostalgia. Early on in the text, its choice of a Osamu Tezuka-inspired manga style to illustrate the brutal put down of student protests during the 13 May incident in 1954 – a pared-down, stylized depiction of the incident – gives us a vulnerable perspective, focalized through the students. The depiction makes explicit the claustrophobia of police brutality and the closing-down of space for student dissent in a panel where the cartoon bodies of the students in an utter panic are pushed up against, crushed, and crowded into the fence. The lines of movement draw our line of sight into the violence and the compression of the crowd highlights how the urban space of dissent was foreclosed. At this crucial point in Singapore's late colonial history where urban space was forcefully regulated – in effect by the assault on student bodies – Liew confabulates a fantastical Tezuka-inspired giant robot into the mix. The robot eventually stops the colonial police violence against the students. The absurdity of this fairy-tale ending to the unrest allows the text to convey the idealism and naivety of the times. It allows for different perspectives on this historical urban space: one that highlights the importance of the freedom of assembly, of public commons, of youth protests. These are aspects of spatial rights that are completely alien to contemporary Singapore. It further recalls the seeds of control that were written into the laws and spatial practices of the country from this colonial moment.

The text is also punctuated with pages of sketches that reveal the process through which these narratives are made possible, and show how the novel is preoccupied with Singapore's urban histories. Drawn in pencil, the sketches portray places that have vanished due to authoritarian modes of urban planning and the exigencies of redevelopment. They are an anti-map of the contemporary iteration of Singapore: Charlie's imperfect memories of how colonial policing functioned in the city, demolished cinemas, entertainment parks, and other buildings, coupled with quick portraits of the people who inhabited them. These sketches then form the basis of Charlie's cartoons. For instance, in depicting the Chinese student protests in the 1950s, the text provides a range of sketches that range from the more realistic to the more cartoon-like (Liew, 2015, 42–43) to reveal Charlie's processes. In this way, the graphic novel functions on a metafictional level and unpacks its confabulatory methodologies. It illuminates a spectrum of representation, of different versions of the same history.

It is not possible here to perform an exhaustive analysis of Liew's multifaceted, dense work, so I turn now to a closer analysis of the most ambitious work that Charlie produces in his later years. Excerpts of "Days of August" are "presented" by Sonny Liew in the final chapter, "The King of Comics." This section of the text is important because it demonstrates how Liew's text is not content to simply stay in the realm of alternate history-making. In this chapter, the frame narrative has Charlie going to San Diego Comic Convention for the first time in his life in an attempt to jumpstart his career. He is sorely disappointed by his reception but happens to pick up a copy of Philip K. Dick's *The Man in the High Castle*, which inspires "Days of August"'s alternate take on Singapore history. In this history, a merger with Malaya never occurs, Operation Coldstore does not take place, and Lim Chin Siong is the leader of Singapore, while Lee Kuan Yew has been forced into exile in Cambodia. What makes "Days of August" effective, however, is just how uncannily similar Lim's contemporary Singapore resembles Lee's. This is to say that Lim's Singapore is no utopia, even as it is as economically successful as Lee's.

In the opening page, we are given an orderly grid of 4x4 panels that mimic a television screen where Albert Winsemius, the United Nations urban planning advisor (modeled on the actual historical figure), is being interviewed. This interview, in a comforting and familiar format, gives us a shorthand version of this alternate history before cutting back to a newscaster who informs us that the interview is to commemorate Lim Chin Siong's birthday. The two-page spread features these panels and superimposes them on a full-page drawing of Singapore's iconic skyline which the weather reporter refers to as their "island paradise." Instead of the burning catastrophe that was suggested by "every other way" but the PAP way, we have the reassurance that the urban landscape is somehow very much the same, negating the spatial threat of a non-PAP universe.

Figs. 22 and 23 Excerpt from *The Art of Charlie Chan Hock Chye* (2015). Credit: Sonny Liew. Used with permission from Epigram Books.

As the comic progresses, a sense of the subtle changes of this alternate universe continues. These are conveyed in terms of urban histories: Bukit Ho Swee, a village of anarchist squatters and the site of a controversial fire which led to the community being rehoused in regulated public housing, is a conservation site in this Singapore. Charlie makes a cameo as a successful artist in this alternate universe who even has a gallery dedicated to his work. In other ways, Lim Chin Siong and Lee Kuan Yew's similarities are highlighted. In another interview depicted in the comic, Lim fends off questions about a "cult of personality" (Liew, 2015, 277) that has arisen around his name. Liew's alternate history in "Days of August" thus reveals the constructed nature of PAP dominance and inevitability as one that is arbitrary. There *were* other paths open to Singapore that would have also resulted in economic stability and prosperity. Liew's text seeks to flesh out these other possible paths and to confabulate alternate narratives of Singapore's history.

This is not to say that the text is simply harboring a fantasy of paths not taken. What it is equally interested in is how storytelling comes to affect accepted realities and histories – what it calls "the power of the word, the image" (Liew, 2015, 282). In "Days of August," the alternate world breaks down due to a specter that resembles a "man in white" – a young Lee Kuan Yew. Charlie's cameo is central to the action since he is the artist who is writing an alternate history comic within the alternate Singapore. In a dizzying turn of events, the doubly fictional Charlie Chan is writing a comic of Singapore's actual history with Lee Kuan Yew in power. This Charlie sees this as a mission to assuage the anger of the alternate reality, his comic within a comic is one where "every panel [is] a prayer, a shot in the dark" (2015, 282). The power of the "true" reality eventually triumphs, destroying the alternate Singapore and sending Charlie and Lim back into the past to pre-independence Singapore in 1955. Only now they have an awareness of their doomed futures – Charlie to a life of invisibility and Lim Chin Siong to one of persecution and ignominy.

In this final section of the novel, we return to the realist visual style with which *The Art of Charlie Chan Hock Chye* began, especially in Charlie's autobiographical comic excerpts, "The Most Terrible Time of My Life," that document pre-independence Singapore. It is a careful graphic echo of the earlier part of the text that lends unity to the work but with one crucial alteration: a complex temporal and narrative awareness that suffuses these historical street scenes with greater weight and importance. There is no nostalgic reworking of the past, but a historic version of Singapore invested with a paradoxical sense of both inevitability and possibility. If artistic confabulation in Singapore means imagining otherwise in compensation for the amnesia of a state-driven narrative and urban landscape, Liew's final challenge to the instrumentalization of nostalgia and Singapore's pre-independence past in official propaganda could not be more bittersweet. Lim and Charlie have returned to 1955 on the day of the Hock Lee Bus Incident, which was a conflict between the British colonial authorities and students and unionized workers.

Charlie, now young again in his own comic, knows that he *would* "be a fool to go down that road again" (Liew, 2015, 289). He says this in reference to both himself and Lim Chin Siong, since, as he tells him, "everything you were. Or are working towards ... it all fails in the end. The P.A.P. and Lee Kuan Yew will win ... and **nothing** we do now can alter the course of this history" (2015, 286, emphasis original here and below). Surrounded by the sights and sounds of pre-independence Singapore, Lim replies with the belief that "these things that we're fighting for ... the **welfare** of the workers, our **freedom**, our dignity ... whatever the costs they're still worth the while, are they not?" (2015, 287). Lim's idealism and conviction are balanced by superimposed text boxes in the voice of the fictional Charlie, who sees the fixed path of Lim's future even as his young self walks away from Charlie, literally down a street in Singapore:

> In those last days, my dreams had grown more vivid. I'd begun to see the future with a new kind of clarity. His arrests and the years he would spend locked up without trial. The attempted suicide. The exile. The bouts of depression that would follow him for the rest of his life. The lost man of Singapore. Largely forgotten until his passing at the age of 63 from a heart attack. (2015, 287)

With complex compositional elements, the comic gives us multiple temporalities and perspectives in the single space of the Singapore street. It makes the keen possibilities of 1950s Singapore even more evident despite Charlie's vision of the future and his refusal to tell Lim all the details.

What *The Art of Charlie Chan Hock Chye* offers with its confabulatory practice here is a far more complex sense of time and space than the teleological conception of Singapore as mapped spatio-temporality allows for. "Days of August" allows for the possibility of individual agency in Singapore's past, to imagine otherwise in spite of the personal and political costs, and for the potential of narrative complexity to transcend official stories. What *could have been* and what *was* are combined in new and significant ways as Charlie and Lim Chin Siong both choose to continue on a path that will lead to failure. Charlie notes, "perhaps I wanted a world where he still made a mark, however briefly. Fought the good fight. A moment in time, a breath, when he was our brightest star" (Liew, 2015, 288). The symbolic nature of Lim's dissent, of his vision for a more compassionate and possibly less autocratic country, is held up as singular in its ability to reimagine the urban landscape and narrative of nation building. Charlie wants to recapture "just a feeling of wanting to draw, to tell stories" without "worrying about whether it was good or bad. If it was going to sell or not" (2015, 291). Both Charlie and Lim are turning away from a mapped path, into a known future where they refuse conventional notions of profit-driven success.

Forced to relive their choices and lives in "Days of August," the characters move from the complexities of past conditional temporality, *what could have been*, to an incomplete present modality. Charlie knows that he will have to

Figs. 24 and 25 Excerpt from *The Art of Charlie Chan Hock Chye* (2015). Credit: Sonny Liew. Used with permission from Epigram Books.

contend with the "harsh reality" of trying to make a living as an artist in Singapore, but seeks in this final moment to dwell on the comics that he has "yet to draw," a life he has "yet to live," and of a Singapore "that is yet to be" (Liew, 2015, 292–93). Thus, even in the ostensible past of the nation, in 1955, "Days of August" emphasizes the openness of Singapore's possible trajectories, linking them to Charlie's rich, creative archive that will be imperfect and mostly unpublished. *The Art of Charlie Chan Hock Chye* takes us through the past conditional temporality to examine and critique the ideological foundations of the Singaporean state, and the compromises that have been made for it to project the spectacle of its success. In "Days of August," *what could have been* is given a poignant and uncanny depiction in this alternate Singapore. And even though the story ends in a realist tenor – our heroes are unable to alter the past – we are also given to understand that there is no fiction stranger or more exciting than the truth of what is to come: the pleasures of reliving, redrawing, and retelling these stories, of discovering anew a yet unbuilt, unimagined existence outside or invisibly alongside Singapore's planned urban spaces.

Dream Storeys

Where *Hotel* and *The Art of Charlie Chan Hock Chye* reimagine Singapore's past, Clara Chow's *Dream Storeys* investigates the near future.[7] Her hybrid text envisions the unbuilt landscapes of Singapore born out of thwarted architectural dreams. In a series of interviews that accompany each short fiction, architects themselves are revealed as confabulators, and in collaboration with Chow, each chapter produces their imagined space for a brief literary moment, one that reconfigures the planned city. These spaces are born out of and seek to resist Singapore's spatial politics of land values, demolitions, development, and redevelopment. They include shopping malls that have expiry dates, a maze-like palace that is always in the process of being built by its inhabitants, an entirely underground city, a dinosaur theme park, print-to-order flats (a parody of the government housing allocation policy of "Build-To-Order" flats or BTOs), a house that records and remembers its inhabitants' every action and word, and an old folks home and an orphanage coexisting in a rambling tree house.[8] In each of first eight chapters, protagonists find themselves in uncanny situations that are inherently spatial conundrums. They arise out of buildings and spaces that Chow has confabulated with the architects she interviews. Each of these spaces shape and exaggerate the behavior of the characters in them: in "The Mall" a woman feels such an attachment to a shopping center to be demolished that she wishes to die with it, while in "The Mountain" a Borgesian play structure is so intriguing that hosts of children disappear in it. Singapore's obsession with infrastructure and underground caverns is taken to its logical conclusion in "Cave Man," where the bulk of the population lives in underground units and a select few are chosen by lottery to spend a few years above ground. The eviction of whole communities is satirized in "Bare Bones," where the entire island's population is made to relocate to outlying islands as the discovery of dinosaur fossils leads the state to convert the entire country into a paleontological theme park. The titular story "Dream Storeys" is a dystopian take on made-to-measure flats which turn out to be nightmarishly identical down to their hipster accessories and design elements.

In her introduction, Chow explicitly links her stories, and stories in general, with the built environment of the island:

> [I]n half a century, Singapore as a nation state has been engaged in the cultural work of telling its government-approved, as well as community-based stories, to itself. The skyline tells a narrative, too: of hard work,

---

7 Clara Chow is a writer-editor who works in Singapore. Her subsequent publications include *Modern Myths* (2018), which was shortlisted for the Singapore Literature Prize. Like Tan Shzr Ee, she was also previously a journalist with *The Straits Times*.
8 See https://www.hdb.gov.sg/cs/infoweb/residential/buying-a-flat/buying-procedure-for-new-flats/modes-of-sale.

sacrifice, prosperity, and progress; and of pragmatism, materialism, and collective amnesia. Depending on who is telling the story.

These, then, are the stories I tell myself. (2017, 3)

Instead of the mapped fictions of Housing Development Board flats, preserved colonial architecture, brand-name architect projects, integrated resorts, and feats of engineering, what Chow gives us are failing buildings, improvised communities, tropical and climate-emergency dystopias, and ways of living together on the island that are ethical and relational, cutting across boundaries of class and race.

The book itself cuts across genres as the potentialities of the buildings discussed in the interviews with architects are then fully fleshed out as fictional spaces. This process further highlights the thin line between a blueprint and a material reality, envisaging what other possible pasts and futures could have been built in Singapore and the wholly unexpected effects this might have had on its inhabitants. The architects and their willingness to imagine otherwise with their intimate knowledge of the local terrain provide the foundational settings for Chow's fictional Singapore. Confabulation works with the half-imagined, the never fully realized, the imperfect plans, the failed projects, and the sketches. These seemingly closed-off possibilities give us other ways of living together as many of the architects further align their philosophies for community living with their unbuilt architectural spaces. *Dream Storeys* is an unorthodox, unauthorized blueprint and dreamscape subverting the categories and rules of the actually existing city as well as attempting to narrate itself out of it. Many of the architects interviewed are interested in questioning the status quo and focusing on how to transform urban planning in fair and equitable ways (Chang Jiat Hwee, qtd. in Chow, 2017, 19). There is a strong sense of planning and designing structures that are conscious of their surrounding environments (Tan Kok Hiang, qtd. in Chow 2017, 164), while some, like Joshua Comaroff, argue for the need to make room for "the strange" (Comaroff, qtd. in Chow 2017, 137). *Dream Storeys* unpacks these spatial relations between architecture and Singaporeans in its short fictions, each one taking on the struggles of characters who are faced with surreal conundrums as Chow plays the architectural fantasies against darker impulses of top-down urban planning that involves control through quotas, standardized buildings, and the demolition of ordinary but beloved buildings.

The most compelling story in the collection, however, is a confabulated tale that is not accompanied by an interview with an architect. It is about a structure that has already been built: the Singapore Flyer – a tourism attraction that was built to mimic the London Eye. Plagued by financial difficulties since its construction in 2008, the structure was the world's tallest Ferris wheel between 2008 and 2014 with 28 air-conditioned capsules (see Lim, 2013). Since its opening, it has had a few high-profile breakdowns, including a memorable one which stranded 173 people for six hours ("Trapped Passengers," 2008). In "The Wheel," Singapore is a hyper-surveilled, carceral state with its oil refineries lying in toxic, polluted ruins and its population rendered inexplicably infertile. Chow was inspired by the artist Chun Kai Feng's installation piece *Ride of a Lifetime!*, a miniature Ferris wheel of wood and perspex whose capsules are prison cells. His artwork, made in the same year that the Singapore Flyer opened, turns the symbol of tourism, spectacle, metaphorical stasis into a more chilling manifestation of state planning and power. Chow begins her dystopian story with this premise:

> There are twenty-eight capsules, each the size of a small bus. They are glorified oil drums, rolling as the giant wheel spins – a clever engineering trick so that we are never upside down, nor reduced to hamsters on a treadmill.
>
> Twenty-eight people in each capsule, walls of metal separating us into cells. Strapped to vertical gurneys, we sleep upright at night. The carpet has been worn bare in patches. In the day, we stand, shifting from balls to heels, heels to balls, trying not to touch anything shiny, metal encasing our meat. Burns, when we get them, take a terribly long time to heal ... the smell of seared flesh shades from fried beef to charcoal. (2017, 175)

Here, the tourist attraction, as in Chun's art, is reduced to its constituent, seemingly pointless parts, a giant wheel that goes nowhere, studded with "glorified oil drums" – one in a series of references to oil in the story. The wheel is in stasis even as it is continuously in motion – a metaphor for economic progress *vis-à-vis* the continued repression of human rights in Singapore. Motion is coupled with imprisonment, and the state's concealment of the longer histories of detention without trial is laid bare through this reverse panopticon, with the prisoners always in view.

This conflation of Singapore's spectacular and iconic architecture with its repression of political dissent through detention without trial under the Internal Security Act is an act of spatial and literary confabulation. Chow's story explores *what could have been* and *what might be* despite officially enforced amnesia regarding these mass political detentions, alleged torture, and repression. It imprints this on the urban landscape, directly critiquing a built structure that serves no purpose but to provide an aerial, cartographical view of the city as well as to function as spectacle in and of itself. "The Wheel" does not attempt a historical reconstruction or oral history. Instead, it feeds many elements of the psychological and physical torture that was inflicted on political detainees, and the long exiles that some of them still suffer through a prism of dystopian and speculative fiction. These stories, which we only have in eyewitness accounts and testimonies, are lifted out of a state-imposed silence in Chow's fiction. The first story that Chow wrote for her debut collection, "The Wheel," is a collision of all the contradictions, whispers, and scars of modern Singaporean history: there are arbitrary imprisonments, the torture of political dissidents, a preoccupation with women's bodies and their fertility, the literalization of a nanny state that takes in children from China as part of an economic agreement.

The story starts with an unlikely prison break and the creation of a temporary utopian colony on the offshore island Pulau Hantu, an escapade that is ultimately shown to be part of an elaborate reality show staged by the state: "*Lord of the Flies* meets *Animal Farm*, leading to a gory end. A cautionary tale against communism or any sort of revolution" (Chow, 2017, 213). In the story's world, there has been a catastrophic industrial accident at the "Clam Oil Refinery on Pulau Bukom," leaving its neighboring islands with contaminated soil and water. The story hints that this may have also contributed to the sterility of the population. In the ensuing years, Singapore and China work out an agreement to have barren Singaporean families raise surplus Chinese babies and, in the process, China begins to heavily influence the country's social policies.

As the escapees journey away from Singapore's mainland to establish a small commune, one of the characters recalls present-day Singapore, our contemporary moment:

> Decades ago, people had come to Pulau Hantu to get away from the stresses of the over-developed mainland. You boarded a ferry at Marina South Pier, letting the sea breeze cover you in mist until your thin clothes are soaked as the little boat wove its way like a gnat past the big Chinese tankers parked offshore, waiting to be loaded or unloaded of containers of goods. Tankers with names like 秋池 (autumn pond), 大球 (big ball), and 新发现 (new discovery). You watch the mainland coast unfurl like a fantascope: the skyscrapers giving way to millionaires' homes on Sentosa Cove, and then to the white cake-like structures of Jurong Island's energy and chemicals industry ... You catch a whiff of bitumen, bunker oil, kerosene and diesel in the air, as Pulau Bukom glides into sight – a sign that you're approaching Hantu. (Chow, 2017, 195)

This detailed parsing of the seascapes and littoral zones of southern Singapore allows us to observe and experience their incongruous layers. Transnational circuits of crude in Chinese tankers, exclusive housing built undoubtedly in part from the profits of the extraction, refining, and trading of fossil fuels, and the refineries themselves are in this instance juxtaposed as closely as they are linked in real life. Even though it is offshore, out of sight most of the time, what gives the petroleum away is the olfactory – the "whiff of bitumen, bunker oil, kerosene and diesel" in the air, in the atmosphere, invisible but present.

When the escapees are recaptured by the state and returned to their rotating jail, the story describes the gruesome specters that haunt one of its main characters, Mae: those who have been hung by the state, those who were collateral damage in their escape. These offshore islands are also haunted by another set of ghosts: those involved in the failed bombing of the Pulau Bukom Shell refinery in 1974, touted as Singapore's first brush with international terrorism. Two members of the Japanese Red Army and two members of the Popular Front for the Liberation of Palestine attempted to blow up the refinery to strike a blow against Western imperialism, and to disrupt the oil supply from Singapore to South Vietnam in solidarity with the revolutionary forces. During their attempt, they deceived and enlisted the help of a Malay fisherman. Chow's story confabulates the interactions between the would-be bombers and the fisherman. Making small talk, the fisherman tells them of the "Garoupa, ikan batang, ikan bawal hitam, toman ... udang" (Chow, 2017, 206) that fill these waters. They bond briefly over this knowledge, suggesting other, anti-colonial ways of reading this historical episode, other ways of seeing these coastal waters, the concealed histories of Singapore's oil, and the wars it was used to fight:

> I think of the Malay fisherman and his scowling, skittish passengers now, as I see the lights of a fishing boat, like phosphorous barnacles, gliding towards the opposite shore.
> They are here. More ghosts. (2017, 207)

This dystopian Singaporean future is haunted by failed anti-imperial, anti-petroleum acts and the detritus of its energy ambitions. Its refineries have shut down, they are "steel ruins, unspeaking remains ... the industrial wasteland" (2017, 214). Neglect, as the story puts it, is also a form of reclamation.

These dystopian details seemed designed to elucidate the possible futures of contemporary Singapore's current anxieties and trajectories. In spite of their escape, the prisoners are eventually either killed or brought back to the wheel. The small glimmer of hope comes as the story ends with a moment of metafictional confabulation – where "The Wheel" makes it apparent that it is imagining a possible reality beyond what the "facts" can give us. One of the characters who finds herself strapped into the Wheel again dreams of the possible fate of the remaining escapee:

> [S]he dreams of Mae in her dinghy, paddling quietly towards the steel ruins, the unspeaking remains of Pulau Bukom and its refineries. She steps on the white sand when she reaches the island, her toes sinking between the twisted twigs of the casuarina trees, the dried-up sponges washed ashore from the coral beds. Pulls her dinghy up towards the high tideline marked by ribbons of seaweed. Disappears into the industrial wasteland. (2017, 213–14)

The use of the present tense in the final moments of the story is particularly significant. What confabulation offers us, in its subversion of the fragments that dominate histories is a strange and open temporality – one that is enmeshed in dream time, in the always-present time of fiction where island cities are multiple and filled with potentialities, where political prisoners might escape from authoritarian regimes and disappear, where unbuilt but potentially buildable utopias reside.

SG50 and SG200: Jubilee and Bicentennial

If Lee in his memoir attempted to relate a teleological story of Singapore's progress from Third World to First, the state was more than happy to provide continuity to his narrative with two major public initiatives following his demise. SG50 in 2015 was ostensibly to celebrate the jubilee of the nation-state's postcolonial independence. SG200 in 2019, four years after Lee's death, attempted to further cement his vision of history by launching a yearlong bicentennial commemoration of the arrival of the British in Singapore. The bicentennial marked what was deemed "one of the key turning points in the Republic's modern history" (Liu, 2019). Under the auspices of the Singapore Bicentennial Office under the Prime Minister's Office, the state coordinated a series of events, exhibitions, public artworks, and so forth. With exhibitions like "Raffles, Scholar or Scoundrel," some of the associated exhibitions and art pieces purported to question the centrality of colonial legacies in the city-state (even as the government insisted, with no irony whatsoever, that the bicentennial meant looking back 700 years into Singapore's history from the 1300s). What might it mean then, for what is possibly the world's most economically successful postcolony to insist upon commemorating its colonial beginnings? In this fraught gesture, we see the ongoing, contested confabulations of the Singaporean state and its urban spaces. If the works of Alfian and Vanderstraaten, Chow, and Liew attempt to remediate the suppression of Singapore's minor and alternate histories, the bicentennial functioned as a top-down recalibration of the Singaporean state's attempt to consolidate its control of the island nation's spatial and temporal narratives.

This strategy, of course, is not new: as I discussed in the introduction to this book, in its urban planning, the state has placed great emphasis on preserving the colonial core of its downtown district and in particular on retaining the statue of its colonial founder by the Singapore River. In this way, the physical manifestation of Singapore's carefully mapped and zoned histories and spaces meet their confluence. Cognizant of the significance of the statue, the bicentennial commemorations famously featured the work of the artist Teng Kai Wei, painting half the statue of Sir Stamford Raffles in order to enable it to blend into the city skyline. This symbolic gesture was ostensibly meant to make Raffles invisible to the public through an optical illusion in order to question his centrality to Singapore's modern mythmaking. In a statement to *The Straits Times*, a spokesperson for the Bicentennial Office called for a greater discussion of other figures in Singapore's history: "As we enter the Bicentennial year, we want Singaporeans to think more deeply about our history – is our story just about one date or one man? The act of Raffles 'disappearing' is an opportunity to engage Singaporeans in an open dialogue about the many other men and women who also arrived on our shore and made significant contributions" (Liu, 2019). The disappearing act of the statue underneath a layer of carefully applied dark gray acrylic paint was only ever meant to be a temporary publicity stunt. As some online commentators pointed out, Teng's work could be read subversively as a commentary on the (post)colonial reality of Singapore's urban spaces where the influence and legacy of the colonial map and elite remain firmly entrenched even as they have become invisible or unremarkable to most.

State-directed bicentennial commemorative events meant that only certain, approved versions of Singapore's longer history could be told, making this a whitewashing of an actual, painful, and potentially productive confrontation with Singapore's precolonial and colonial history. The state could not help but make the colonial founding of Singapore the linchpin of its explications: "our history is a 700-year journey going back 500 years before 1819, and forward 200 years to 2019. 1819 was a turning point in that journey that set us on a new trajectory."[9] As Nien Yuan Cheng pointed out in an online opinion piece, "the Singapore Bicentennial committee and its partners have the unenviable job of having to foreground Raffles and 1819 while at the same time hastily reassuring the public that no, 'Singapore's history is more than just one date, or one man'. The Singapore Story wants its cake (1819) and to eat it too (700 [years])" (2019). In effect, it seemed as if the committee sought to redefine the word "bicentennial" to encompass seven centuries of history, some of which had little to do with the modern postcolonial state itself.

In his speech launching the bicentennial year, Prime Minister Lee Hsien Loong was more honest about the British colonial legacy:

> 1819 marked the beginning of a modern, outward looking and multicultural Singapore. Without 1819, we may never have launched on the path to nationhood as we know it today. Without 1819, we would not have 1965, and we would certainly not have celebrated the success of SG50. 1819 made these possible. And this is why the Singapore Bicentennial is worth commemorating. (2019b)

Singapore may be one of the few postcolonies that credits its (post)colonial status to its initial colonization – an irony that appears to be lost on its leaders. Lee's fixation on 1819 is no mistake, he is in fact simply elucidating the clear links between colonial laws, urban plans, governance, and elite forms of government and Singapore's contemporary state. The "decisive and indelible imprint that the British left on Singapore" that he notes, in "the rule of law, the parliamentary system of government, even the language I am speaking" (Lee, 2019b) are discursive forms that have been used to continue to repress, control, and censor dissenting views and alternate spatializations. This narrative persists with slickly produced interactive audiovisual exhibitions, and the co-opting of personal and collective memories to consolidate the power of the state.

---

9 See the Singapore Bicentennial Official Website, https://www.sg/sgbicentennial/.

A case in point was the commemoration's "signature event": "From Singapore to Singaporean: The Bicentennial Experience @ Fort Canning." This audiovisual, theatrical, and filmic extravaganza was set, again seemingly without irony, in a former British military installation. In an echo of how many colonial buildings in the city center have been gutted and repurposed, the creators of this multimedia exhibit remodeled the interior of the spaces to create purpose-built sets and produce a carefully scripted, immersive version of Singapore's history. Helmed by Michael Chiang, a playwright, and Beatrice Chia-Richmond, a theater director, who have both had experience directing the annual National Day Parade, the two-part experience was a familiar arc of mystical beginnings, colonial vision, wartime suffering, and manifest destiny. "The Time Traveller" was divided into five acts (Beginnings, Arrival, Connectivity, Occupation, Destiny) like a classic play, while the accompanying "Pathfinder" was a series of non-guided exhibits set in a park featuring maps, artifacts, and other more static objects. "The Time Traveller" employed live actors, surround screens and sound, and elaborate water and light features to provide what Gene Tan, the Executive Director of the Singapore Bicentennial Office, called a history lesson translated "to the mainstream audience in an emotional way" ("Creating the Bicentennial Experience," 2019).

Faced with these sophisticated modes of state storytelling, confabulatory gestures in Singaporean writing and art are even more urgent. Alfian and Vanderstraaten's theatrical confabulations, Chow's architectural subversions, and Liew's engagement with the paths not taken in Singapore's pre-independence struggles are but a selection of the ongoing artistic interventions that challenge the Singaporean state's (post)colonial narratives.

Conclusion: Return to Eden

The image began appearing on 11 June 2018, in various online news outlets and social media feeds. The photograph was banal: three Asian men, two wearing suits with a pudgy, baby-faced man in the center wearing a black Mao suit. Yet the headlines made it clear – this was an historic photograph since it was one of the first times that the North Korean dictator Kim Jong Un had been pictured in the thoroughly contemporary genre of the selfie. Posted on the Instagram account of Singapore's Foreign Minister Vivian Balakrishnan, the caption included the hashtags "#jalanjalan" and "#guesswhere" (the former translates as "walkwalk" in Bahasa Malay). The backdrop to the selfie was a profusion of flowers in Singapore's Gardens by the Bay, its meticulously designed techno-botanical spectacle an ideal setting for the North Korean's leader's unlikely foray into online self-promotion. Later that evening, Kim was seen touring Marina Bay Sands surrounded by what media outlets like CNN, BBC, and Al Jazeera described as seemingly ecstatic crowds (Gallo, 2018). The next day, the cameras were again in attendance when Kim took a stroll with the US President Donald Trump around colonial-era buildings in the offshore resort island of Sentosa. When North Korean television crews finally edited a 42-minute propaganda feature of his visit to the city-state, little if any censorship was necessary (Choe, 2018). The North Korean media seemed more than pleased to air clips of Singapore's gleaming buildings, orderly streets, and welcoming crowds, depicting Singapore as an ideal model for its own development.

The North Korean–United States Singapore Summit and the planning process that surrounded it are peak examples of the perfection of Singapore's control over its urban spaces and its populace. In just two weeks, the state was able to gazette two separate spaces in downtown Singapore and on the offshore island of Sentosa as Special Event Areas. Under the extensive Public Order Act, first enacted in 2017, the state increased its wide-ranging powers to police Singapore's spaces and particularly those demarcated for special events. These included measures to search vehicles and persons entering these areas and further the prohibition of multiple items in the restricted zone. Some of the items, like explosives, arms, and flammable materials, were banned for clear safety issues. Most of the list of outlawed materials, however, reflected a clear attempt to suppress freedom of expression and assembly in the space:

> An item capable of attaching a person to an object or another person, or preventing removal of any locking or connecting device
> An aerosol paint container or other implement or substance that is capable of being used to mark graffiti
> A loud hailer
> Any flag or banner which is larger than one meter by one metre, or has a handle longer than one meter
> Any public address system, electronic equipment, broadcast equipment or similar device which may interfere with broadcast equipment or similar devices being used by the event organizer or police officers. (Government Gazette, electronic edition, 3 June 2018, Public Order Act, Chapter 257A)

The gazette was an effective tool that capitalized on the exceptional nature of the Trump–Kim summit to justify its highly restrictive rules. It made legible the spatial restrictions that were already present in much of Singapore's urban spaces, where governmental permission must be granted for assemblies, protests, street art, vigils, and artistic performances that do not neatly fall within the acceptable notions of the city-state's charted existence. The restrictions against textual materials such as flags, banners, and spray paint clearly limited the means of political expression within the designated zones down to the minutest detail. The ban on loud hailers and other means of amplification was a legal reminder of the continual silencing of non-state voices in these spaces. Additional measures to search and examine every person entering the zone further subjected bodies in these spaces to surveillance and policing. The speed and transparency of these legal maneuvers, and the population's acquiescence, point simply to the efficient machinery of an already securitized and planned space. These measures were an augmentation of the tensions, inequalities, and panoptic suppression that exist to keep Singapore's ecologies, spaces, and citizens in check.

Shatkin points out that other states that would adopt the real Singapore model as their goal might need to consider more than just a ruthlessly centralized urbanization plan:

> While many of Singapore's achievements in the areas of economic growth and provision of basic needs have been laudable, the consequences of the means through which these achievements have been realized raise pressing questions. Singapore's transformation has been premised on the following: the subjugation and co-optation of civil society to the interests of the state; the severe curtailment of alternative claims to urban space outside of the state and the corporate economy; the imposition of a comprehensive regime

of state social control; the assertion of state hegemony in determining the aesthetic and functional form of the city; and the bending of the meaning of history and culture to the interests of the state. (2014, 135)

The control of material, symbolic, and discursive spaces in Singapore is inextricably linked in the way the state exercises its power. Hence, the fields of literature, film, and conceptual art, fields that often seek to complicate and challenge the overly one-dimensional narratives and authoritarian laws dispensed by the state, have been the most vulnerable to the long arm of censorship and oversight.

Dissident art, film, and writing in Singapore is for the most part subsumed by the glitz and orderliness of the city-state. Indeed, in this case, numerous photo ops and looping media coverage depicted one of the few nations in the world that could host the controversial Trump–Kim summit with so little resistance from its citizens and expatriate subjects. The venue for the summit itself, also within a special event zone with identical restrictions, was the Capella Resort on Sentosa Island, designed by the British architectural firm Foster + Partners. Fittingly, the building hosting the meetings was an amalgamation of British colonial military buildings from the 1880s and carefully integrated contemporary developments that featured a six-star hotel and villas amidst more tropical flora.

As the Singapore developer Stephanie Kwee notes, the careful restoration of the colonial buildings and their integration with the luxury development was meant to be "a modern interpretation of colonial architectural language" (Prystay, 2008). The Capella Resort is an orderly (neo)colonialist space *par excellence* – its colonial histories carefully integrated with a tropical, elitist additions (conceived of by Lord Foster's architecture firm). Foster + Partners described the site as

> Comprising a six-star hotel, villas and a centerpiece garden courtyard, the project frames two carefully restored historic colonial buildings and it follows the natural contours of the site, cascading down the tiers of the hillside as it dissolves into a 12-hectare tropical sanctuary.
>
> The masterplan and the scale of the new elements respectfully relate to the former military Tanah Merah buildings, which dominate the overall composition and provide a gateway to the resort. (2009)

The aesthetic deference to colonial architecture echoes the conservation of iconic colonial-era buildings across mainland Singapore. Newer projects, like the revitalization of the National History Museum and the opening of the National Art Gallery in the colonial-era Supreme Court, preserve and venerate these colonial spaces and integrate them into the contemporary cityscape (see Ng Yong He, 2019). These structures and spaces are a far cry from the housing estates, ruins, graveyards, excavation sites, and memory-infused spaces examined and imagined by the writers and artists in my study. Counter-cartographical texts like the ones I have examined in this book represent both subtle and clear divergences from the state-dictated, colonially inflected mapping of the country.

The Trump–Kim summit was an event which made evident how Singapore now markets itself on a global stage as a city that has seamlessly integrated its histories of colonial planning, architecture, and legal systems into a cosmopolitan, globalized, authoritarian city-state. Mapped Singapore, planned Singapore, (post)colonial Singapore intersect in these depictions of the city-state. As Cheryl Narumi Naruse points out, Singapore has long been framed in terms of its strategic utility on a global stage, securitized, touristic, and economic:

> In contemporary understandings, the commonsense notion of "strategic" implies that with the right investments, individuals and businesses can take advantage of Singapore's geography in ways that can maximize capital accumulation because it is placed in the center of major capital flows. (2017, 239)

Singapore as a cartographically legible model is writ large on the global map – the city-state markets itself as the ideal scale model for efficient, capitalist authoritarianism. True to its colonial history, it prides itself on being strategically located, a historical interface and node between West and East, between the USA and North Korea among others.

Thus, domestically mapped Singapore, which has powerful capabilities to control dissent in tangible and spatial ways, further reshapes and burnishes Singapore's international reputation for order, predictability, and a manicured tropicality. I began this book with a discussion of the contemporary pinnacle of this planning: the eco-development and botanical spectacle of Gardens by the Bay, built on sand seized from regional neighbors and festooned with plants imported from all over the world. An earlier, smaller symbol of this carefully conceived control and its strategic deployment is the botanic and political performance of "orchid diplomacy" (Whang and Lim, 2019). This is a practice which sees special hybrid orchid species bred specifically for visiting dignitaries. The first VIP orchid, as they are known, was created for the wife of one of Singapore's colonial governors in 1956. Subsequent hybrids have been presented to various heads of state and famous figures, but most significantly to numerous members of the British royal family. This floral exercise of diplomatic influence partly stems from the history of Singapore's national flower: the hybrid orchid Vanda Miss Joaquim, named after the nineteenth-century Singaporean-Armenian horticulturalist Agnes Joaquim, who bred it, Singapore's first hybrid bloom. The flower was chosen in 1981 as the national flower for its "bright colours, resilience, hardiness and free-flowering nature [which] are qualities that reflect the Singapore spirit."[1] The shaping of a

---

1 This description is from the NParks online site "Flora & Fauna Web," https://www.nparks.gov.sg/florafaunaweb/flora/2/5/2539.

manufactured vision of a tropical ecology is unmistakable in the co-optation of even a flower's genomic makeup for the national narrative of planning.

At this juncture, it is timely to turn to a speculative short fiction by the writer-activist Ng Yi-Sheng that imagines a counter-factual version of Singapore's colonial history which weaves the unlikely elements of plant sentience, botanical warfare, and anticolonial resistance.[2] The text "Agnes Joaquim, Bioterrorist" was published in the first speculative fiction anthology published in Singapore, *Fish Eats Lion* (2012). Ng reimagines the life of Agnes Joaquim through the genre of magical realism. At the center of the story is an orchid that achieves sentience and has an anticolonial agenda. Agnes becomes a freedom fighter because:

> This was what the flower wanted of her; she knew it. For she had heard its commands over the last month, even as she scolded the cook or folded the bedclothes of her nieces and nephews. She stroked the petals of the specimen that sat on her lap, remembering that in her veins ran its fiery sap, transferred via the touch of its spongy roots, its slender stalk, and its gossamer labellum. And in her ears rang the flower's words, over and over like a malfunctioning gramophone: "Only you can change the world." (Ng, 2012, 35–36)

The story's depiction of the orchid collapses the boundaries between plant and human. The "fiery sap" is conflated with the blood in Agnes's veins and the plant's "spongy roots, its slender stalk, and its gossamer labellum" suggestive of human genitalia. It is no coincidence that the flower sits in Agnes's lap as she strokes it like a pet. This coupling of human and orchid disrupts heteronormative ideas of reproduction and fertility (Agnes ultimately dies from a uterine tumor) and works to build non-familial solidarity and kinship in the face of colonial violence.

In a condensed epic of anticolonial reprisals that resituate and reinterpret the politics of Singapore's "strategic" global location, Agnes and the orchid tackle imperial violence writ large on a global scale. Agnes's "seeds of dissension and chaos" (Ng, 2012, 39) let us reimagine historical and contemporary uses of plants and gardening. With her botanical superpowers, she performs a series of clandestine global journeys that turn the Singaporean state's importation of temperate plants and climes on its head. In acts of transnational anti-imperial solidarity, she makes contact with "local radicals who fought against the powers of centralized governments" (2012, 39). Sultans, empresses, tsars, and US presidents die amid and due to overgrown plants: "asphyxiated by a creeper," "half-dissolved in a massive pitcher plant," "flesh turned into

---

2 Ng Yi-Sheng a Singapore-based poet, fiction writer, playwright, researcher, and LGBTQ activist. He was educated in the US and the UK. He won the 2008 Singapore Literature prize for his debut poetry collection and has since published nonfiction works, additional collections of poetry, and a collection of short fantasy and science fiction stories, *Lion City* (2018).

mango wood," or "miserably fused together through a fretwork of bougainvillea" (2012, 39, 40). Each instance of botanical violence is a graphic replay of Agnes's own fusing with the orchid, suggesting the inseparability of plant from human despite the latter's attempt at forms of control.

The text details alternate forms of botanical knowledge that eschew the ideas of control and Empire. As a displaced Armenian Jewish woman, the text imagines Agnes learning to swear in Chinese dialect (not the imperial Mandarin) as she becomes a political activist and builds networks with a range of ethnic communities: "She'd even become familiar with the servants, persistently quizzing them on their knowledge of local herbal remedies. Rumour had it that she'd even ventured into their distant villages, seeking out sinsehs, bomohs and Ayurvedic healers to glean their botanic wisdom" (Ng, 2012, 37). Agnes's use of indigenous botanical knowledge is in direct opposition to the instances of imported and controlled botany that we have seen in Gardens by the Bay or in texts like Kwan's novel.

Moreover, it is suggested that Agnes is somehow involved in the production of a botanical compound, a drug called "joaquimine." The drug is the antithesis of opium as it "sharpens one's sense of focus, driving its abusers towards new purpose in life" (Ng, 2012, 40). Ng's story dwells in the marginal spaces and communities of the Empire as the drug transforms them:

> It soon became common to see dockyard coolies in Clifford Pier arguing over their plans for constructing hybrid electric steamships, or else pipa girls in Chinatown, huddled over the writing of Karl Marx in the original German. Shadow universities began to crop up, run by secret societies and mosques, where gangsters and farmers' daughters discussed every branch of the sciences and the arts in a motley creole based on English, Arabic, Mandarin, Tamil, Teochew and Malay. (2012, 40)

The text's unlikely juxtapositions of magical realist plant life and subaltern, laboring bodies create powerful utopian alternatives to colonial history. The creation of a new "motley creole" based on the polyphony of languages in the contact zone attempts to incorporate difference into an imagined civil society that became impossible under colonialism. The spaces of "shadow universities" and "secret societies" are mutable, nomadic, and unmappable.

The story even manages to demolish a famous colonial landmark in Singapore: the historic and luxurious Raffles Hotel. Before her untimely death from uterine cancer (a fate that befell the historical Agnes Joaquim), Agnes manages to infiltrate the British monarch's room in the hotel and, inexplicably, change the queen's mind about colonialism. The queen and the hotel are enveloped in "an explosive growth of giant purple orchids" suggesting a resurgence of a form of deviant tropicality as "botanic horrors penetrated every storey of the edifice with an excrescence of creeping tendrils. Guardsmen openly wept as they attempted to penetrate the foliage, hacking with their parangs at the greenery" (Ng, 2012, 33). This vivid scene of combat against nature appears to be Singapore's own conflict with its bioregion writ large. This is a secret fear of a kind of native, tropical excess, "an excrescence of creeping tendrils" and "botanic horrors" against which state or colonial violence is the only riposte. This overgrowth is figured as a successful anticolonial rebellion that transcends the colonially mapped and controlled space of late nineteenth-century Singapore.

Agnes's "bioterrorism" and the conflation of her body and the orchid recalls Haraway's point that "staying with the trouble requires making oddkin; that is, we require each other in unexpected collaborations and combinations, in hot compost piles. We become-with each other or not at all. That kind of material semiotics is always situated, someplace and not noplace, entangled and worldly" (2016, 4). Haraway's injunctions echo the funeral scene of the titular heroine in "Agnes Joaquim, Bioterrorist," where figures in "a sea of humanity" each hold "something in common, a token of farewell to their heroine: a single flower" (Ng, 2012, 43). Far from being a simple funeral ritual, Ng's text suggests the possibility of making new kin through the figure of Agnes, who is in the end both flower and woman. Even at her death, the flowers have multiplied and bloomed, and their hallucinogenic effects on the humans lead to insuppressible anticolonial movements.

As Queen Victoria returns to London, the image of this botanical excess recurs in the center of Empire at the end of the short story: the queen dies by "bursting into blossom" in the middle of London. The story ends with a remarkable image: "the seeds blew from her body, taking root instantly in the cobblestoned streets of snow. And across the city, a million orchids bloomed" (Ng, 2012, 45). This final image of the imperial body transformed into a million hybrid, tropical flowers recasts botany, gardening, and nature as a counter-cartographical form of transcorporeal anticolonialism. The short fiction provides us with an orchid that eschews colonial borders, boundaries, and planning, one that refuses state-driven narratives which instrumentalize it as an inert, aesthetically pleasing form of diplomacy and a pliable national symbol. It further enlarges its anticolonial ambit to transnational contexts which rework and complicate the imperial mapping of global botanical networks. Ng's story is a subversive text that critiques developments like Gardens by the Bay and more popular forms of fiction like *Crazy Rich Asians*. "Agnes Joaquim, Bioterrorist" wrestles with the state's constant anxiety about environmental issues such as rising sea levels, overgrowth of jungles, that leads it to the micromanagement of tree planting and domed "sustainable" gardens.

Gardens by the Bay manifests this ambivalence in a distorted fashion in the basement of the Cloud Forest biome. Here, much like in the City Gallery that I described in this book's introduction, an official narrative of Singapore's Masterplan to cope with the city-state's vulnerability to climate change is mapped out with great detail. The state attempts to control the extent of its territorial borders through a series of land reclamation projects and with a system of barrages and sea dams. Thus, the visitors' experiences of the climate-controlled montane plant treasures are capped with the ominous film on climate change. Again, as Sonny Liew illustrates in *The Art of Charlie Chan Hock Chye*, there are only two pathways highlighted in this Masterplan: one of control and one of unabated catastrophe. The anthropologist Natasha Myers points out that this experience is one of "Edenic beauty [...] tightly coupled with fantasies of apocalypse" (2016, 20). Similarly, Matthew Schneider-Mayerson begins his consideration of Singapore in the Anthropocene with an indictment of this audiovisual presentation in which "Singapore's technonature [is] a response to and salvation from its own dystopian forecasts" (2017, 167). Undermining the very botanical basis of (post)colonial Singapore's success and returning us to an alternative imagined colonial and decolonial past, Ng's story moves us away from the narrative of dystopian botanical tourism that the Gardens uses as "edu-tainment." "Agnes Joaquim, Bioterrorist" forces us to pay attention to the planned, manicured flowers and wonder about their potential for a place-based, disruptive, anticolonial tropicality beyond the state planners' strictures.

Earlier in this book I posited that the Cambodian-American filmmaker Kalyanee Mam's film *Lost World* forces us to "grieve with" the land. We do so through the fisherwoman Phalla Vy's shattering realization that her native ecologies have been irrevocably stolen and destroyed for Singapore's development. This theft and destruction are the culmination of ongoing (post) colonial realities and state power that extend to land-making and botanical spectacle in Singapore. Mam's film invites us to "grieve with" Phalla and thus undermines the success of Gardens by the Bay as an exemplar of planning and control. This so-called eco-development is a performance and a critical lens through which to understand the rest of the city. As Eng-Beng Lim puts it,

> the naturalization of botanical performance is key to this fantasy production, a way to secure the illusion that everything made-up is also natural and sustainable, including the complex ideology of postcolonial governance and neoliberal capitalism, and the actual practice of ecopreservation driving this project. (2014, 452)

The work of the artists, writers, and filmmakers that I have examined in this study wrestle against the picture-perfect vistas and carefully calibrated routes of spaces such as these in the rest of the island. Returning to Kim Jong Un and Vivian Balakrishnan's selfie, one cannot help but note the simultaneous spectacles of tropicality and luxury that camouflage and enhance the smooth and seamless passage ("#jalanjalan," indeed) of the North Korean dictator in the city-state. Kim's tour through the lush Gardens by the Bay and the gleaming Marina Bay Sands Integrated Resort, and his meeting with Trump bring to the fore the uneven (post)colonial geographies of these spaces. Frequently lauded as a model city and a postcolonial exception, Singapore poses as an augmented, future perfect version of our global spaces.

What art and writing can be made in these tightly controlled contexts? The practitioners that I have examined have a slightly different, if not more urgent query: what art and writing *must* be produced in these contexts? They do so from a minoritized vantage point, in a precarious context where Singapore's apparent success is celebrated by the illiberal governments of larger countries in Asia and beyond who seek to learn from its so-called soft authoritarianism (see Means, 1996). In the face of state amnesia, what might excavations of histories long suppressed or disappeared produce? Against the centralization of power, what repeated circumventions are necessary to elucidate the contours of control? What routes and trajectories of wayfinding are crucial in challenging increasing spatial controls? And, finally, how does one imagine *what could have been* and what might yet be, in a city where so much space and history has already been tightly mapped out? The rich textual, artistic, and filmic possibilities that I have drawn from in this study provide a sharp counterpoint, what I am calling a counter-cartography, an anti-map of the world's most mapped country.

In 2017, as I walked through Gardens by the Bay, 12 years after its inception, the plants were lush, having grown in and thrived under the careful cultivation of an army of migrant workers and local gardeners. Surrounded by this contemporary iteration of a colonial botanic garden, I recalled "Agnes Joaquim, Bioterrorist" and considered Ng's story as a way to read Singapore's past, present, and possible futures otherwise. I paused to examine the innards of the climate-controlled conservatories that held the optimal, carefully calibrated environment for a bevy of imported plants. In this most highly regulated of spaces, I noticed that the interior of the Cloud Forest tower, the structure that held the temperate plants, was covered in green, brown, and black stains. Moss, mildew, rust, and mold had accumulated on the insides of the structures where the moist plant roots and leaves met concrete and metal – testimony to the immense humidity that these materials must contend with if the cooled interior continues to be sealed against the sultry exterior.

These biotic and abiotic forms were not easily tamed. They did not make for good photographs, and certainly were not part of the Master Plan. Neither would they have made it into any marketing materials or speeches. It is crucial to see these forms of unplanned nonhuman life and the residues of chemical reactions as a form of revolt, in addition to the artistry and writing that I have highlighted in this book. They testify to the silent and ongoing failure of mapping, of complete control, and of the production of flawless tropical spectacle. At the heart of Singapore's fabulous techno-botanical miracle, its globally oriented spectacle and model, is a strange, damp, moldy concrete building. The persistence, spread, and tenacity of fungal hyphae and iron oxides are keen reminders of the resistance of the unmappable.

Works Cited

Agamben, Giorgio. 2005. *State of Exception*. Translated by Kevin Attell. Chicago: The University of Chicago Press.
Ahmed, Sara. 2006. *Queer Phenomenology*. Durham, NC and London: Duke University Press.
Alatas, Syed Hussein. 1977. *The Myth of the Lazy Native: A Study of the Image of the Malays, Filipinos and Javanese from the 16th to the 20th Century and Its Function in the Ideology of Colonial Capitalism*. London: Cass.
Alfian, Sa'at. 1998. *One Fierce Hour*. Singapore: Landmark Books.
Alfian, Sa'at. 1999. *Corridor*. Singapore: SNP Editions.
Alfian, Sa'at. 2008. *A History of Amnesia*. Singapore: Ethos Books.
Alfian, Sa'at. 2011. *Cooling-Off Day*. Singapore: Ethos Books.
Alfian, Sa'at. 2012. *Malay Sketches*. Singapore: Ethos Books.
Alfian, Sa'at. 2016. "A Censorship Manifesto" (2000). In *Histories, Practices and Interventions: A Reader in Singapore Contemporary Art*, edited by Jeffrey Say and Seng Yu Jin, 167–77. Singapore: LASALLE College of the Arts.
Alfian, Sa'at, and Marcia Vanderstraaten. 2015. *Hotel*. Unpublished script.
Anderson, Benedict. 2016. *Imagined Communities: Reflections on the Origin and Spread of Nationalism*. Verso.
Ang, Pauline. 2011. "Future Memory: Of Demolished Architecture & Forgotten Memories." Futurememory.sg. December. Accessed 9 Mar 2012.
Arts and Heritage Development Division. 2018. *Renaissance City Plan III*. Singapore: Ministry of Information, Communications and the Arts.
Awadalla, Maggie, and Paul March-Russell. 2013. "Introduction: The Short Story and the Postcolonial." In *The Postcolonial Short Story: Contemporary Essays*, edited by Maggie Awadalla and Paul March-Russell, 1–14. London: Palgrave Macmillan.
Bakhtin, Mikhail. 1981. *The Dialogic Imagination: Four Essays by M.M. Bakhtin*. Austin: University of Texas Press.
Bal, Charan. 2015. "Dealing with Deportability: Deportation Laws and the Political Personhood of Temporary Migrant Workers in Singapore." *Asian Journal of Law and Society* 2, no. 2: 267–84.
Barnard, Timothy and Corrine Heng. 2014. "A City in a Garden." In *Nature Contained: Environmental Histories of Singapore*, edited by Timothy Barnard, 281–306. Singapore: National University of Singapore Press.

Barr, Michael D. 2005. "Assimilation as Multiracialism: The Case of Singapore's Malays." *Asian Ethnicity* 6, no. 3: 161–82.

Barr, Michael D., and Carl A. Trocki, eds. 2009. *Paths Not Taken: Political Pluralism in Post-War Singapore*. Singapore: NUS Press.

Bishop, Ryan, John Phillips, and Wei-Wei Yeo. 2003. *Postcolonial Urbanism: Southeast Asian Cities and Global Processes*. New York: Routledge.

Bishop, Ryan, John Phillips, and Wei-Wei Yeo. 2004. "Beyond Description: Singapore Space Historicity." In *Beyond Description: Singapore Space Historicity*, edited by Ryan Bishop, John Phillips, and Wei-Wei Yeo, 1–16. London: Routledge.

Certeau, Michel de. 2002. *The Practice of Everyday Life*. Translated by Steven Rendall. Berkeley: University of California Press.

Chan, Kenneth. 2010. "Maid to Serve: Representations of Female Domestic Workers in Singapore Cinema." *Moving Worlds: A Journal of Transcultural Writings* 10, no. 4: 56–70.

Cheah, Pheng. 2006. *Inhuman Conditions: On Cosmopolitanism and Human Rights*. Cambridge, MA: Harvard University Press.

Chen, Anthony et al. 2017. "Film Community Position Paper, 21st December 2017." Retrieved from https://www.imda.gov.sg/-/media/imda/files/inner/pcdg/consultations/consultation-paper/public-consultation-on-proposed-amendments-to-the-films-act/film-community_1st-submission.pdf.

Cheng, Nien Yuan. 2019. "The Singapore Bicentennial: It Was Never Going to Work." *New Mandala*, 6 March. https://www.newmandala.org/book-review/raffles-renounced-towards-a-merdeka-history/.

Cheong, Suk-Wai. 2012. "No Walk in the Park. Escalating Costs Fueled by Building Frenzy Dogged Gardens by the Bay." *The Straits Times*, 30 June.

Chia, Adeline. 2010 "Funds Cut: Is It Censorship?" *The Straits Times*, 7 May.

Choe, Sang-Hun. 2018. "North Korea Film Glorifies Kim's World Debut, with Trump in Starring Role." *New York Times*, 15 June. https://www.nytimes.com/2018/06/15/world/asia/north-korea-kim-trump-film.html.

Chong, Terence. 2010. "'Back Regions' and 'Dark Secrets' in Singapore: The Politics of Censorship and Liberalisation." *Space and Polity* 14, no. 3 (1 December): 235–50. https://doi.org/10.1080/13562576.2010.532952.

Chong, Terence. 2012. *The Theatre and the State in Singapore: Orthodoxy and Resistance*. London: Routledge.

Choong, William. 2013. "Hard Truths about Singapore's Defence." *The Straits Times*, 17 March.

Chow, Clara. 2017. *Dream Storeys*. Singapore: Ethos Books.

Chua, Beng Huat. 1994. *That Imagined Space: Nostalgia for the Kampong in Singapore*. Singapore: Dept. of Sociology, National University of Singapore.

Chua, Beng Huat. 1995. *Communitarian Ideology and Democracy in Singapore*. New York: Routledge.

Chua, Beng Huat. 1997. *Political Legitimacy and Housing: Stakeholding in Singapore*. New York: Routledge.

Chua, Beng Huat. 2003. "Multiculturalism in Singapore: An Instrument of Social Control." *Race & Class* 44: 58–77.

Chua, Beng Huat. 2011. "Singapore as Model: Planning, Innovations, Knowledge Experts." In *Worlding Cities: Asian Experiments and the Art of Being Global*, edited by Ananya Roy and Aihwa Ong, 29–54. London: Blackwell.

Chye, Brandon. 2018. "Exporting Planning and Expertise: A Small City-State's Claim to Fame through Urban Development." *Oxford Urbanists*, 1 June. https://www.oxfordurbanists.com/magazine/2018/5/31/exporting-planning-and-expertise-a-small-city-states-claim-to-fame-through-urban-development/.

Comaroff, Joshua. 2015. "Built on Sand: Singapore and the New State of Risk." *Harvard Design Magazine* 39, special issue "Wet Matter." https://www.harvard-designmagazine.org/articles/built-on-sand-singapore-and-the-new-state-of-risk/.

Crampton, Jeremy W. 2006. "An Introduction to Critical Cartography." *ACME: An International E-Journal for Critical Geographies* 4, no. 1: 11–33.

"Creating the Bicentennial Experience." *Channel NewsAsia*, 3 December 2019. https://www.channelnewsasia.com/watch/creating-bicentennial-experience-1487411.

Curless, Gareth. 2014. "Archival Research in Singapore." *The Imperial and Global History Network* (23 June). http://imperialandglobal.exeter.ac.uk/2014/06/archival-research-in-singapore/. Accessed 15 Nov 2015.

De Koninck, Rodolphe. 2017. *Singapore's Permanent Territorial Revolution: Fifty Years in Fifty Maps*. Cartography by Pham Thanh Hai and Marc Girard. Singapore: NUS Press.

Deleuze, Gilles, and Félix Guattari. 1986. *Kafka: Toward a Minor Literature*. Translated by Dana Polan. Minneapolis: University of Minnesota Press.

Deleuze, Gilles, and Felix Guattari. 1987. *A Thousand Plateaus: Capitalism and Schizophrenia*. Translated by Brian Massumi. Minneapolis: University of Minnesota Press.

De Rozario, Tania. 2016. *And the Walls Come Crumbling Down*. Singapore: Math Paper Press.

Devan, Janadas. 1999. "My Country and My People: Forgetting to Remember." In *Our Place in Time: Exploring Heritage and Memory in Singapore*, edited by Kwok Kian Woon, Chong Cuan Kwa, Lily Kong, and Brenda Yeoh, 21–33. Singapore: Singapore Heritage Society.

Doggett, Marjorie. 1957. *Characters of Light*. Singapore: Donald Moore.

Eco, Umberto. 1994. "On the Impossibility of Drawing a Map of the Empire on a Scale of 1 to 1." In *How to Travel with a Salmon and Other Essays*. Translated by William Weaver, 95–106. New York: Harcourt, Brace.

Economic Review Committee. 2003. *Report of the Economic Review Committee: New Challenges Fresh Goals – Towards a Dynamic Global City*. Singapore: Ministry of Trade and Industry.

Eng, Teo Siew. 1992. "Planning Principles in Pre-and Post-Independence Singapore." *Town Planning Review* 63, no. 2: 163–85.

Evers, Hans-Dieter. 2016. "Nusantara: History of a Concept." *Journal of the Malaysian Branch of the Royal Asiatic Society* 89, no. 1 (2016): 3–14. doi:10.1353/ras.2016.0004.

Foster + Partners. 2009. "Capella Resort." https://www.fosterandpartners.com/projects/capella-resort/.

Foucault, Michel. 1984. "Of Other Spaces, Heterotopias." *Architecture, Mouvement, Continuité* 5: 46–49.

Frow, John. 1997. *Time and Commodity Culture: Essays in Cultural Theory and Postmodernity*. Oxford: Oxford University Press.

Gallo, William. 2018. "Selfies, Cheers Greet Kim in Singapore." *Voice of America*, 11 June. https://www.voanews.com/a/kim-takes-selfies-receives-cheers-ahead-of-meeting-with-trump/4433617.html.

Gan, Elaine, Anna Tsing, Heather Swanson, and Nils Bubandt. 2017. "Introduction: Haunted Landscapes of the Anthropocene." In *Arts of Living on a Damaged Planet:*

Ghosts and Monsters of the Anthropocene, edited by Anna Lowenhaupt Tsing, Elaine Gan, Heather Anne Swanson, and Nils Bubandt, G1–14. Minneapolis: University of Minnesota Press.

George, Cherian. 2017. *Singapore, Incomplete: Reflections on a First World Nation's Arrested Political Development*. Singapore: Woodsville News.

Goh, Daniel P.S. 2014. "The Little India Riot and the Spatiality of Migrant Labor in Singapore." *Society & Space*. https://societyandspace.org/2014/09/08/the-little-india-riot-and-the-spatiality-of-migrant-labor-in-singapore/.

Goh, Daniel P.S. 2015. "Singapore, the State, and Decolonial Spatiality." *Cultural Dynamics* 27, no. 2 (July): 215–26. https://doi.org/10.1177/0921374015585225.

Gómez-Barris, Macarena. 2017. *The Extractive Zone*. Durham, NC: Duke University Press.

"Government Making Weekly Rest Day Mandatory For Foreign Domestic Workers a Progressive Move." *Transient Workers Count Too*, 5 March 2012. http://twc2.org.sg/2012/03/05/government-making-weekly-rest-day-mandatory-for-foreign-domestic-workers-a-progressive-move/.

Han, Fook Kwang, Warren Fernandez, and Sumiko Tan. 2015. *Lee Kuan Yew: The Man and His Ideas*. Singapore: Marshall Cavendish.

Haraway, Donna J. 2016. *Staying with the Trouble: Making Kin in the Chtulucene*. Durham, NC: Duke University Press.

Harley, J.B. 1988. "Maps, Knowledge, and Power." In *The Iconography of Landscape*, edited by Denis Cosgrove and Stephen Daniels, 277–312. Cambridge: Cambridge University Press.

Harvey, David. 1997. "Contested Cities." In *Transforming Cities: Contested Governance and New Spatial Divisions*, edited by Nick Jewson and Susanne MacGregor, 17–24. New York: Routledge.

Harvey, David. 2008. "The Right to the City." *New Left Review* 53, September. https://newleftreview.org/issues/II53/articles/david-harvey-the-right-to-the-city.

Harvey, Penelope, Casper Bruun Jensen, and Atsuro Morita, eds. 2016. *Infrastructures and Social Complexity: A Companion*. London: Routledge.

Harvey, Sophia Siddique. 2007. "Nomadic Trajectories: Mapping Short Film Production in Singapore." *Inter-Asia Cultural Studies* 8, no. 2 (June): 262–76. https://doi.org/10.1080/14649370701238730.

Harvey, Sophia Siddique. 2008. "Mapping Spectral Tropicality in *The Maid* and *Return to Pontianak*." *Singapore Journal of Tropical Geography* 29, no. 1: 24–33.

Heng, Michelle. 2012. "Tan Pin Pin: The Hidden Depths of Memory." Iremember.sg. 30 March. Accessed 9 Mar 2012.

Ho, Louis, and Mayee Wong. 2012. "The Sticker Bomber and the Nanny State: Notes from Singapore." *Evental Aesthetics* 1, no. 3: 10–22.

Holden, Philip. 2013. "Unmaking Sense: Short Fiction and Social Space in Singapore." In *The Postcolonial Short Story: Contemporary Essays*, edited by Maggie Awadalla and Paul March Russell, 49–63. London: Palgrave Macmillan.

Holden, Philip. 2016. "'Is it manipulative? Sure. But that's how you tell stories': The Graphic Novel, Metahistory and the Artist in *The Art of Charlie Chan Hock Chye*." *Journal of Postcolonial Writing* 52, no. 4: 510–23.

Hong, Lysa. 2008. "Whose Invisible City? Articulating Singapore's Pasts in Invisible City." *s/pores* 2, no. 1. https://s-pores.com/2008/01/invisible/.

Huang, Shirlena, and Brenda S.A. Yeoh. 2007. "Emotional Labour and Transnational Domestic Work: The Moving Geographies of 'Maid Abuse' in Singapore." *Mobilities* 2, no. 2 (1 July): 195–217. https://doi.org/10.1080/17450100701381557.

Hutcheon, Linda. 1989. "Historiographic Metafiction, Parody, and the Intertextuality of History." In *Intertextuality and Contemporary American Fiction*, edited by P. O'Donnell, and Robert Con Davis, 3–32. Baltimore: Johns Hopkins University Press.

ila. 2019. "A Fluid Borderless Past." *Singapore Unbound*, 23 September. https://singapore-unbound.org/blog/2019/8/26/sg24fvdmfdsgkj9z5cldl3ygkurw4f.

Ingold, Tim. 2000. "To Journey Along a Way of Life: Maps, Wayfinding and Navigation." In *The Perception of the Environment: Essays on Livelihood, Dwelling and Skill*, 219–42. London: Routledge.

Jaensubhakij, Ruth. 2017. "This Is How the Little India Riot in 2013 Has Changed the Area for Better or Worse." *Mothership*, 30 June. https://mothership.sg/2017/06/this-is-how-the-little-india-riot-in-2013-has-changed-the-area-for-better-or-worse.

Jameson, Fredric. 1991. *Postmodernism, or, The Cultural Logic of Late Capitalism*. Durham, NC: Duke University Press.

Jiang, Genevieve. 2008. "Homeless … Hopeless." *The New Paper*. http://news.asiaone.com/News/The+New+Paper/Story/A1Story20081209-106536.html. Accessed 10 Jan 2010.

Jones, Evan. 2018. "'Refugees Not Welcome Here': As ASEAN Chair, Singapore Must Take the Lead." *Hong Kong Free Press*, 7 January. https://www.hongkongfp.com/2018/01/07/refugees-not-welcome-asean-chair-singapore-must-take-lead/.

"Jurong Rock Caverns." *Surbana Jurong*. https://surbanajurong.com/sector/jurong-rock-caverns/.

Kaur, Satveer, Naomi Tan, and Mohan Jyoti Dutta. 2016. "Media, Migration and Politics: The Coverage of the Little India Riot in *The Straits Times* in Singapore." *Journal of Creative Communications* 11, no. 1 (1 March): 27–43. https://doi.org/10.1177/0973258616630214.

Khiun, Liew Kai. 2015. "'I Am Limpeh (Your Father)!' Parodying Hegemony, Anti-Nostalgic Cultural Insurgency and the Visual Amplification of Lee Kuan Yew in Late Authoritarian Singapore." *Journal of Creative Communications* 10, no. 1 (1 March): 21–38. https://doi.org/10.1177/0973258615569949.

Khoo, Gaik Cheng. 2013. "Where the Heart Is: Cinema and Civic Life in Singapore." In *New Suburban Stories*, edited by Martin Dines and Timotheus Vermeulen, 97–108. London: Bloomsbury Academic.

Koh, Buck Song. 2012. *Perpetual Spring: Singapore's Gardens by the Bay*. Singapore: Marshall Cavendish Editions.

Koh, Fabian. 2018. "Illegal Procession: Activist Refuses to Pay Fine, Gets Jail." *The Strait Times*, 4 October. https://www.straitstimes.com/singapore/courts-crime/illegal-procession-activist-refuses-to-pay-fine-gets-jail.

Koh, Wan Ting. 2017. "Pink Dot 2017 Draws Thousands Despite New Restrictions." *Yahoo News Singapore*, 1 July. https://sg.news.yahoo.com/pink-dot-2017-draws-thousands-despite-new-restrictions-152411039.html.

Kong, Lily. 1995. "Music and Cultural Politics: Ideology and Resistance in Singapore." *Transactions of the Institute of British Geographers* 20, no. 4: 447–59. www.jstor.org/stable/622945.

Kong, Lily. 2012. "Ambitions of a Global City: Arts, Culture and Creative Economy in 'Post-Crisis' Singapore." *International Journal of Cultural Policy* 18, no. 3 (1 June): 279–94. https://doi.org/10.1080/10286632.2011.639576.

Koolhaas, Rem. 1995. "Singapore Songlines: Portrait of a Potemkin Metropolis or Thirty Years of Tabula Rasa." In *S, M, L, XL*. New York: Monacelli Press.

Kusno, Abidin. 2017. "Southeast Asia: Colonial Discourses." In *Routledge Handbook of Planning History*, edited by Carola Hein, 218–39. London: Routledge.

Kwan, Kevin. 2013. *Crazy Rich Asians.* New York: Doubleday.
Lee, Hsien Loong. 2019a. "PM Lee Hsien Loong at the Launch of the Singapore Bicentennial." Prime Minister's Office Singapore, 28 January. https://www.pmo.gov.sg/Newsroom/PM-Lee-Hsien-Loong-at-the-launch-of-the-Singapore-Bicentennial-Jan-2019.
Lee, Hsien Loong. 2019b. "PM Lee Hsien Loong at the Official Opening of Jewel Changi Airport." Prime Minister's Office Singapore, 18 October. https://www.pmo.gov.sg/Newsroom/PM-Lee-Hsien-Loong-Official-Opening-Jewel-Changi-Airport.
Lee, Kuan Yew. 1995. "Speech by Mr. Lee Kuan Yew, Senior Minister at the Launch of the National Orchid Garden." Speech delivered at the Singapore Botanic Gardens, Singapore, 20 October.
Lee, Kuan Yew. 2000. *From Third World to First: Singapore and the Asian Economic Boom.* London: Harper Collins.
Lefebvre, Henri. 1991. *The Production of Space.* Translated by Donald Nicholson-Smith. Oxford: Blackwell.
Leow, Joanne. 2013. "Echoing the City: Notes on Re-Watching Tan Pin Pin's *Singapore GaGa.*" *ISSUE 2* 2: 41–50.
Liew, Sonny. 2015. *The Art of Charlie Chan Hock Chye.* Singapore: Epigram Books.
Lim, Charles. 2015. *SEA STATE: Charles Lim Yi Yong.* Edited by Shabbir Hussain Mustafa. Singapore: National Arts Council.
Lim, Charles. 2019. *SEA STATE.* www.charleslimyiyong.com.
Lim, Cheng Tju. 1997. "Singapore Political Cartooning." *Southeast Asian Journal of Social Science* 25, no. 1: 125–50.
Lim, Eng-Beng. 2014. "Future Island." *Third Text* 28, no. 4–5: 443–53.
Lim, Jessica. 2013. "How to Spin the Revenue?" *The Straits Times,* 19 June. https://www.straitstimes.com/singapore/how-to-spin-the-revenue.
Lim, Lydia. 2007. "Put Ministers' Pay in Perspective." *The Straits Times,* 5 April.
Lim, Tin Seng. 2017. "Land from Sand: Singapore's Reclamation Story." *biblioasia* 13, no. 1: 16–23. Retrieved from https://biblioasia.nlb.gov.sg/files/pdf/BiblioAsia%20Apr-Jun%202017.pdf.
Lim, William S.W. 2011. *Incomplete Urbanism: A Critical Urban Strategy for Emerging Economies.* Singapore: Asian Urban Lab.
Lim, Yan Liang. 2015. "Record 28,000 Gather at Hong Lim Park for Annual Pink Dot Rally." *The Straits Times,* 3 June. https://www.straitstimes.com/singapore/record-28000-gather-at-hong-lim-park-for-annual-pink-dot-rally.
"Little India Riot: Violence Sparked by Accident, Alcohol 'Major Factor', Says COI." *The Straits Times,* 30 June 2014. https://www.straitstimes.com/singapore/little-india-riot-violence-sparked-by-accident-alcohol-major-factor-says-coi.
Liu, Gretchen. 2001. *Singapore: A Pictorial History.* Richmond, UK: Curzon.
Liu, Vanessa. 2019. "Statue of Sir Stamford Raffles in Boat Quay 'Disappears' for Singapore Bicentennial." *The Straits Times,* 2 January. https://www.straitstimes.com/singapore/statue-of-sir-stamford-raffles-at-boat-quay-disappears-for-singapore-bicentennial.
Loh, Kah Seng. 2009. "Kampong, Fire, Nation: Towards a Social History of Postwar Singapore." *Journal of Southeast Asian Studies* 40, no. 3: 613–43.
Loh, Kah Seng. 2010. "Encounters at the Gates." In *The Makers & Keepers of Singapore History,* edited by Loh Kah Seng and Liew Kai Khiun, 21–22. Singapore: Ethosbooks and Singapore Heritage Society.

Loh, Kah Seng. 2013. *Squatters into Citizens: The 1961 Bukit Ho Swee Fire and the Making of Modern Singapore*. Singapore: NUS Press.

Loh, Kah Seng, and Kenneth Tan. 2016. "Convergence and Slippage between Film and History: Reviewing *Invisible City*, *Zahari's 17 Years* and *Sandcastle*." In *Singapore Cinema: New Perspectives*, edited by Kai Khiun Liew and Stephen Teo, 219–42. London: Routledge.

Lowe, Lisa. 2015. *The Intimacies of Four Continents*. Durham, NC: Duke University Press.

Lynch, Kevin. 1960. *The Image of the City*. Cambridge, MA: MIT Press.

Mam, Kalyanee. 2018. "Open Story." *Lost World*. https://emergencemagazine.org/story/lost-world/.

Manpower Ministry, "Foreign Workforce Numbers." 2015. http://www.mom.gov.sg/documents-and-publications/foreign-workforce-numbers.

Massey, Doreen. 2005. *For Space*. London: Sage.

Means, Gordon Paul. 1996. "Soft Authoritarianism in Malaysia and Singapore." *Journal of Democracy* 7, no. 4 (1 October): 103–17. https://doi.org/10.1353/jod.1996.0065.

Mignolo, Walter D., and Madina V. Tlostanova. 2006. "Theorizing from the Borders: Shifting to Geo- and Body-Politics of Knowledge." *European Journal of Social Theory* 9, no. 2: 205–21.

Miksic, John N. 2013. *Singapore and the Silk Road of the Sea, 1300–1800*. Singapore: NUS Press.

Ministry of National Development Singapore. 2013. *A High Quality Living Environment for All Singaporeans: Land Use Plan to Support Singapore's Future Population*. Singapore: Ministry of National Development.

Muñoz, José Esteban. 2009. *Cruising Utopia: The Then and There of Queer Futurity*. New York: NYU Press.

Mutalib, Hussin. 2011. "The Singapore Minority Dilemma." *Asian Survey* 51, no. 6 (December): 1156–71.

Mydin, Iskander. 2013. "Foreword." *Singapore and the Silk Road of the Sea, 1300–1800*. Singapore: NUS Press.

Myers, Natasha. 2016. "From Edenic Apocalypse to Gardens against Eden: Plants and People in and after the Anthropocene." In *Infrastructure, Environment, and Life in the Anthropocene*, edited by Kregg Hetherington, 115–48. Durham, NC: Duke University Press.

Naruse, Cheryl Narumi. 2017. "Singapore as Strategic Location: Setting and Positionality in Goh Poh Seng's *If We Dream Too Long* and Lydia Kwa's *Pulse*." In *Singapore Literature and Culture: Current Directions in Local and Global Contexts*, edited by Angelia Poon and Angus Whitehead, 237–55. London: Routledge.

Ng, Yi-Sheng. 2012. "Agnes Joaquim, Bioterrorist." In *Fish Eats Lion*, edited by Jason Erik Lundberg, 31–45. Singapore: Math Paper Press.

Ng Yong He, Gregory. 2019. "If You Talk Like a Coloniser and Eat Like a Coloniser," *New Naratif*, 10 August. https://newnaratif.com/if-you-talk-like-a-coloniser-and-eat-like-a-coloniser/.

Nichols, Bill. 2001. *Introduction to Documentary*. Bloomington: Indiana University Press.

Noor, Farish A. 2011. "'Racial Profiling' Revisited: The 1915 Indian Sepoy Mutiny in Singapore and the Impact of Profiling on Religious and Ethnic Minorities." *Politics, Religion & Ideology* 12, no. 1 (1 March): 89–100. https://doi.org/10.1080/21567689.2011.564404.

Nora, Pierre. 1996. "General Introduction: Between Memory and History." Translated by Arthur Goldhammer. In *Realms of Memory: Rethinking the French Past*, edited by Lawrence D. Kritzman, 1–20. New York: Columbia University Press.

Ooi, Can-Seng. 2010. "Political Pragmatism and the Creative Economy: Singapore as a City for the Arts." *International Journal of Cultural Policy* 16, no. 4 (1 November): 403–17. https://doi.org/10.1080/10286630903118071.

Ortmann, Stephan. 2009. "Singapore: The Politics of Inventing National Identity." *Journal of Current Southeast Asian Affairs* 28: 23–46.

Panagia, Davide. 2009. *The Political Life of Sensation*. Durham, NC: Duke University Press.

Peterson, William. 2001. *Theatre and the Politics of Culture in Contemporary Singapore*. Middletown: Wesleyan University Press.

Pickles, John. 2004. *A History of Spaces: Cartographic Reason, Mapping and the Geo-Coded World*. London: Routledge.

Poon, Angelia. 2009. "Introduction: 1990–Present." In *Writing Singapore: An Historical Anthology of Singapore Literature*, edited by Angelia Poon, Philip Holden, and Shirley Lim, 359–79. Singapore: NUS Press.

Prystay, Cris. 2008. "Mixed Marriages, Historic Buildings' Modern Makeovers." *Wall Street Journal*, 5 September. https://www.wsj.com/articles/SB122054828740900349.

Rae, Paul. 2011. "Freedom of Repression." *Theatre Research International* 36, no. 2 (July): 117–33. https://doi.org/10.1017/S0307883311000204.

Rahim, Lily Zubaidah. 1998. *The Singapore Dilemma: The Political and Educational Marginality of the Malay Community*. Kuala Lumpur: Oxford University Press.

Rahman, Noorashikin Abdul. 2010. "Managing Labour Flows: Foreign Talent, Foreign Workers and Domestic Help." In *Management of Success: Singapore Revisited*, edited by Terence Chong, 199–216. Singapore: Institute of Southeast Asian Studies.

Rajah, Jothie. 2012. *Authoritarian Rule of Law: Legislation, Discourse and Legitimacy in Singapore*. Cambridge: Cambridge University Press.

Ratliff, Evan. 2007. "Google Maps Is Changing the Way We See the World." *WIRED*, 26 June: 154–59. https://www.wired.com/2007/06/ff-maps/.

Reisz, Emma. 2003. "City as Garden: Shared Space in the Urban Botanic Gardens of Singapore and Malaysia, 1786–2000." In *Postcolonial Urbanism: Southeast Asian Cities and Global Processes*, edited by Ryan Bishop, John Phillips, and Wei Wei Yeo, 123–50. New York: Routledge.

"Riot in Little India: Spark and Fuel." *Yawning Bread*, 10 December 2013. https://yawningbread.wordpress.com/2013/12/10/riot-in-little-india-spark-and-fuel/.

Safdie Architects. 2011. "Design of the Year 2011." *President's Design Award Singapore*. https://pda.designsingapore.org/presidents-design-award/award-recipients/2011/marina-bay-sands-integrated-resort-singapore.html.

Savage, Victor R., and Brenda S. A. Yeoh. 2013. *Singapore Street Names: A Study of Toponymics*. Singapore: Marshall Cavendish.

Schneider-Mayerson, Matthew. 2017. "Some Islands Will Rise: Singapore in the Anthropocene." *Resilience: A Journal of the Environmental Humanities* 4, no. 2: 166–84.

Scott, A.O. 2018. "Review: 'Crazy Rich Asians' Is a Party with a First-Rate Guest List." *New York Times*, 14 August. https://www.nytimes.com/2018/08/14/movies/crazy-rich-asians-review.html.

Scott, James C. 1990. *Domination and the Arts of Resistance: Hidden Transcripts*. New Haven: Yale University Press.

Scott, James C. 1998. *Seeing Like a State: How Certain Schemes to Improve the Human Condition Have Failed.* New Haven: Yale University Press.

Shaheed, Farida. 2012. Letter of the United Nations Special Rapporteur in the Field of Cultural Rights to Lee Hsien Loong, Singapore, 29 May. https://spcommreports.ohchr.org/TMResultsBase/DownLoadPublicCommunicationFile?gId=21390.

Shatkin, Gavin. 2013. "Reinterpreting the Meaning of the 'Singapore Model': State Capitalism and Urban Planning." *International Journal of Urban and Regional Research* 38, no. 1: 116–37. https://doi.org/10.1111/1468-2427.12095.

"Singaporean Ministers Can Decide What Is Fake News." *The Economist*, 6 February 2020. https://www.economist.com/asia/2020/02/06/singaporean-ministers-can-decide-what-is-fake-news.

"The Singapore Exception." *The Economist*, 18 July. https://www.economist.com/special-report/2015/07/18/the-singapore-exception.

"Singapore: Executions Continue in Flawed Attempt to Tackle Drug Crime, Despite Limited Reforms." Amnesty.org, 11 October 2017. https://www.amnesty.org/en/latest/news/2017/10/singapore-executions-continue-in-flawed-attempt-to-tackle-drug-crime/.

Singapore Government. 1920. *Foreshores Act 1920: 2020 Revised Edition.* https://sso.agc.gov.sg/Act/FA1920.

Singapore Government. 2012. *Public Order Act 2009: 2020 Revised Edition.* https://sso.agc.gov.sg/Act/POA2009.

Soja, Edward. 1989. *Postmodern Geographies: The Reassertion of Space in Critical Social Theory.* London: Verso.

Sorluan, N.G. 2008. "Your Backyard, My Front Door." *The Straits Times*, 7 September.

Stoler, Ann Laura. 2016. *Duress: Imperial Durabilities in our Times.* Durham, NC: Duke University Press.

Tan, Guan Zhen. 2017. "Seelan Palay Arrested outside Parliament House Only Highlights Chia Thye Poh More." *Mothership*, 2 October. https://mothership.sg/2017/10/seelan-palay-arrested-outside-parliament-house-only-highlights-chia-thye-poh-more/.

Tan, Kenneth Paul. 2012. "The Ideology of Pragmatism: Neo-Liberal Globalisation and Political Authoritarianism in Singapore." *Journal of Contemporary Asia* 42, no. 1 (1 February): 67–92. https://doi.org/10.1080/00472336.2012.634644.

Tan, Kenneth Paul. 2013. "Forum Theater in Singapore: Resistance, Containment, and Commodification in an Advanced Industrial Society." *Positions: East Asia Cultures Critique* 21, no. 1 (16 March): 189–221.

Tan, Kenneth Paul. 2016. "Choosing What to Remember in Neoliberal Singapore: The Singapore Story, State Censorship and State-Sponsored Nostalgia." *Asian Studies Review* 40, no. 2 (2 April): 231–49. https://doi.org/10.1080/10357823.2016.1158779.

Tan, Pin Pin, dir. 2004. *Singapore GaGa.* Singapore.

Tan, Pin Pin. 2005. "Films Act: Film-Makers Seek Clarification." *The Straits Times*, 11 May.

Tan, Pin Pin, dir. 2007a. *Invisible City.* Singapore.

Tan, Pin Pin. 2007b. "Tan Pin Pin on Self-Censorship, Memories and Our Views of History." By Ken Kwek and Peh Shing Huei. *The Straits Times*, 6 July.

Tan, Pin Pin, dir. 2013. *To Singapore, With Love.* Singapore.

Tan, Shzr Ee. 2006. *Lost Roads: Singapore.* Singapore: SNP Editions.

Tan, Tarn How. 2017. "1987's Scar Literature and Scar Art." *Tan Tarn How Too*, 4 June. https://tantarnhow.wordpress.com/2017/06/04/1987s-scar-literature-and-scar-art/.

Teh, David. 2012. "Charles Lim's Informatic Naturalism: Notes on *SEA STATE 2*." *CHARLES LIM: SEA STATE 2: As Evil Disappears*. Singapore: Future Perfect.

Teo, You Yenn. 2018. *This Is What Inequality Looks Like*. Singapore: Ethos Books.

Teo, Youyenn. 2011. *Neoliberal Morality in Singapore: How Family Policies Make State and Society*. New York: Routledge.

Tiang, Jeremy. 2016. *It Never Rains on National Day*. Singapore: Epigram Books.

"To Johor Bahru with Love: 350 S'poreans Watch MDA-Banned Film across Causeway." *The New Paper*, 21 September 2014. http://www.tnp.sg/news/johor-bahru-love-350-sporeans-watch-mda-banned-film-across-causeway.

Tong, Kelvin, dir. 2015. *Grandma Positioning System*. Singapore: Boku Films.

"Trapped Passengers Evacuate Singapore Ferris Wheel." *Reuters*, 23 December 2008. https://www.reuters.com/article/uk-singapore-flyer-idUKTRE4BM3KF20081223.

Valles, Eric Tinsay. 2012. "On the Commercialisation of Creativity in the Merlion State." In *The Creativity Market: Creative Writing in the 21st Century*, edited by Dominique Hecq, 190–205. Bristol: Multilingual Matters.

Watson, Jini Kim. 2008. "The Way Ahead: The Politics and Poetics of Singapore's Developmental Landscape." *Contemporary Literature* 49, no. 4 (Winter): 683–711.

Watson, Jini Kim. 2011. *The New Asian City: Three-Dimensional Fictions of Space and Urban Form*. Minneapolis: University of Minnesota Press.

Watson, Jini Kim. 2016. "Aspirational City." *Interventions* 18, no. 4 (3 July): 543–58. https://doi.org/10.1080/1369801X.2015.1126193.

Watson, Jini Kim. 2018. "Separate Futures: Cold War Decolonization in Mohamed Latiff Mohamed's *Confrontation* and Sonny Liew's *The Art of Charlie Chan Hock-Chye*." *Discourse* 40, no. 2: 165–87. https://doi.org/10.13110/discourse.40.2.0165.

Watson, Jini Kim, and Gary Wilder, eds. 2018. *The Postcolonial Contemporary: Political Imaginaries for the Global Present*. New York: Fordham University Press.

Wee, C.J.W.-L. 2007. *The Asian Modern: Culture, Capitalist Development, Singapore*. Hong Kong: Hong Kong University Press.

Whang, Lay Keng, and Lim Siu Ann. 2019. "Flower Power." *NParks Buzz* 43, no. 4. https://www.nparks.gov.sg/nparksbuzz/issue-43-vol-4-2019/gardening/flower-power.

Wong, Souk Yee, and Tay Hong Seng. 2002. "Esperanza." In *5 Plays from Third Stage: A Collection of Five Singaporean Plays*, edited by Anne Lim and Suan Tze Chng, 99–129. Singapore: Third Stage.

World Wildlife Foundation. 2014. *Living Planet Report 2014*. Switzerland: WWF International.

Yap, Arthur. 2013. *The Collected Poems of Arthur Yap*. Singapore: NUS Press.

Yee, Alex Thiam Koon, Richard T. Corlett, Soo Chin Liew, and Hugh Tan. 2011. "The Vegetation of Singapore: An Updated Map." *Gardens' Bulletin Singapore* 63 (1 January): 205–12.

Yeo, Wei-Wei. 2004. "Of Trees and the Heartland: Singapore's Narratives." In *Beyond Description: Singapore Space Historicity*, edited by Ryan Bishop, John Phillips, and Wei-Wei Yeo, 17–29. London: Routledge.

Yeoh, Brenda S.A. 1996. *Contesting Space: Power Relations and the Urban Built Environment in Colonial Singapore*. Kuala Lumpur: Oxford University Press.

Index

Note: page numbers in italics refer to illustrations.

Agamben, Giorgio 10
Ahmed, Sara 76, 83, 84, 86, 87
Alfian, Sa'at 14, 21, 92, 106n9, 115, 116, 117
   Malay Sketches (2012) 93, 106, 107–14
   and Marcia Vanderstraaten, *Hotel* (2015) 21, 123, 125–34, *130, 133,* 148, 150
Anderson, Benedict 1–2
Ang, Pauline 9
Ang Swee Chai 70, 71
Anti-British National Liberation War (1948–1960) 62
the arts 12–17
Awadalla, Maggie, and Paul March-Russell 107

Bakhtin, Mikhail 21, 90
Bal, Charan 65
Barisan Sosialis 70, 135
Barnard, Timothy P., and Corinne Heng xix
Barr, Michael 106
   and Carl A. Trocki 120
Bishop, Ryan, John Phillips, and Wei Wei Yeo 4, 8, 9
Boo, Junfeng, *Sandcastle* (2010) 63
Borges, Jorge Luis 103n7, 143
Bukit Brown cemetery 59–60

Cambodia, sand harvesting 41–2
   see also Mam, Kalyanee, *Lost World*

Capella Resort 153
Certeau, Michel de 2, 24n15, 97, 105, xviii
Chan, Cheow Thia 51
Chan, Kenneth 67n3
chance, concept of 23–4
Changi Airport 71, 98, xx
Changi prison 73, 99, 100–1
Chen, Anthony, *Ilo Ilo* (2013) 67
Chen, Anthony, et al. 16
Chia, Thye Poh 63
Chia-Richmond, Beatrice 150
Chiang, Michael 150
Chng, Suan Tze 67
Chong, Terence 15, 67
Chow, Clara, *Dream Storeys* (2017) 21, 123, 143–7, 148, 150
chronotopes 21, 30–1, 46, 90, 93, 97, 103, 109–12, 125
Chua, Beng Huat 7, 10, 50, 112–13, xiii, xvi, xx
Chun, Kai Feng, *Ride of a Lifetime!* 145
Chye, Brandon 10n5
circumvention 61–87
   definition 3, 20, 68–9, 84, 93, 123
   see also Tan, Pin Pin, *To Singapore, With Love*
city planning
   mapping Singapore xvi–xvii, *xvii,* 4–12
   Master Plans xvii, xviii, 4, 6, 13, 95, 110–11, 117, 121, 159

171

colonialism, legacy of xviii, 13, 18, 51–2, 114, 119
    see also city planning; Raffles, Sir Stamford
Comaroff, Joshua 28, 144
confabulation
    definition 3, 21, 121–2, 123
    see also Alfian, Sa'at, and Marcia Vanderstraaten, *Hotel*; Chow, Clara, *Dream Storeys*; Liew, Sonny, *The Art of Charlie Chan Hock Chye*
counter-cartographical reading
    definition 19, 23, 24–5
    see also circumvention; confabulation; excavation; wayfinding
Crampton, Jeremy W. 2
Crazy Rich Asians (film, 2018) 157, xv
Curless, Gareth 62

De Koninck, Rodolphe 5–6, 29, 116, xiii, xvi
De Koninck, Rodolphe, Julie Drolet, Marc Girard, and Pham Thanh Hai 5
De Rozario, Tania 83n13
    And the Walls Come Crumbling Down (2016) 20–1, 61, 68, 82–7
death penalty 18, 64, 126–8
decolonization (1963) 62, 135–6
    see also independence; merger with and separation from Malaysia
Deleuze, Gilles, and Felix Guattari 22, 108, 109
Devan, Janadas 46
Doggett, Marjorie, *Characters of Light* (1957) 51–2, 52n11
domestic workers 65–7, 128–9

Eco, Umberto 2–3, 11–12, 116
Eng, Teo Siew xvii
Ethnic Integration Policy (EIP) 109n13
excavation
    definition 3, 20, 68–9, 93, 123
    see also Lim, Charles Yi Yong, *SEA STATE*; Tan, Pin Pin, *Invisible City*
exiles 61–4, 68, 69–73, *70*, 82, 135, 145

filmmaking 16

Foreign Maids Scheme
    see domestic workers
Foreshores Act 36
Foucault, Michel 112
Frow, John 48, 53, 103n7

Gan, Elaine et al. 44
Gardens by the Bay 28, 41, 42–4, 78, 151, 154, 156, 157–9, xiii–xvi, *xiv*, *xvi*, xxi
    Cloud Forest 43, 157, 159, xiv, *xvi*
    design by Grant Associates xiv
    Flower Dome xiv
    Supertrees xiv
Goh, Daniel P.S. 6, 77
Golding, Henry xv
Gómez-Barris, Macarena 38
Guattari, Felix, and Gilles Deleuze 22, 108, 109

Han, Tan Juan 53
Haraway, Donna 43, 157
Harley, J.B. 2
Harvey, David 5
Harvey, Penny, Casper Bruun Jensen, and Atsuro Morita 41
Heng, Corinne, and Timothy P. Barnard xix
Heng, Michelle 47
Ho, Juan Thai 61, 69–70, *70*, 71
Hock Lee Bus Incident 140
Holden, Philip 107n12, 136, 137
Hong, Lysa 53, 53n12
Hong Lim Park 64
Housing Development Board flats 7, 96, 111, 113, 137, 144
Huang, Shirlena, and Brenda Yeoh 129
Humanitarian Organization for Migration Economics (HOME) 64
Hutcheon, Linda 122

ila 30, 54n13
    "A Fluid Borderless Past" (2019) 54–9
    bekas (2019) 55, 57–9, *58*
independence (1965) 5, 13, 32, 39, 48n8, 51, 52, 62, 123
    see also decolonization; merger with and separation from Malaysia

Indigenous people 39, 49, 54, 106–7, 109
Ingold, Timothy 21, 91, 93, 104

Jackson Plan (1822) 109n13, xvii
Jameson, Fredric 91–2
Japanese occupation of Singapore 54, 62, 73, 79, 129–30, 132
    see also Alfian, Sa'at, and Marcia Vanderstraaten, *Hotel*
Jee Leong Koh 54
Jewel, Changi Airport xx
Johore Battery 99
Jurong Island 31–2, 56, 146

Khoo, Eric, *No Day Off* (2006) 67n3
Khoo, Francis 70, 71, 72–4, 74n7, 137
Khoo, Gaik Cheng 15n11
Kim, Jong Un 151–2, 153, 154, 158
Koh, Gilbert, "Garden City" 27n1
Koh, Wan Ting 64
Kong, Lily 13, 72
Koolhaas, Rem 5, xiii
Kuo, Pao Kun 17
Kusno, Abidin xviii
Kwan, Kevin, *Crazy Rich Asians* (book) xv
Kwee, Stephanie 153

Land Acquisition Act (1966) 4–5, 5n1
Land Acquisition Ordinance (1920) 4
land reclamation 27–9
    see also Lim, Charles, *SEA STATE*
Lee, Hsien Loong xx, 149
Lee, Kuan Yew 10, 119–21, 122, 129, 135, 139, 140–1, xix
    From Third World to First (2000) 119, 123, 148
Lee Tzu Pheng, "My Country and My People" 27n1
Lefebvre, Henri 2, 3, 7, 10–11, 21, 22, 30–1, 123
legislation 4–5, 16–17, 36, 63–4, 151–2
Leong Liew Geok, "Trees Are Only Temporary" 27n1
LGBTQ rights and spaces 18, 64, 76, 83–4, 155n2
    see also De Rozario, Tania, *And the Walls Come Crumbling Down*
Li, Xinli, "In Our Time" 114–17, *115,* 123

Liew, Sonny, *The Art of Charlie Chan Hock Chye* 15, 21, 122–5, *124,* 134–42, *139, 142,* 148, 150, 158
Lim, Charles Yi Yong 28, 53, 55
    SEA STATE (2005–) 20, 30, 31–9, *33–5, 37, 40,* 44, 53
Lim, Chen Sian 49
Lim, Cheng Tju 134
Lim, Chin Siong 135, 139, 140–1
Lim, Eng-Beng 158
Lim, Tin Seng 28
Lim, William S.W. 9
Loh, Kah Seng 7, 7n2, 62–3, 72, 111n15
Lowe, Lisa 121
Lynch, Kevin, *The Image of the City* (1960) 91–2

Malay identity
    see ila, "A Fluid Borderless Past"
Malayan Emergency
    see Anti-British National Liberation War
Mam, Kalyanee, *Lost World* 20, 29, 30, 39–44, *40,* 58, 158
mapping 3–4
Marina Bay 9–10, 28, xiii, *xiv*
Marxism 13–14, 66–7, 136
Massey, Doreen 18, 20, 23–4, 31, 94, 98, 104
Master Plans
    see city planning
Md Mukul Hossine, *Me Migrant* (2016) 67n4
MD Sharif Uddin, *Stranger to Myself* (2017) 67n4
memory 92, 103n7
    see also Alfian, Sa'at, *Malay Sketches*; Liew, Sonny, *The Art of Charlie Chan Hock Chye*; Tan, Pin Pin, *Invisible City*; Tan, Shzr Ee, *Lost Roads: Singapore*
merger with and separation from Malaysia 10, 54, 62, 72, 125n1, 135
    see also decolonization; independence
Mignolo, Walter D., and Madina V. Tlostanova 1
migrant workers 64–7, 76–7
    see also Tiang, Jeremy, "National Day"
Miksic, John N. 59

173

military
  British 100, 150, 153
  Japanese 54, 62, 73, 79, 129–30, 132
  Singaporean 79, 96, 100–1, 107, 110–11, 115–16
  United States 39
Muigai, Githu 106–7
Muñoz, José Esteban 83–4, 85–6, 87
music 69, 72–3, 136
Mutalib, Hussin 106–7
Mydin, Iskander 59
Myers, Natasha 158

Naruse, Cheryl Narumi 154
National Arts Council 14, 17
National Day Parade 75, 76, 79, 150
Ng, Yi-Sheng, *Fish Eats Lion* (2012) 155–7, 158, 159
Nichols, Bill 69
Nien, Yuan Cheng 149
Noor, Farish 126
Nora, Pierre 92
North Korean–United States Singapore Summit 151–2, 153, 154, 158

Operation Spectrum 13–14, 66, 136
Ortmann, Stephan 72

Pak Ramlan, interviewed by ila 56
Panagia, Davide 71
People's Action Party (PAP) 5, 7n2, 15, 29, 62, 120, 123, 135, 139–40, 192, xix–xx
  consolidation of power 135
Peterson, William 66–7
Pickles, John xviii
Polunin, Ivan 49–51, *50–1*, 52
Poon, Angelia 12n6, 13
Public Entertainments and Meetings Act (1958; revised 2001) 14–15
Public Order Act (2017) 16n12, 63, 151–2

queer spaces
  see De Rozario, Tania, *And the Walls Come Crumbling Down*

racial quota housing system 7, 87, 109, 111, 114, 144

Rae, Paul 14–15
Raffles, Sir Stamford 52, 103n8, 122, 126, 148–9, xvii, xviiin3
Raffles Hotel 156
Rahim, Lily Zubaidah 106n10
Rahman, Noorashikin Abdul 65
Rajah, Jothie 16, 62
Ratliff, Evan 2

Safdie, Moshe 8, 9–10, 9n4
Said Zahari 70
Savage, Victor, and Brenda S.A. Yeoh 104
scar literature 63
Schneider-Mayerson, Matthew 158
Scott, A.O. xv
Scott, James C. 4, 11, xviii
sea states (World Meteorological Organization) 34–5
See, Martyn 72
Seelan Palay 63
Sentosa Island 48n7, *49*, 146, 151–2, 153
separation from Malaysia
  see merger with and separation from Malaysia
Sepoy Mutiny (1915) 126
Sharma, Haresh, *Model Citizens* (2012) 67
Shatkin, Gavin 5, 8, xx, 152
Sim Chiyin 63
Singapore City Gallery, scale model of Singapore 11–12, *12*, 78, 123
Singapore Flyer 144–5
Singapore Master Plan
  see city planning, Master Plans
Soja, Edward 30
Sook Ching Massacre 54, 57
Stoler, Ann Laura 23, 28–9
student protests 53, 70, 135, 138, 140
The Substation 17, 45
Swettenham, Sir Frank 107

Tan, Gene 150
Tan, Jing Quee 70
Tan, Kenneth Paul 13, 15
Tan, Pin Pin 17, 20–1, 30, 45n5, 55, 79n11
  9th August (2006) 79n11
  In Time to Come (2017) 17, 46, *115*
  Invisible City (2007) 30, 44–53, *49*, *50*, *51*, 53n12, 55, 74

Moving House (2001) 46
Singapore GaGa (2004) 45, 45n6
To Singapore, With Love (2015) 61, 68, 69–74, *70*
Tan, Royston 15n11
Tan, Shzr Ee, *Lost Roads: Singapore* (2006) 21, 92, 93, 94–106
Tan, Tarn How 63
Tan, Wah Piow 70
Tay, Hong Seng 67
Teh, David 35
Teng, Kai Wei 148
Teo, You Yenn 7–8, 66n2
The Third Stage 13–14
  Esperanza 66
Tiang, Jeremy 15, 20–1, 74n8
  It Never Rains on National Day (2015) 74, 79
  "National Day" 61, 68, 74–82
  "Sophia's Party" 75, 81
  State of Emergency (2017) 63
Tong, Kelvin
  Grandma Positioning System (2015) 21, 89–94, 107, 115, 116, 117
  The Maid (2005) 67n3, 90n1
Transient Workers Count Too (TWC2) 64, 75
Trump, Donald 151–2, 153, 154, 158

United States, military presence in the Asia Pacific region
  see military
Urban Redevelopment Authority, City Gallery 11, 116, 123

Valles, Eric Tinsay 15n10
Vanderstraaten, Marcia, and Alfian Sa'at, *Hotel* 21, 123, 125–34, 148, 150

Wang, Sha 122–3
Watson, Jini Kim 10, 19n14, 23, 45–6, 136, xx
wayfinding
  definition 3, 93–4, 123
  see also Tong, Kelvin, *Grandma Positioning System* (2015)
Wee, C.J.W.-L. 19n14
Wilder, Gary 23
Wong, Souk Yee 67

Yap, Arthur 27–8
Ye, Fong 122–3
Yeoh, Brenda 104, 129, xvii–xviii